CELLULOID HEROES
DOWN UNDER

CELLULOID HEROES DOWN UNDER

Australian Film, 1970–2000

Theodore F. Sheckels

   Westport, Connecticut
London

Library of Congress Cataloging-in-Publication Data

Sheckels, Theodore F.
    Celluloid heroes down under : Australian films, 1970–2000 / Theodore F.
    Sheckels.
       p.   cm.
    Includes bibliographical references.
    ISBN 0–275–97677–7 (alk. paper)
    1. Motion pictures—Australia—History. I. Title.
PN1993.5.A8 S54   2002
791.43′75′0994—dc21   2002020586

British Library Cataloguing in Publication Data is available.

Copyright © 2002 by Theodore F. Sheckels

All rights reserved. No portion of this book may be
reproduced, by any process or technique, without the
express written consent of the publisher.

Library of Congress Catalog Card Number: 2002020586
ISBN: 0–275–97677–7

First published in 2002

Praeger Publishers, 88 Post Road West, Westport, CT 06881
An imprint of Greenwood Publishing Group, Inc.
www.praeger.com

Printed in the United States of America

The paper used in this book complies with the
Permanent Paper Standard issued by the National
Information Standards Organization (Z39.48–1984).

10 9 8 7 6 5 4 3 2 1

Copyright Acknowledgments

The author and the publisher gratefully acknowledge permission for use of the following material:

Revised excerpts from Theodore F. Sheckels, " 'New Wave' Cinema's Redefinition of Australian Heroism," *Antipodes* 12.1 (June 1998): 29–40.

Contents

Preface		vii
Chapter 1	Australian Film, 1970–2000	1
Chapter 2	The Hero of Old	11
Chapter 3	The Revised Hero	31
Chapter 4	A Woman's Role	75
Chapter 5	The Aborigines' Role	119
Chapter 6	Youth: The Basis for Heroism to Come	137
Chapter 7	Playing with the Concept	169
Chapter 8	Eccentrics	189
Chapter 9	Conclusion	221
Appendix: The People behind Australian Film, 1970–2000		225
Bibliography		235
Index		241

Preface

My interest in Australian film grows out of my interest in Australian literature and, more broadly, what those in academe once called "Commonwealth Literature." In the early 1980s, this body of literature—from such English-speaking places as Canada, Jamaica, Trinidad, Ghana, Nigeria, South Africa, Kenya, India, and Australia—was rarely taught in the United States, especially to undergraduates. Those of us who taught it were trying to introduce students to a rich body of literature and to the cultures of these Commonwealth nations. There has emerged a consensus among this group that film is a highly effective way of introducing students to Australian culture, indeed a more effective way than through poems, plays, and novels.

In the early 1980s, such films as *Breaker Morant* (1980), *My Brilliant Career* (1979), *Gallipoli* (1981), and *The Chant of Jimmie Blacksmith* (1978) were brought to the screen. Because two of them were based on novels, we could ask students to read *My Brilliant Career* by Miles Franklin and then discuss Gillian Armstrong's film adaptation, and read Thomas Keneally's *The Chant of Jimmie Blacksmith* and then discuss Fred Schepisi's adaptation of it. These films are still very much a part of how professors introduce students to Australia, with later films added to the list.

I still use film in teaching Australian literature. I found, however, that I could not possibly screen as many motion pictures as I wanted even in a two-semester survey of the British Commonwealth. So, several years ago, I proposed an honors course entitled "Celluloid Heroes Down Under." Our undergraduate honors courses are one-shot offerings. If the course is successful, one is encouraged to propose it as a course available to all students. Thus, the honors program enriches the entire curriculum. "Celluloid Heroes" then became a film studies course entitled simply "Australian Film."

I have taught the subject in several ways: following chronology, tracing themes, and investigating a particular director's work. I have discovered, however, that the way I approached the subject the first time around—by defining how the films and the culture they reflect define heroism—both provides the best introduction to Australian culture and gives students the best "handle" on a daunting number of feature films. I have sketched that approach in an essay that appeared in *Antipodes* in 1998. This book expands on that sketch.

My argument in this book, a subject I discuss more fully in Chapter 1, is that the films of the 1970–2000 period define a heroism that is much like that of the bushrangers (outlaws living in the bush), ockers (often crude, beer-guzzling rowdies), and rural laborers celebrated in some of the earliest films of the period. This heroism is revised in such a way that the rough edges are sanded away. This heroism is distinctly male; although available to women, there are frequently barriers placed in their way. This heroism is also distinctly "White"; and although available to aborigines, stereotypes and the victimization of aborigines prevent both White and Black directors from depicting the heroism that is there. The films of the 1970–2000 era not only present this heroism, but they also question it by raising what-if questions, by placing heroes in some imagined future and by offering characters who are eccentric to it either because they represent an unhealthful exaggeration of some of the heroic characteristics or because they embody a positive quality that the dominant culture has excluded.

Celluloid Heroes Down Under supports this argument by examining one hundred feature-length films (one made exclusively for television and three made for both television and cinematic release) and, because of its importance, one short film. I would suggest that 100 (or 101) films represent a numerically sufficient "database" for my study. The total number of films produced during the period is probably close to 700, so 100 represents a 15 percent sampling—sizable enough assuming the films are representative.

The sampling is indeed representative because it includes films that were commercially successful as well as ones that were not; films that were critically acclaimed as well as ones that were panned; and, most important, variety. Among the 100 are period pieces such as *My Brilliant Career* and *Gallipoli*, "more European" films such as *Man of Flowers* (1983) and *The Last Days of Chez Nous* (1992), and examples of the many Hollywood genres that were followed—and in some cases adapted—in the 1980s. Two other factors did affect my sampling: the first was availability (obviously, I had to see the film to critique it); the second was the film's relevance to my thesis. This criterion, of course, might cause some to question the representativeness of my sampling, so let me address this issue directly.

I would suggest that if the entire corpus of Australian film could be examined, one would find very few films that contradict what I argue in this book. One would find some films that only peripherally deal with the question of heroism, and one would find a few films that are irrelevant to my thesis. The latter group I am convinced is small. As for the former, I chose not to deal with these because a discussion of them would weaken the book. Let me clarify what I mean by that statement: not weaken the thesis, but weaken the book by extracting messages from films that are rather obviously not those films' primary messages.

I would also suggest that, with just a handful of exceptions, I deal with the films that those who study Australian cinema would salute as the most noteworthy productions. The exceptions—I will let the "experts" name their own—were either unavailable to me or, in my judgment, peripheral or irrelevant—but not contradictory—to the argument I am trying to make.

In selecting films, I, like everyone else who has written on the subject, had to deal with the nagging question of what an Australian film is, a question that has bedeviled not only scholars but government funding agencies who wished to promote only Australian products. There are at least seven elements one might look at in determining if a film is Australian: (1) the national origin or current citizenship or current home of the producer(s); (2) the national origin or current citizenship or current home of the director; (3) the source of funding; (4) the national origin of the technical support personnel; (5) the film's setting; (6) the film's source—be it a novel, play, legend, or original screenplay; and (7) the national origin or current citizenship or current home of the principal or supporting performers. I do not intend to use these criteria and insist, arbitrarily, that for a film to be Australian, it must meet 3 of the 7 critera. I would, however, like to suggest how four have proven problematic and three not so.

The Director. Nicolas Roeg (*Walkabout* [1971]) and Tony Richardson (*Ned Kelly* [1970]) are British; Ted Kotcheff (*Wake in Fright* [1971]) is Canadian. They are not Australian. Jane Campion is a bit more problematic. She is from New Zealand, but received her training in film at the Australian Film, Radio, and Television School (AFRTS), and she has lived for long periods in Australia. Then, there are the several Australian directors—such as the famous Bruce Beresford, Peter Weir, Gillian Armstrong, Fred Schepisi, and the less famous Jim Sharman—who have worked both in Hollywood and "Down Under."

Money. During the 1980s, when the cost of making a film skyrocketed and the funding mechanism became not grants but tax write-offs, producers had to take money from wherever it was available. Thus, there was a great deal of American money behind Australian films, as well as French money, which heavily supported *The Piano* (1993) and *Muriel's Wedding* (1994).

Setting. *Far East* (1982) and *The Year of Living Dangerously* (1982) were set in South Asia. *Crocodile Dundee* was half set in New York City.

Performers. During the 1980s, when sizable profits were necessary to cover sizable costs and please investors, success in Australia was not enough. A film had to do well outside of Australia, especially in the United States. To attract American audiences, producers and directors began using American performers in key roles. Sometimes, all key roles would go to non-Australians (*Quigley* [1990]) and sometimes just one (*The Man from Snowy River* [1982]).

The other three characteristics have proven less problematic. Producers, at least the ones who truly worked on the films, have characteristically been Australian, as have the technical personnel. In fact, one of the reasons Australia has attracted a fair number of "offshore" Hollywood productions is because of the quality of its technical personnel. The AFRTS, criticized by some for not attending sufficiently to either film history or film theory, has certainly graduated many fine craftspeople. Finally, the sources of the films have usually been Australian.

Critical consensus has adopted three early problematic films—*Ned Kelly*, *Walkabout*, and *Wake in Fright*—as being Australian despite directors and casts. The subject matters have been enough in all three cases. Critical consensus has also determined which films by the likes of Beresford, Weir, Armstrong, Schepisi, and Sharman are Australian and which are not. Thus, *Driving Miss Daisy*, *The Dead Poets' Society*, *Little Women* (1994), *Barbarosa*, and *The Rocky Horror Picture Show* are not Australian. These critical decisions, to which I yield, leave us with the case of Jane Campion. Most seem willing to discuss her as Australian, but they see *Sweetie* (1989) as more Australian than *The Piano* or *An Angel at My Table*, but *The Piano* as more Australian than *An Angel at My Table* (1990). The first distinction makes sense because *Sweetie* is set in Australia; the second is not clear, because both seem equally remote from Australia. Having made these distinctions, however, scholars embrace Campion as "Australian enough" for consideration in studies such as this one. I will follow suit.

Three other decisions need to be explained. I have included the miniseries *A Town Like Alice* (1981) as if it were a feature film. I do so because I think this particular miniseries, popular both in the United States and in Australia, is culturally resonant. I do so also because the line between feature film and miniseries is a rather blurred one in Australia. The blurring is because, in the 1980s, many projects that would have been feature films in the 1970s were done—and done well—as television miniseries. These projects were quite frequently of the period-piece type, not in a Hollywood genre. So, projects that might have been the successors to *The Getting of Wisdom* (1977) and *My Brilliant Career* were done for television, not the cinema. And some, such as *Robbery under Arms* (1985), were done for both. Once the miniseries proved to be a worthy form, some projects developed with a determination regarding the venue rather late in the production's life.

I have included the short film *Night Cries* (1989) also. Short- and medium-length filmmaking is very much alive in Australia, and there is some blurring between medium-length and feature-length, especially among feminist filmmakers. The blurring, however, is not the rationale for including *Night Cries*; it is quite simply that this particular short film is important because on the screen it captured the life experience of aborigines from their own perspective.

In each of the chapters (2–8) that focus on films, I have chosen to discuss them one by one in chronological order, offering what almost might be read as separate sketches of the motion pictures. I chose to proceed in that manner for two reasons, both related to my readers. I thought some readers might like to consider, on their own, how the cinema evolves with respect to the questions raised in these seven chapters. I do not focus on that evolution, but I wanted to facilitate someone else's examination of it by discussing the films in chronological order. I also knew some readers would want to use this book as a quasi-reference work, looking up what I have to say about a particular film just as they look up what others have said. I am pleased that the studies by Neil Rattigan and David Stratton facilitate this use of their studies by devoting a chunk of easily located text to a given film. I wanted this book to be comparably easy for others to use in this manner.

ACKNOWLEDGEMENTS

All of these decisions were fully mine, as this book evolved from what a group of students and I discussed several years ago to the study's current form. I did, however, benefit from the comments of the students in that honors course as well as students enrolled in several sections of my Australian film course in the years that have followed. I thank them.

I also thank Cynthia L. Hartung, the reference assistant in charge of interlibrary loan requests, and others in Randolph-Macon College's McGraw-Page Library for helping me acquire the many books and selected journal articles on Australian film. What they acquired for me was supplemented by reading I did in the Australian Film, Television, and Radio School library (the Jerry Toeplitz Library) in the Sydney suburb of North Ryde and the ScreenSound Australia Library in Canberra. In these two libraries, I was able to view numerous Australian films. I thank Michele Burton and her staff at the Jerry Toeplitz Library for their courteous assistance. I thank Peter Kunz and his associates at the ScreenSound Australia Library for theirs. I also thank Peter for his help in selecting illustrations for this book and his guidance as I acquired the necessary permissions to use those photographs. Chapter 1 represents a reworking of some of the ideas I presented in an article in the journal *Antipodes*. I thank its current editor, Nicholas Birns, for permission to repeat several paragraphs from that 1998 essay.

I thank Frank Bladwell for sharing his thoughts on Australian film with me over a delightful dinner in Sydney. Frank, a retired actor and school teacher, spends some of his spare time now teaching classes in film (Australian as well as from Hollywood) to community members. I thank John and Annette Warfield

Hughes for suggesting additional films I "had to see" and include in the study. Annette is one of my former students. She is now a senior litigator in Melbourne, and she and John offered their suggestions (scribbled on a napkin by John) after a wonderful meal at their suburban home. I thank my dear friend Kathleen Mackin Sweeney for suggesting additional films and reading and commenting on a draft version of this book. I turned to her for assistance with this project because of her knowledge and love of film as well as her gift at catching both the unclear as well as the pretentious and the pedantic in academic writing. Also very helpful was the careful editing of Athan Metsopoulos at Greenwood Press. I thank him as well as editor Eric Levy, who has helped steer this project forward.

I also thank Randolph-Macon College for granting me a sabbatical leave during the January term and the spring semester of 2001 to do the bulk of the work on this book. My final thanks goes to the the Rashkind Family Endowment, which, through the college, offers grants to faculty members, primarily for travel during sabbatical periods to do research; because of its generous grant, I was able to travel to Australia, work at the Jerry Toeplitz Library at the "film school" in Sydney, and work at the ScreenSound Australia Library Archives in Canberra.

Chapter 1
Australian Film, 1970–2000

Several who have chosen to write on Australian film have noted the large number of feature films produced in Australia between 1970 and 2000, a number that the population of Australia does not come anywhere near to justifying. This explosion requires an explanation, and I will provide a brief one in the following paragraphs. It also has inspired a number of attempts to impose some order on this huge output. I will review the various schemes in this chapter, suggesting what they offer and what they lack. In general terms, what they lack is a focused, coherent picture of Australian film. After reviewing these schemes, I will suggest that this large body of film does represent a focused endeavor—that being to present Australia to itself and the world by celebrating and interrogating a heroism that embodies the national culture.

The turn of the century saw an upsurge in Australian nationalism that produced some of the nation's most famous works of literature. The 1970s saw another upsurge, but, this time, the government was involved, and the government decided that the nation needed a clear, positive definition of who it was. Rather than rely on literature to offer this definition, the government decided on film. Through film, an industry in which Australia had been a pioneer, the nation would define itself. This definition would be offered for national and international consumption.

Both the federal government and some state governments put a fair amount of money toward this goal. This early money is behind the revival of the film industry in the 1970s; it made possible some of the masterpieces of Australian film produced during the 1978–1982 period. After this period, the mechanism used to provide public support of film changed. Rather than outright grants, the government provided tax incentives to investors. Initially, very generous incentives caused the number of films to mushroom. The investors wanted the tax benefits, but they also wanted a return on their investment. Guaranteeing a return seemed to mean imported stars, higher production values, and many more special effects. All of these "necessities" drove up the cost considerably. To cover this higher cost and still return a profit, films had to make the "lion's share" of their money abroad, in particular in the United States. Because the films had to appeal to the American market, more of the elements that had caused the cost of making a movie to rise were needed. They also—arguably—had to become more explicitly pitched at the American market. That pitching meant—arguably—an end to the attempt to define Australia and share that vision nationally and internationally.

Then, the political climate changed in Australia. The amount of money being lost in tax revenue struck some as too high, and, as a result, progressively the tax incentives were reduced and, finally, by the end of the 1980s, eliminated. Then, the government resumed the practice of subsidizing but on a much smaller scale. The total number of film projects funded was relatively small, and the percentage of costs met by the subsidy was small as well. This policy resulted in a slowdown in the industry. However, the films that were made, because they had to attract investors, still had many of the "Hollywood" elements of the motion pictures turned out in mind-boggling numbers during the 1980s. The result was the production of fewer, but better, films.

Throughout the entire thirty-year period, the government expressed in various ways its desire that the films produced "be Australian." Sometimes, the emphasis seemed to be on the content; sometimes, on the personnel involved. Clearly, the government did not want to subsidize—directly or through tax incentives—films unless they benefited the nation culturally or economically. One of the liveliest debates in Australian film commentary is over whether the films, after a point, ceased being Australian. I would suggest that, at their core, the films remained Australian well into the 1990s.

Films made in Australia were no longer culturally or economically Australian by the late 1990s due to the globalization of the film industry. Under this regime, films are made wherever the technological capabilities are high and the costs are low. Largely because of the educational programs of the Australian Film, Television, and Radio School (AFTRS), technological capabilities are quite high at both the large Warner Brothers complex near Brisbane and the Fox complex in Sydney. Production costs are also low in Australia, aided by an exchange rate that has recently not favored the Australian dollar. There is also a wide range of sites in Australia—city, beach (tropical, subtropical, and temperate), mountains, farmland, grazing land, and desert—in addition to a quality of light that appeals to many cinematographers. As a result, many films are being produced in Australia now, and whether they are "offshore" productions or, in some way, Australian productions is very difficult to say. Consider recent films such as *Matrix* and *Moulin Rouge*. Would anyone seeing them think them Australian unless they knew where and with what technical expertise they were filmed?

The globalization of the industry may not eliminate films we would recognize as Australian, but it does require a new understanding of what constitutes an Australian film. Consequently, globalization provides one studying the subject with a convenient *terminus ad quem*, with the beginning point being the films made when industry and government decided that the Australian film industry would have a renaissance in the 1970s.

This renaissance is chronicled fairly well in Andrew Pike and Ross Cooper's *Australian Film, 1900–1977* and Scott Murray's *Australian Film, 1978–1992*. Some sense of the critical response to this body of work can be gleaned from Elizabeth Jacka's bibliographical essay in *The Oxford Guide to Film Studies*. Given all that is already in print on Australian film, one might wonder why another study is useful. My contention is that, although what is in print offers very useful insights into Australian film, this body of work presents a rather fragmented picture rather than finding and exploring a single thread that unifies the hundreds of films into a focused enterprise.

First there are popular accounts that celebrate Australian film rather than examine it critically. David White's *Australian Movies to the World* is this sort of account. Especially useful are its profiles of the more prominent directors and actors. Equally celebratory is Diane Collins' *Hollywood Down Under*. As her subtitle suggests, she deals with the entire history beginning in 1896, not just the post-1970 period. Both books offer many bits of Australian film trivia that actually do enhance one's appreciation of individual films.

More scholarly are several attempts to "control" the large output of films by placing them into thematic categories. A good schema ought to be based on a consistent principle, be exhaustive, minimize overlapping, and offer both a general thesis and a thesis about each category. Peter Kemp's "Developing Pictures: Australian Cinema (1970–1995)" points to four themes: growing up, stirring (restlessly upsetting the status quo), getting intimate, and claiming identity. His first theme is the easiest to grasp, as is the third, although, insofar as it deals with a wide range of male-female relationships and associated problems, it seems too broad. The second and fourth themes are not that easy to grasp. The second mixes together films such as *Petersen* (1974), *Mad Max II* (1981), *Sweetie* (1989), and *Romper Stomper* (1992); the basis for the mix is not entirely clear; possibly, they feature a character or group of characters who stir things up. If so, there are other examples I can cite, including *The Getting of Wisdom* (1977), which is about growing up, and *Shame* (1988), which is about violently abusive male-female relationships. The third theme, then, seems to overlap with others. The fourth seems to overlap a great deal with the first, since, in growing up, one is also finding an identity. Films such as *The Getting of Wisdom*, *My Brilliant Career* (1977), and *Puberty Blues* (1981) seem to fit equally as well in the fourth and the first. There is, however, a strongly implied overall thesis offered in Kemp's article: that Australian film chronicles the developing human story. One does, however, wonder how films such as *The Cars That Ate Paris* (1974) and *Far East* (1982) fit this thesis and this scheme.

Brian McFarlane's *Australian Cinema* offers a schema that is tied to Australian culture as opposed to stages of human development. McFarlane proceeds empirically, and, after looking at the nearly four hundred films produced between 1970 and 1985, he finds six thematic preoccupations. First, many films focus on the Australian male's identity. Be he ocker or underdog, the Aussie male has a strong antiauthoritarian streak. Second, many films focus on Australia as a nonurban place. Third, an increasing number of films focus on the Australian city and the social problems found there. Fourth, many films focus on relationships, be they beteween parent and child, man and woman, or male mates. Fifth, many Australian "new-wave" films such as Michael Pattinson's *Street Hero* (1984), Don McLennan's *Hard Knocks* (1980), and Bruce Beresford's *Puberty Blues*, deal with teenagers. And sixth, many films focus on the past, whether it be the 1890s or World War I.

McFarlane's scheme is useful as a corrective to those who, for example, conceive of Australian film as multiple views of the outback. His six thematic foci suggest that new-wave films may be more diverse than a quick glance would suggest. The scheme, however useful, falls short of being a powerful one, because McFarlane does not offer a generalization or a set of generalizations about the films as a group. He might have asked: What does the existence of these six themes suggest about Australia at this point in its history, or, what do the themes suggest about the enterprise of Australian filmmaking? The scheme, in addition, does not offer discrete categories. A film such as Geoffrey Wright's *Romper Stomper*, for example, would fit in four of the six categories because it deals with male identity among young people also involved in romantic and "mateship" relationships in the city. Also, some Australian films of note do not readily fit in any. Weir's *The Last Wave*, (1977) for example, is not primarily about male identity, and its Sydney location is rather incidental. It is set in the present, does not involve youth, and its primary focus is not relationships. Or Beresford's *The Fringe Dwellers* (1986): it is nonurban, and it touches on relationships of different sorts and features a young woman as a major character; but its primary concern, the results of racism in Australia, does not fit into any of McFarlane's six categories.

More exhaustive is the work of David Stratton. He wrote two full-length studies of Australian film: *The Last New Wave* and *The Avocado Plantation*. In the former, Stratton observed the variety of films being produced in Australia in the 1970s, but because of the lack of variety, he did not feel compelled to offer a classification scheme. Not so in the latter, which covers the 1980s, which he sees as a very different decade—primarily because Australian films had to emulate Hollywood to cover costs and make a profit. The content of the films did not become, in Stratton's view, wholly American; one can, however, see the American influence. He classifies the great variety "grown" on the avocado plantation and largely shipped elsewhere into eleven content-based categories: true stories, big country, lovers, wild side, adapted from books or plays, about justice, featuring guns, horror, comedy, made for kids, and about youth. Indeed, these categories do seem to cover the territory. They are not, however, discrete categories. Beresford's *Puberty Blues*, for example, is adapted from a book, is about youth, and takes us on a walk on the wild side; Phillip Noyce's *Heatwave* (1982) is about justice and lovers and is partially based on a true story. In addition, Stratton makes no unifying argument about the films of the 1980s except that the number and variety are prodigious and that there is a strong Hollywood influence. His *Avocado Plantation* does, however, provide a wealth of inside information about the making of the 1980s films and is therefore a "must read" for Australian film fans.

Also focused on the 1980s is Tom O'Regan's "The Enchantment with Cinema" He fails to include many films in his discussion because he uses the rather traditional categories of the genre film, the art film, blockbusters, and television miniseries. Or perhaps he has numerous Hollywood genres in mind for the first category making it rather large and unwieldy. His scheme does, however, shift the focus from the content of the films to the director's choice among artistic options. This perspective was anticipated by director Tim Burstall in his brief 1985 essay "Twelve Genres of Australian Film." A more elaborate description of the large body of films from the director's perspective is provided by Susan Dermody and Elizabeth Jacka in the second volume of their *The Screening of Australia*. (The first volume considers the film industry, noting how changes in budgeting and funding resulted in greater commercialization in the 1980s; the sequel, *The Imagining Industry*, argues that further commercialization in the very late 1980s has virtually eliminated any Australian elements in the films made in the nation.) In the second volume of *The Screening of Australia*, Dermody and Jacka offer an elaborate typology for the choices directors made. Directors could choose to make the beautifully filmed period piece that the Australian Film Commission (AFC) seemed to love (what Dermody and Jacka term the "AFC Genre") or they could select social realism or pure commercialism or they could pursue what Dermody and Jacka term "the Australian Gothic." Directors might do a "sexual mores film" or a "male ensemble film." They might direct a film featuring a strong female role or a film exploring human subjectivity. If these eight aesthetic categories were not enough, directors could choose to be eccentrics.

This schema calls our attention to the aesthetic and ideological contrast between such period pieces as Peter Weir's *Picnic at Hanging Rock* (1975) and Simon Wincer's *Phar Lap* (1983) and the gritty social realism of Don McLennan's *Hard Knocks* and Bruce Beresford's *The Fringe Dwellers*. This schema also reveals the culturally fascinating contrast between males in groups, as in Peter Weir's *Gallipoli* (1981), and females alone, as in Igor Auzins' *We of the Never Never* (1982), characteristic of these films. Although the schema Dermody and Jacka construct points out these and several other interesting trends and contrasts in Australian cinema, the schema proves problematic when one sees how many films fit into several of the nine categories. Take Gillian Armstrong's *My Brilliant Career*, for example: Dermody and Jacka cite it as a prime example of the AFC Genre (despite the AFC's refusal to fund it). In addition they cite it as belonging to that group of films featuring strong female roles. Or consider Beresford's *Puberty Blues*: It has elements of social realism, explores sexual mores, and features a strong female role. When many of the films of the new wave fit into more than one aesthetic category, one has to question the usefulness of the categories. Also, the lack of logical precision in the Dermody and Jacka schema is troubling: some of the categories are genres; some refer to emphases the director has chosen.

Implicit in many of the studies reviewed thus far is the contrast between the 1970s and the 1980s. James Ricketson's 1985 essay "Poor Movies, Rich Movies" contrasts the decades based on how much it costs to produce a film. More elaborate is the four-stage chronological schema offered by Glenn Lewis in *Australian Movies and the American Dream*: taking off, consolidation, king hits and critical successes, and lost in America, the last stage dealing with 1984 onward.

Still more elaborate is the schema offered by Scott Murray in "Australian Cinema in the 1970s and 1980s," a chapter in his *Australian Cinema*. He uses recognizable "Hollywood" genres and Australian variants of them as his categories. Thus, in the 1970s, he points to sex comedies—such as Tim Burstall's *Alvin Purple* (1973) and *Petersen*—the similar, but more Australian, ocker comedies—such as Tim Burstall's *Stork* (1971) and Bruce Beresford's *The Adventures of Barry McKenzie* (1972)—and period films—such as Peter Weir's *Picnic at Hanging Rock*, Gillian Armstrong's *My Brilliant Career*, and Ken Hannam's *Sunday Too Far Away* (1975). These are the films that most commentators, such as Jack Clancy in his chapter on film in John Carroll's *Intruders in the Bush*, focus on. Murray also points out one important eccentric film, Dr. George Miller's *Mad Max* (1979). (I follow the practice of some others by distinguishing the Miller of *Mad Max* fame from the George Miller of *The Man from Snowy River* (1982) fame by referring to the former, who is a medical doctor, as "Dr. George Miller.") After 1980, Murray paints a strikingly different picture: thrillers such as Russell Mulcahy's *Razorback* (1984); action–adventure films such as George Miller's *The Man from Snowy River*, Simon Wincer's *Quigley* (1991), and Dr. George Miller's *Mad Max II*; and comedies such as Peter Faiman's *Crocodile Dundee* (1986), Nadia Tass' *Malcolm* (1986), and Yahoo Serious' *Young Einstein* (1988). According to Murray, there were still period films such as Bruce Beresford's *Breaker Morant* (1980) and Peter Weir's *Gallipoli*, and there were, for the first time, Australian films that explored sexuality and relationships seriously—films such as Jane Campion's *The Piano* (1993) and Gillian Armstrong's *High Tide* (1987). Finally, Murray explores social realist films such as Richard Lowenstein's *Strikebound* (1984) and Geoffrey Wright's *Romper Stomper*.

The contrast that Murray strikes between the 1970s and the post-1980 period is a useful one. Thanks to it, we see, first, the greater variety of the later period and, second, the increased reliance on the part of Australian directors on venerable film genres. As Australian new-wave cinema matured, it seems to have offered audiences more, but what it offered was to a large extent more of the usual Hollywood fare. Stuart Cunningham's 1985 essay "Hollywood Genres, Australian Movies" makes much the same point. It is well worth noting that Australian directors seemed to be using Hollywood formulas because the American influence on Australian film does indeed complicate it as a nationalistic one after 1985. However, as Brian McFarlane notes, Australian films do not neatly fit into genres such as these. Furthermore, pigeonholing Australian films into familiar American genres obscures the relationship between these films and the Australian culture that informs them and may prevent one from seeing how the Australian film transforms the genre as it uses it—thereby "Australianizing" it. For example, Tom O'Regan argues that *Strictly Ballroom* (1992) and *The Adventures of Priscilla: Queen of the Desert* (1994) Australianize the musical genre (*Australian* 1).

The schemes examined thus far have been lists of themes or lists of aesthetic choices or lists of genres premised on the 1970s and the 1980s being very different decades as far as Australian film is concerned. McFarlane's comment suggests another premise for a list. The basis for that premise is in the history that I recounted at the beginning of this chapter. The government poured money into the enterprise because it was thought that film could present to Australia and the world what the nation and its people were. Put another way, it was thought that film could define and then present Australia's culture.

Neil Rattigan's *Images of Australia* begins with such a premise. According to Rattigan, the films of the new wave offer Australians and the world at large images of Australians rooted deeply in its culture. The films represent a reconsideration of these images. Thus, they focus on the bush as place (a topic Ross Gibson's 1988 essay "Formative Landscapes" discusses at length), the bushman, the pioneer, the Australian and New Zealand Army Corps (Anzac) fighting man, and the ocker. In addition, many films focus on the American as an ambiguously attractive and unattractive image. What Rattigan's cultural assumption gains him is a thesis concerning why so many films were produced during the 1970s and 1980s. The phenomenon was not due solely to the ready availability of government funds; rather, it reflected a cultural need for a satisfying national image. Unfortunately, Rattigan's schema does not do justice to the range of films produced during the period. Many films—for example, those focused on women or teenagers—simply do not fit into his very adult, male categories. We either have to accept the argument that some films answered a cultural need while others were merely entertaining or were eccentric, or revise our understanding of what is going on, culturally, in Australian new wave cinema in order to include more of its creative output.

Rattigan's work—and any work that talks about Australian myths—is indebted to Russel Ward's *The Australian Legend*. Ward's "classic" study has, however, been questioned in recent years. The essays in Carroll's *Intruders in the Bush* debunk these myths, particularly those concerning the bush, as does Bob Hodge and Vijay Mishra's *Dark Side of the Dream*. These debunking studies suggest that the myths of the bush, the bushman, and so on, may be as much the product of wishful thinking as reflections of a historical reality. Be they urban dreams or rural realities or, most likely, a little of both, these myths did clearly influence both Australian literature and Australian film.

These myths, however, were not the only influence on Australian film when its makers tried to respond to a cultural need. John Tulloch's *Australian Cinema* discusses the films of the previous "wave" during the 1920s and 1930s. These films curiously reflected the very same myths Rattigan talks about. Tulloch argues that what complicates all of these films is that, rather than existing in a univocal manner in the culture, these myths are always voiced with entailed interpretations. These interpretations will emphasize different aspects, and they may be flattering or they may be critical: they will rarely be politically neutral. And the films of two decades will therefore speak in many voices, some of them contradictory. What Tulloch has to say about the 1920s and the 1930s is equally true of the new wave. O'Regan's *Australian National Cinema* acknowledges that culture comes into film with such interpretations. He also alerts us to the very important material conditions under which filmmaking existed in the 1970s and 1980s. These conditions, as well as certain demographic facts, make a "national cinema" a problematic venture in Australia. Furthermore, the myths that will of course be a part of any such endeavor usually are privileged and marginalized based on such social characteristics as class, religion, race, gender, and sexual orientation. This dynamic further complicates the effort, especially because the voices of those marginalized will, in a free society, eventually be heard, rejecting or qualifying the culture's dominant ideology as embodied by those myths. Finally, O'Regan notes that the very idea of nationhood in Australia is problematic because of its youth, its several influxes of people, and its strong state-based identities that, for example, make some think of themselves as Queenslanders first, Australians second. If one does not know what the nation is, how does one create a national cinema? he asks.

The fact is, however, that a national cinema of sorts is what the filmmakers in the post-1970 period did indeed create. It is a cultural endeavor characterized very much by the problems Tulloch and O'Regan point out, but it is a cultural endeavor nonetheless. Rattigan's *Images of Australia* asks the correct question: what cultural function do these films serve? However, the answer is both simpler and more complex than the one he provides. Yes, the films are indeed sending a message about Australia to Australians and the world at large. However, I would argue that the message is not that Australians are the people who have historically inhabited the outback, which is where they are rooted;

rather, it is that Australians are potentially a certain type of person with identifiable characteristics. These characteristics may be more distinct in the outback than elsewhere, but they are present wherever because they are what makes Australians Australian. These characteristics constitute a kind of heroism that is at the core of the culture.

Australian film in the post-1970 period presents this heroism. Because its historical manifestations are too rough or too crude or too violent for post-1970 tastes, Australian film usually presents this heroism in a sanitized version. This heroism is furthermore usually presented as male and "White." Thus, many films grapple with how, and if, this defining heroism "fits" women and aborigines. This heroism is usually seen in adults. Thus, many films look to the world and lives of youth, speculating about whether this heroism—and with it, a particular conception of the Australian nation—will survive. Films also probe the heroism, asking how it would be perceived under various futuristic scenarios. Finally, some films question the heroism either by showing and satirizing extreme cases or by noting critically some positive qualities that the dominant heroic code seems to exclude.

In the chapters that follow, I will explore this single focus of this large body of films. I will examine the hero of old, noting his rough edges (Chapter 2) and then show how many films sanitize this figure so that he is compatible with modern sensibilities (Chapter 3). In Chapter 4, I will consider how women fit into this heroic code and in Chapter 5 how aborigines fit. In Chapter 6 I will look at films focused on youth and ask whether the qualities of youth and the qualities of the world that youth inhabit are such that the revised or sanitized Australian hero will survive in this generation. In Chapter 7, I will look at films that play what-if games with the concept, testing its viability under future conditions such as anarchy and alien invasion. Finally, in Chapter 8, I will look at films that critique this heroism by offering us eccentric heroes, who are "out there" either because they have taken the Australian code to an extreme or because they, despite their nobility, do not fit the code and are therefore culturally excluded.

This study considers one hundred post-1970 films and a short subject. In the preface I discussed why I selected the films I did. Here, just let me repeat that any attempt to discern what film(s) might be communicating about a culture must be based on an examination of not just the elite works or the best works, but also the popular and the flawed. Thus, in the pages that follow, one will find discussions of "classics" such as *My Brilliant Career*, *Breaker Morant*, and *Gallipoli* as well as more popular successes such as *Mad Max II* and *Crocodile Dundee*. One will also find discussions of less successful, but nonetheless culturally interesting, films such as *Dogs in Space* (1987), *Dead-End Drive-In* (1986), and *Dallas Doll* (1993). All of the films considered in this study are part of an effort to define and communicate "Australianness" to audiences at home and abroad. Most—but not all—are good films. All, however, are part of the culture that the post-1970 films offer and then probe.

Chapter 2

The Hero of Old

Any definition of the Australian hero that one might offer runs the risk of being reductive. However, I need to run that risk if this study is to be something other than analyses of one hundred Australian films (and a short subject). I do ask the reader to keep in mind that any given hero is more than just a composite of the characteristics I will shortly enumerate. To underscore that point, I ask the reader to consider, together for a moment, the bushranger hero Captain Starlight from Donald Crombie and Ken Hannam's *Robbery under Arms* (1985) and the bushranger hero Mad Dog Morgan from Philippe Mora's *Mad Dog Morgan* (1976). These are two of the films I will analyse in this chapter, so more will be said about these heroes shortly. For the moment, note how Sam Neill portrays Starlight as a dashing and sophisticated fellow who, like Robin Hood, robs the rich to serve the suffering poor. Note how Neill's portrayal contrasts with Dennis Hopper's portrayal of Morgan. Morgan is drawn to crime because of his own bitter impoverishment. His prison experience, which includes homosexual rape and branding, hardens him; so, upon his release, he seeks his criminal revenge. Because many Australians shared Morgan's dislike for authority, he becomes a popular hero, as Starlight also does. However, Morgan's scruffiness, brutality, and near insanity clearly distinguish him from the very urbane Starlight.

The heroes of old discussed in this chapter are indeed quite different, however, they do exhibit twelve shared traits. First, they love freedom. Thus, not surprisingly, these heroes are both antiauthoritarian (second trait) and anti-British (third trait). Australia's vast expense of uninhabited land perhaps give them the space they need to be free. They therefore value the land and are in touch with it (fourth trait). The horses that allow them to traverse the land are also loved (fifth trait), although it is worth noting that the horses' appeal may have as much to do with their speed as their personalities. Thus, the fast horse–loving trait of earlier heroes will become the fast car–loving trait of later ones. The heroes of old love their mates (sixth trait), creating "mateship" as an important defining characteristic of the Australian culture as a whole. These heroes are also intensely competitive (seventh trait); they love to drink (eighth trait), are rather anti-intellectual (ninth trait), and are rather sexist (tenth trait). Somewhat surprisingly, given Australia's sad legacy of oppression of its aboriginal peoples, these heroes are not especially racist. They feel that they—and the people they serve or exemplify—are very much underdogs (eleventh trait). And, win as they might many times, they are rather fatalistic (twelfth trait). They feel that, in the end, they are doomed to suffer and lose.

Even though in this chapter, I treat eight films in the order in which they were released, I present this kind of heroism in two different categories of Australian films: the first covers the nineteenth century; the second the twentieth century. This chronological division should show how the heroism continues, even as the material circumstances of life change because the nineteenth-century arenas and the earliest of the twentieth-century arenas feature criminals, whereas the remaining twentieth-century arenas feature workingmen. The films that depict traditional heroism in a nineteenth-century setting are Tony Richardson's *Ned Kelly* (1970), Philippe Mora's *Mad Dog Morgan*, and Donald Crombie and Ken Hannam's *Robbery under Arms*; and the films that depict this heroism in a twentieth-century setting are Bruce Beresford's *The Adventures of Barry McKenzie* (1972), Ken Hannam's *Sunday Too Far Away* (1975), Donald Crombie's *The Irishman* (1978), Tim Burstall's *The Last of the Knucklemen* (1979), and Kevin Dobson's *Squizzy Taylor* (1982).

NED KELLY (TONY RICHARDSON, DIRECTOR, 1970)

The story of bushranger Ned Kelly has been presented—in different media—many times. One of Australia's premiere films from the 1920s centers on the Kelly gang's saga; so does one of its more recent novels, Peter Carey's *The True Adventures of Ned Kelly*. Both Kelly's character and most of his criminal adventures would be inherited by any filmmaker and assumed by any Australian audience because his story is so well known.

Such was the situation British director Tony Richardson faced in 1970 when bringing Ned Kelly to the screen. This film has not won much acclaim in Australia, probably because the audience had expectations Richardson did not meet. The audience expected Kelly to be a burly Irishman, with chips on his broad shoulders against the condescending squatters and the English-mannered police. Instead, Richardson—probably to make money internationally for his film company—gives them scrawny Mick Jagger (lead singer of the British rock group The Rolling Stones) in the lead role (Pike and Cooper 250–51).

If the casting is designed to appeal to the international market, the script seems attuned to the Australian. I say this because the script seems to assume that both the events and Kelly's motivation are already known to viewers. For example, one of the earliest events in the movie has Kelly and his gang freeing stock from a holding pen. We really do not know why unless we already know Kelly's story and why in the ongoing battle between squatters (who were typically "better-born" English and had acquired title to large tracts of land) and settlers (who were typically "base-born" Irish and had staked out much smaller parcels), squatters had adopted the practice of seizing any settler's livestock that had wandered onto once-common grazing land that the squatters now owned and were enclosing. Kelly was freeing these captured animals—and the squatters' own stock to boot. The movie fails to make this scene and others clear for viewers who do not already know the legend.

The motion picture's quality, however, is not the issue here. Rather, the issue is how the Australian hero—in this case, the notorious bushranger Ned Kelly—is depicted. Ned Kelly and Captain Starlight, the hero of Crombie and Hannam's *Robbery under Arms*, are the two best-known Australian bushrangers. As we will see later in this chapter, the two have many traits in common. However, there are crucial distinctions of origin and class. Ned Kelly is an Irish Australian, not an expatriate Brit; Ned Kelly is a lower-class settler, not a displaced nobleman.

Kelly is a believer in freedom. He wants to be left alone to farm the land his family has settled. And, when events lead him into progressively more and more serious criminal acts, he wants freedom from imprisonment more than anything else. The enemies in Kelly's eyes are the police, who act in a very English manner, and the squatters, who are typically English (not Irish) in origin and also act in a very English manner.

Kelly and those who join him are a roughneck group compared to the Marstons in *Robbery under Arms*. Drink plays a role in their lives, although Richardson's film does not stress it; matters that one might term "intellectual" play virtually no role. The land and the horses they ride roughly across it are at the center of the Kelly gang's life, but what the movie stresses is their movement into a life of revenge and crime when the police, the squatters, and distant authorities conspire to deny them this life. Thus, a war between social classes is at the root of the Kelly gang's defiance. It is joined with revenge when these authorities act in any way against Ned's mates. Ned is loyal to his mates, among whom are his siblings. He is also loyal to his mother. Although it is not especially clear in the movie, much of Ned's criminal activity is directed at freeing his mother from prison, having been sent there on somewhat trumped-up charges as an accessory to Ned's crimes.

The gang competes in battle against these conspiring others. The numbers against the Kellys increase; the weaponry used against them becomes increasingly more sophisticated; and they deal routinely with betrayals, since they can count on the loyal support of most but not all of their fellow Irish-Australian settlers. The odds are clearly against the Kellys. The audience senses that it is only a matter of time before they lose. They are underdogs, and, sooner or later, the manpower or firepower against them will lead to their defeat. Until then, they will compete. The crimes will become more daring, and the defiance and the bravado associated with that defiance will increase.

Ned competes to the bitter end. He, perhaps crazed into an egomaniacal state, decks himself in a suit of handmade armor. The suit does indeed protect him from the gunfire of the authorities; however it does not prevent his sense of hearing from being assaulted and shots to his unprotected legs from dropping him to the rail bed, from which he is captured. Later, he will be executed at Melbourne gaol, a site that is still, to this day, a tourist attraction because it was the site of the hero Ned Kelly's death.

THE ADVENTURES OF BARRY McKENZIE (BRUCE BERESFORD, DIRECTOR, 1972)

Richardson's *Ned Kelly* takes us back to nineteenth-century Australia. Like many Australian films, including most discussed in this chapter, it looks retrospectively at the traditional hero. From this viewpoint, the hero seems noble, although most directors insist on giving that nobility an "edge," which causes us to question the hero's stability and, by extension, the heroism's stability. Other films of the 1970s and 1980s offer a different viewpoint: they look at the present time and present a hero who seems, at least at first glance, very different. This hero, rather than robbing from the rich and giving to the poor, gains television stardom by dropping his trousers and pouring curry powder down those pants and on his genitalia to spice up his lovemaking.

When the Australian film industry was resuscitated with the help of government funding in the 1970s, the films that initially proved the industry's viability were the ocker comedies *Alvin Purple* (1973) (directed by Tim Burstall) and *The Adventures of Barry McKenzie* (directed by Bruce Beresford). Both *Alvin* and *Barry* will have sequels. These farcical films present, center stage, the Australian ocker, a type which, as we will soon see, exhibits just as many of the characteristics of the traditional hero as Ned Kelly and others yet to be discussed in this chapter, but with a comic coarseness that causes cringes of embarrassment from those trying to present Australian film as a worthy enterprise (Pike and Cooper 265). The ocker's popularity at the box office gives us the incongruous string of Bruce Beresford's *Barry McKenzie Holds His Own* (1974); Fred Schepisi's *The Chant of Jimmie Blacksmith* (1978)—discussed in Chapter 5; John Duigan's *Dimboola* (1979); Bruce Beresford's *Breaker Morant* (1980)—discussed in Chapter 3; John Eastway's *Melvin: Son of Alvin* (1984); Graeme Clifford's *Burke & Wills* (1985); and George Miller's *Les Patterson Saves the World* (1987). This string alternates ocker comedies with the polished period pieces Susan Dermody and Elizabeth Jacka termed the "AFC Genre" (*The Screening* 2: 117). The fledgling film industry, then, exhibits what seems to be an incongruity. However, when one examines the ocker hero, one finds that he has much in common with the traditional heroes of these AFC Genre films. In fact, some have suggested that the ocker comedies are not as bad in retrospect as "film authorities" have suggested (Hinde; O'Regan, "Cinema Oz").

The Adventures of Barry McKenzie may well be the best of these ocker comedies. In it, we learn many Australian slang expressions for vomiting and urinating and are offered etymological explanations for some—for example, "chunder" (which is allegedly "watch under" said rapidly) as one on a higher deck might say to those on the lower ones before becoming seasick over the rail. We also are given much gratuitous sex and much gratuitous talk about sex, including renditions of "One-Eyed Trouser Snake" sung by Barry Crocker who plays Barry McKenzie. These elements, as well as to the looseness of the plotting and the weakness of some of the gags, are what prompts the cringes.

There is, however, much in the saga of Barry's journey to England that is "heroic" in the sense in which I am using the term. He very much enjoys the freedom with which he takes on the United Kingdom, a freedom that is only occasionally cramped by Aunt Edna (played by yet another Barry, Barry Humphries) who accompanies him. In the course of this journey, the movie satirizes the British time and again. The pomposity of the British customs officer, the way the British taxi drivers and landlords exploit visiting Aussies, British beer, British racism, the British *nouveaux riches*, the British "hippie" counterculture, and the British advertising and television industries are all "sent up" by the film. The taxi driver, for example, takes Barry to his London hotel (the "Kangaroo Court Motel") via Stonehenge and Scotland; and the hippies, whose songs comically ooze the late 1960s counterculture, conspire to exploit Barry as an authentic Australian folksinger and rake in the profits. Given the film's pronounced anti-British attitude, it is somewhat surprising that the motion picture did well at the box office in the United Kingdom. Its success there is probably because the film's type of humor was familiar to British audiences—and popular—through many British comedies.

The film sends up things that are not exclusively British. The intellectual mumbo jumbo of pop psychology is parodied, as are the cerebral rumblings of an Australian would-be writer who intends to pen a philosophy of surfing. So, the anti-British thrust of the film is matched by an anti-intellectual thrust. And, sometimes, the jokes are at the expense of Barry's fellow Australians in England. Their love of beer is apparent in Barry's attempt to smuggle tubes (cans) of Foster's into the country, as well as in the mates' Gulliver-like extinguishing of the television studio fire by urinating on it while chugging one tube after another. The most revealing beer-drinking scene occurs at a Young Conservatives Social Barry attends with an English girl named Sara whom Aunt Edna and Sara's parents are trying to fix up with Barry. In the front room are boorish English young women and men, the latter of whom spout supposedly funny anti-Australian lines at Barry; in the back room are Foster's-chugging Aussies. Both the English and the Australians are being stereotyped and satirized, but we as viewers tend to share Barry's feelings as he enters the back room: "Human beings at last!" The satire directed against the Australians seems less to denigrate them and more to characterize them—and affirm them—as beer-loving (Rattigan 46–47).

Barry and the Australian males are also presented as sexist. Shortly after arriving at the Kangaroo Court Motel, Barry and his mates plot the seduction of "hot" Australian sheilas (women) and "loose" foreign fight attendants. Later in the film, Barry approaches a distressed Australian girl, asking her if "she bangs like a dunny door [outhouse]." We tend to forgive this sexism somewhat—probably because Barry is so inept as a seducer and lover. His sexism seems stupid and benign, not at all threatening.

Throughout the movie, Barry and his Austalian mates, in general, seem in a "one-down" position to the British. They are in this underdog position, from which they comically compete, because of a combination of their flaws and English condescension. We see that they are in this position in the way the taxi driver exploits Barry's lack of familiarity with England and in the insulting remarks made to Barry at the Young Conservatives Social. We also see it when Barry is given a script to read advertising a brand of cigarettes—a script loaded with double entendres concerning oral sex, which Barry is oblivious to. We also see the one-down position and the British condescension toward it when Barry goes on the television show "Midnight Oil," which is focusing that evening on how Australians, notwithstanding the uncouth stereotype, are doing wonderful work in the arts. The television show hostess' condescending intellectual, "artsy" language and Barry's Australian slang combine to defeat communication, leading the hostess to declare that she can't see Barry's point. Annoyed by her attitude, Barry drops his pants on live television to show her "his point." He and his mates are dismissed by the police as "crude colonials," but we cannot help but think Barry won the day, especially when his exposing himself is heralded by the media as an important breakthrough moment for television, and Barry is offered his own weekly program.

"Bazza" McKenzie inhabits a very different world from that inhabited by Ned Kelly or any of the other traditional heroes discussed in this chapter. But, once we get beyond the surface differences, Barry is much like Ned Kelly and the others. Love of horses (or their urban twentieth-century substitutes) does not play any role in *The Adventures of Barry McKenzie*; however, most of the other characteristics of the traditional hero do exhibit themselves as Barry romps his way from episode to episode.

SUNDAY TOO FAR AWAY (KEN HANNAM DIRECTOR, 1975)

Whereas the critical take on *The Adventures of Barry McKenzie* is mixed at best, that on Ken Hannam's *Sunday Too Far Away* is almost unanimously favorable. From its showing in the marketplace at Cannes to its fairly long run in

The shearers in *Sunday Too Far Away* (1975). Photo courtesy of National Film and Sound Archives. Permission granted by South Australian Film Corporation.

Australian theaters, the film was very well received. Unfortunately, it is not as well-known in the United States as it deserves to be.

The film is set in 1955. The central character is a record-setting gun (top) sheepshearer named Foley played by Jack Thompson. Foley has always rung the shed (sheared the most sheep) throughout his entire career. But now, advancing in years, he is challenged by a rival named Arthur Black. The film is loosely plotted, but the thread that holds it together is the competitiveness between Foley and Black—in fact, competition is so all-encompassing that there is even a comic competition to see how fast the man can hand wash their clothes. Since laundry is done in the nude, we watch two men shake their butts to banjo accompaniment as they scrub the soil out of their drawers and singlets (undershirts).

Much of the film, however, is devoted to depicting how Foley and his fellow shearers live. They drift from shed to shed (the building set aside for shearing), enjoying the freedom of new places to work, live, and drink. And they do all three, exhibiting a great deal of camaraderie, because after all, they are mates. They demonstrate that mateship when they vote to ban the cockie (owner of the station) from the shearing pens because his overseeing presence makes them nervous. Foley, seeing the cockie spying on the shearers through a crack in the wall, even pretends to have injured a stud ram's private parts just to force the cockie out of hiding. The shearers further demonstrate their mateship when they vote to replace the cook. Foley again plays a leading role, "borrowing" lemon extract from the cockie's pantry so that the cook will become intoxicated and, therefore, easier to toss out of the job. This particular group of shearers was thrown together by a rather desperate contractor. Thus, they are an odd group, not a group that might in other circumstances become mates. But, differences aside, they play the role of mates while doing this job. And, for the most part, they seem to love their job. Foley, in fact, leads the men in spending their leisure time inspecting the sheep they will shear the next day.

As already demonstrated, antiauthority sentiment characterizes these mates. Led by Foley, they defy the cockie and they defy the contractor, who is a former shearer. Class conflict is implicit in the former if not in both (O'Regan, *Australian* 263). Excessive drinking also characterizes these mates, especially on Saturdays, resulting in the comic depiction of their hangovers come Sunday. Sexism is yet another characteristic. When the cockie's daughter, who caught Foley borrowing the lemon extract from the pantry, blackmails Foley into allowing her to watch the shearers work, the music turns discordant—as if to suggest that her presence is an alien one. The men seem to stress the physicality and the bloodiness of the process during the run she witnesses, as if they are trying to drive her away. They seem uncomfortable with anything feminine. In fact, when one of the younger shearers named Beresford is found writing a letter to his wife, he's accused of being "a queer." One is not sure whether his affection or his literacy draws the men's unfounded accusation and scorn. Curiously, there was supposed to be a developing romantic relationship in the film between Foley and the cockie's daughter. It was edited out. Some argue that this last-minute editing weakened the film because it retained a scene in which she sees Foley crying at the thought of aging and then did not connect her witnessing this emotional moment to anything else in the film (Pike and Cooper 287). Be that as it may, the editing was consistent with the film's antifeminism.

Foley and his mates stick together—against the cockie, against the cook, against the contractor, against the cockie's daughter. The men's cohesiveness is perhaps because they very much feel looked down on. Two points in the film reveal how they felt—with justification—put down and, led by Foley, would not tolerate such treatment. The first involves Old Garth. He is very much a failure: his marriage has failed, his son has become a window dresser (and therefore effeminate) in Sydney, he has become an alcoholic, and he can no longer keep pace with the other shearers. When he dies and the mortician comes for his body with an open-bed truck, not the more costly hearse, Foley reacts angrily. He and the other men compel the mortician to take Garth's body back in the cab of the truck, not in its cargo area. The second involves the government's revocation of the shearers' prosperity bonus, which prompts the men to strike. Foley, having failed for the first time ever to ring the shed and having dissolved in tears and laughter as he confronts the fact that he is aging, is inclined to walk away when much younger strikebreakers are brought in to challenge the outnumbered shearers. Instead, Foley leads the men—less Arthur Black, who is never quite the true mate—in verbally confronting the strikebreakers (an assault a mate labels "piss weak"), and then he leads the men in physically confronting the strikebreakers in a slow-motion barroom brawl. We see Foley hit a man named Frankie Davis, who at the film's beginning had bragged that he had bested Foley at shearing; but we do not see the ultimate outcome of the brawl. We do read on the screen at the end of the movie that the shearers ultimately proved victorious in the strike. So, the shearers, underdogs by age and by number, led by hero Foley, triumph.

Nonetheless, there is a strong sense as the film ends that such triumphs will not continue. Old Garth died a broken man; Foley lost his battle with Black; this group of shearers—suggested to be typical of a fading breed—barely hangs together; and Foley cries at the passing of time and the fading of his prowess—as the cockie's daughter watches. The film mixes in its conclusions a triumphant note with a fatalistic one.

MAD DOG MORGAN (PHILIPPE MORA, DIRECTOR, 1976)

Philippe Mora is somewhat unusual among Australian film directors. Most directors follow the conventions of formal realism. When directing a period piece, they create the illusion that we, the viewers, are back in a previous era; when directing a more contemporary piece, they create the illusion that we are there in present-day Sydney or Melbourne. These directors do not draw attention to the film as film and thereby raise questions such as how seriously to take the film's message. Mora, on the other hand, does draw the viewers' attention to this very question. In *Mad Dog Morgan*, as well as in *The Return of Captain Invincible* (1983), which will be discussed in Chapter 8, he forces viewers to ask how seriously they are to take the film's hero. Is the hero being celebrated? Parodied? Both?

I would argue that in the case of *Mad Dog Morgan*, the answer is both. This creates a tension for the viewers. They clearly see Daniel "Mad Dog" Morgan as a hero in the mold of Captain Starlight and Ned Kelly; however, they also detect the mania of that hero, something incipient in Kelly's armor-clad defiance of police automatic gunfire. American actor Dennis Hopper's portrayal of Morgan heightened this mania (Pike and Cooper 300; Rattigan 109). The dynamic, I think, has the Australian audience being put in a position from which they both accept the heroism, because it embodies Australian values, and reject it, because it is both too uncivilized and too crazed for the present day.

Early moments in the film cause viewers to associate Morgan with the oppressed: the initial music is aboriginal; we meet Morgan who is living with the

Chinese in the gold mining region of Victoria and then witness a racist attack on these Chinese. Having already associated Morgan with the oppressed, we readily accept his turning to thievery because he is impoverished. An unnamed oppressor has created the social circumstances that result in poverty for those of Morgan's class and ethnicity. And the oppression gets worse. Morgan is captured, imprisoned, branded, and raped—with those in charge at the prison laughing while they watch the gang rape. We also find out that Morgan's term and those of others have been unduly lengthened by the oppressing authorities because the state needs "cheap" labor for roads and other civic improvements.

Actor Jack Thompson (who played Foley in *Sunday Too Far Away*) plays Sargent Smith, a police officer who becomes determined to capture Morgan once he is out of prison and involved in criminal activities once again. Sargeant Smith and a parodic rendition of an anthropology professor both insist that bushrangers such as Morgan are different. Smith notes how the bushrangers are like aboriginals in their ability to disappear into the bush and survive there; the professor conjectures that bushrangers are an evolutionary throwback. Neither Smith nor the professor see their judgments as favorable ones. In fact, both reek of racism. As a result, our sympathy is even more with Morgan and against such condescending authorities. And, if Mora has not done enough to tilt viewers' sympathy toward Morgan, the scene in which the professor declares that he wants to have Morgan's scrotum cut off and made into a tobacco pouch has viewers finding themselves taking an antiauthoritarian stance akin to Morgan's.

Perhaps this sympathetic view of Morgan prevents viewers from noticing how brutal his acts of vengeance are and how drunk and deranged he sometimes is. As the plot unfolds, Morgan does enough alleged good to keep his brutality in the corners of viewers' consciousness. He shares his spoils with the poor. He embraces the aboriginal Billy (David Gulpilil) as his equal, as his mate. He learns about the land from Billy, just as he learns to throw the boomerang. He attracts other mates to his entourage, and he is loyal to those who are loyal to him but brutal toward those who betray him. Morgan, because of his generosity, his sense of justice, and his fame for defying authority, gains a great deal of support among the common folks of New South Wales. Like Ned Kelly, Morgan is their hero.

Morgan, like Kelly, does become a little full of himself once his name becomes known. He fancies that he looks like Abraham Lincoln. He asks a family he is robbing at gunpoint if they had seen his image in a wax museum in Melbourne. And he accepts the challenge voiced against him by the Victoria police and decides to cross from New South Wales into Victoria, where the police believe they, unlike the inept New South Wales force, can capture Morgan within twenty-four hours. One can detect in Morgan's march toward Victoria not only his ego but also his competitive drive. He will not hide from the force that has been mounted against him; he will face these Victorian troops head-on.

That decision ultimately proves fatal, although one might argue that Morgan's drunkenness has more to do with his capture than the Victorian police's skill. But before we reach this end, we begin to see a disturbing picture of Morgan. Beyond the point of fatigue, almost exhausted, Morgan begins having bizarre nightmares every time he falls asleep. He seems very much on the brink of insanity. Perhaps we are to believe that the authorities have driven Morgan to this near-deranged state.

However, as one looks back over the film, there is evidence that something is wrong with Morgan long before the climactic minutes. His boasting, his brutal acts of revenge, and even his confusion when approached by a naked woman all suggest that he is not quite "right" long before his nightmares begin. In addition, there is a peculiar quality to some of the lines American actor Dennis Hopper delivers in the role of Morgan: they seem either tongue-in-cheek or poorly improvised. Thus, one wonders whether Mora intends his film to be a serious depiction of heroism, a parody, or both. Extant critical treatment of the motion picture suggests the former and, to the extent critics acknowledge some of the film's quirks, they attribute them to poor filmmaking. I tend to think Mora is aware of how he is presenting this bushranger hero and, somewhat ahead of his time, is offering a film that in a postmodern manner straddles the line between the serious and the parodic. A similar treatment of the hero in Mora's *The Return of Captain Invincible* suggests to me that we are dealing here with a playful director, not a poorly scripted or acted movie.

THE IRISHMAN (DONALD CROMBIE, DIRECTOR, 1978)

Donald Crombie's *The Irishman* is melodramatic, not playful. Its beautiful cinematography by Peter James enhances the melodrama, whereas the too noticeable score by Charles Marawood pushes the melodrama too strongly on the viewer (McFarlane in Murray, *Australian Film* 17; Rattigan 160). Crombie, however, is clearly not engaging in parody; rather, he is offering a textbook example of the AFC Genre in which some of the stylizations of that genre are quite simply overdone.

The story is that of Paddy Doolan, a teamster. The background is a time of transition in Australia from the reliance on horses to the use of motorized vehicles. Paddy is caught at that moment, unwilling to adapt. Also caught at that moment are Paddy's two sons, Will and Michael, who are also experiencing all of the "normal" turmoil of escaping from the influence of their parents and becoming their own men.

Paddy (Michael Craig) very much loves his work. He loves the freedom of the road and the freedom of taking his team from job to job, mastering each one in turn. He is competitive, and, given our first view of Paddy and the noble Clydesdales that comprise his team, we assume he has usually been trium-

Paddy Doolan (Michael Craig) and son Michael (Simon Burke) in *The Irishman* (1978). Photo courtesy of National Film and Sound Archives. Permission granted by Anthony Buckley.

phant. He is the teamster, par excellence. And he loves the horses he labors with, just as he loves the beer and the family he savors when he returns from another teamster triumph.

The appearance early in the film of a younger man named Eric Haywood (Bryan Brown), who has traded in his team for a lorry, proves to be ominous. Paddy ends up in a fistfight with Haywood, motivated partially by the younger man's business challenge and partially by the younger man's influence over Paddy's sons, who have been urging their father to buy a lorry (as well as get electricity for the house).

The audience, given its perspective from 1978, knows how the horses versus the lorries battle will end. Therefore, Paddy quickly falls from the triumphant heights we meet him at and becomes an underdog in a fight that he will inevitably lose. Along the way, he loses his sons and his wife. Will (Lou Brown) rejects his father's offer of a partnership in the family business and goes off to work for Haywood; Michael (Simon Burke), disturbed by the turmoil within his family and disillusioned with his father, goes off to work for an arrogant station owner named Dalgleish. Michael is clearly looking for a surrogate father figure in Dalgleish, but when he discovers in Dalgleish a destructive pride much like that of his father, Michael goes off to the lumber camps to find Paddy.

Paddy has gone there because one evening his wounded pride, aided by alcohol, caused him to destroy his family. Wounded by what he saw as Will's betrayal of him when the boy went to work for Haywood, Paddy angrily curses his son as a "Judas" and a "mongrel." When Paddy's wife tries to intervene, Paddy strikes her. Will strikes his father, causing Paddy to mercilessly beat Will. Then, Michael jumps in to save Will from further brutality. Finally, with his anger spent, Paddy leaves home.

Before we return to the story of Michael and Paddy, we should note the sexist context in which Paddy's assault on his wife occurs. Although the oppression of women is not a major theme in the film, it is nonetheless noticeable: in Paddy's assault and also in the earlier comments of a Mrs. Clark, a frustrated neighbor woman who tells Will that she feels suppressed—like nothing more than a brood mare—in what she labels "a man's world." The oppression is also evident in Will's seduction of Bobo, an aboriginal girl the Clarks have evidently adopted. When their liaison and the fact that she is pregnant with Will's child are discovered, he flees rather than assuming responsibility. That he feels remorse when Bobo dies while miscarrying the child hardly compensates for his seduction and abandonment of the girl, who is doubly oppressed as female and as aboriginal.

Toward the film's end, we feel that Paddy is also quite oppressed—by the changing times and by his pride and what that pride has caused him to do. He says he is leaving his Venus Battery home for Queensland to sell the team. But he cannot bring himself to sell the horses. So, he drifts from job to job, being replaced repeatedly by the more efficient trucks. When Michael catches up with Paddy, Paddy is a broken man. Nonetheless, he offers his younger son a partnership in the family business: "Doolan and Son, Teamsters." Before Michael has the opportunity to persuade his father to return home, a lorry runs Paddy and his team off the road and over a bridge. Paddy dies when he crashes on the rocks below.

Paddy loses his battle, as he must. Small, melodramatic touches of consolation are offered by Michael as the movie ends. Michael insists that Paddy's tombstone read "Patrick Doolan, Teamster"; he also tells his mother that Paddy was indeed heading off to sell the team and then home to her when the fatal accident occurred.

Fatalism is one of the defining traits of the traditional Australian hero: he typically fights on, knowing that eventually he will lose (O'Regan, *Australian* 235). In *The Irishman*, Crombie offers a broader fatalism, for there is a strong sense communicated in the film that the very idea of this kind of hero is fading. We heard that note also in *Sunday Too Far Away* and will hear it as well in Tim Burstall's *The Last of the Knucklemen*.

THE LAST OF THE KNUCKLEMEN (TIM BURSTALL, DIRECTOR, 1979)

Many of the films, especially ones of the AFC Genre, that first brought Australia to the attention of the movie-going world were male ensemble films.

Sunday Too Far Away is a good example, as is Tim Burstall's *The Last of the Knucklemen*. Because the earlier film focuses so much on the character Foley, we get less of the ensemble than we do in the latter, in which the central character named Tarzan (Gerard Kennedy) is not as dominant. As a result, we get a richer look at the male-defined culture of Australia in *The Last of the Knucklemen*.

The men in *Knucklemen* are not shearers; rather, they are miners at a wildcat mine near Andamooka. They live together in a bunkhouse. And, again unlike *Sunday Too Far Away*, which stages much of the action at the site (i.e., the shearing shed) where the men work, *Knucklemen* stages much of the action at the site where they spend their off-work time.

As the film begins, we think the defining tension will be between Tarzan and a man from another work gang named Carl, who has challenged Tarzan to a fistfight. That fight will eventually almost take place, but, by that time, the true defining tension will have long since developed between Tarzan and Pansy (Michael Preston). Thus, the climactic fight will pit Tarzan against Pansy, not Carl.

We meet Pansy at the very beginning of the film. He gets into a scuffle with his university-educated, city-bred supervisor and knocks him unconscious. Although Pansy was clearly in the wrong, the men all quit when Pansy is fired—exhibiting mateship. They do so because Pansy is their mate and, probably, because they share some of Pansy's anti-intellectual, antiurban attitude. In the course of Pansy's fight with the supervisor, Pansy calls him a poofter (vague Australian slang for either a homosexual or someone sufficiently effeminate to maybe be one). Pansy's mates also share his prejudice against all poofters.

Tarzan's role in the film is to keep these men in line. Fortunately, he is sufficiently one of them to have their respect and be able to do the job. Only Pansy resists, but he is alone in his resistance because Tarzan is a mate, not an outsider.

The bunkhouse where the men live is very present in the film, which departs from what was becoming the Australian cinematic norm and makes very little use of the surrounding landscape (Rattigan 175). We witness the drinking, the pornography, and the gambling there. Gradually, the characters become individuated. Besides Pansy and Tarzan, three others are of note. One is an ex-monk. The mates give him a hard time when he will not join them in what almost seems to be the obligatory (in such Australian movies) male nude swimming scene and when he will not join them as they visit the itinerant prostitutes who have come to the mining town. Also, when he does not fully join in the drinking, they baptize him, in Latin, with beer. The ex-monk's presence in the bunkhouse permits Burstall to sketch more fully what characterizes its dominant male culture—unabashed pride in one's male body; sex for sex's sake; beer.

The second interesting character is a rather quiet man named Tom. He also does not fully join in the mates' fun and games. However, they let him be until he defends the ex-monk when he refuses to go visit the prostitutes and declines to go himself because he wants to read and reread a letter he just received from his child. Pansy threatens to get even with Tom later, but for what is ambiguous—for defending the ex-monk, for being sentimental about the letter, or for not joining in with the men in their demonstration (perhaps proof) of their masculinity.

The third interesting character is an old man nicknamed Methusaleh. There are, throughout the movie, hints that he is ill and dying. Nonetheless, he talks about his upcoming retirement, for which he has saved $3,000. Pansy talks Methusaleh into a card game. As the stakes get higher and higher, Tarzan tries to stop the game. But the men do not let him: the gambling culture proves stronger than Tarzan. The game ends with Pansy's winning—his straight flush beating four kings—all of Methusaleh's savings. When Tarzan expresses his displeasure, saying they are all mates, Pansy rejects the very idea of mateship. Pansy says he is looking out for "number one." Shortly thereafter, the old man discovers quiet Tom's true identity. Tom is the "Karate Bandit," for whom there is—coincidentally—a $3,000 reward. Methusaleh, however, does not put his need for money ahead of mateship; he does not turn Tom in for the reward.

Pansy, meanwhile, looking out for "number one," tries to arrange the fistfight between Tarzan and the outsider Carl. Pansy, handling the bets, will take a cut. Pansy also discovers Tom's identity and conspires with Carl to turn Tom in for the reward. That he has done so becomes known just as the fight between Tarzan and Carl is about to begin. At that point, Pansy and Carl jointly become the enemies. Tom takes on Carl—as it turns out, for the money, and Tarzan takes on Pansy—just to teach him a thing or two about being mates. Tarzan easily wins, and Tom shows why he is called the "Karate Bandit" when he bests the much brawnier Carl. Tom then gives his winnings to Methusaleh, the true mate who did not turn him in; and all of the loyal mates conspire to help Tom escape before the authorities arrive.

Like both Foley in *Sunday Too Far Away* and Doolan in *the Irishman*, Tarzan communicates a sense that his heroism is nearly over. He is aging; thus, Carl thought Tarzan no longer invincible. And the film's title does label Tarzan as "the last." There is then a dose of fatalism offered by Burstall's film. However, it is far more optimistic than Crombie's *The Irishman*, for Tarzan wins and, more important, mateship wins. In fact, the bunkroom culture that Tarzan embodies—for good or for ill—wins. At least for the moment, the men who freely roam from mine, to mine defying authority, putting down intellectuals, loving their drink, visiting their whores, and, most important, being loyal to their mates and their valorized hero Tarzan prove triumphant.

SQUIZZY TAYLOR (KEVIN DOBSON, DIRECTOR, 1982)

Kevin Dobson's *Squizzy Taylor* is set in the 1920s in Melbourne. Thus, the setting is quite different from the ones in the other three films about criminals discussed to this point. Those films—*Ned Kelly* and *Mad Dog Morgan*—all take place in the nineteenth century and all in the countryside and small towns of Victoria and New South Wales. Squizzy (David Atkins) might then be characterized as what the bushranger type might be like if transformed, in a time-and-place machine, to the next century and the big city. And like the bushranger of old, Squizzy was legendary and largely viewed positively by the masses. That positive view had, however, nothing to do with stealing from the rich and giving to the poor; rather, it stemmed from his humble origins, the corruption and arrogance of the authorities, and the way the newspapers presented him as defying that authority. Squizzy terms himself a "newspaper hero." What he does not mention, however, is the extent to which he personally manipulated the newspapers so they would present him to the masses in a positive light.

Squizzy is thus more modern than even the twentieth-century heroes Foley and Tarzan insofar as he knows how to work with the media. He is also, perhaps, more modern insofar as he looks out primarily for "number one." Having said that, one also needs to note that once Squizzy has built his urban gang, he refers to them as his mates and looks after them as mates.

The plot of Dobson's film is sometimes difficult to follow: perhaps the screenplay writer Roger Simpson and the director assume that the audience already knows the outlines of Taylor's life; perhaps the film plays off of the audience's familiarity with the true story in much the same way Tony Richardson's *Ned Kelly* does. Basically, Squizzy parlays his way to the top of the Melbourne underworld through a canny combination of conspiring with fellow crooks, manipulating police and media to serve his ends, and double-crossing anyone and everyone when he has the power to do so. He competes, using whatever tools are necessary to gain ultimate control of the city's rackets. If one valorizes criminals—and Australia certainly does that to some extent—then one can so valorize Squizzy because he is good at playing the criminal game.

As long as he plays it well, he has the freedom of power and money. He can defy, even mock, the authorities that he is outwitting. He can delight in the fact that he, who had very little to start with, now has the city of Melbourne at his command; he can delight in the fact that he, with very little education, has consistently outsmarted the better-educated agents of law enforcement and the newspapers. On his way up, Squizzy was very much the underdog, and, before his life begins unraveling, he can delight in his underdog's triumph. Perhaps a literal reflection of Squizzy's underdog status is his height—5'2", something he is very aware of, maybe even pathologically so.

Women play an important part in Squizzy's story. It is difficult to pin down his attitude toward them: at times, they are possessions and thus objectified; at other times, they are people he genuinely cares about. The story of Dolly (Jacki Weaver) illustrates this conflict within Squizzy well. Early in his criminal career, Dolly is the sometimes-lover whom Squizzy pimps for. She seems special to him, but, nonetheless, he has no problem using her body as a commodity to gain money. When Squizzy conspires with crime boss Stokes to double-cross another crime boss, Whiting, Whiting's partner Cutmore gets revenge on Squizzy by having Dolly gang-raped. Squizzy then violently retaliates, but his motivation is unclear: Does he seek revenge because Dolly, whom he cares for, was brutalized? Or does he seek revenge because Dolly, his property, was trespassed upon? The answer is not clear: Squizzy seems to waver between a sexist view of women and a more enlightened one. Similarly, he seems to genuinely love his wife Ida, but does not think twice about characterizing her unflatteringly as a mull (a common woman) in conversation with his mates.

This wavering suggests that, try as he might to create the illusion of control, Squizzy is really as much acted upon as acting. In fact, some of his success as a gangster is due to the debilitating rivalry in the Melbourne police force between two detectives: Piggott and Brophy. The one views Taylor as evil; the other as a useful agent who can be manipulated to do the police's bidding. The conflict between these views paralyzes the police. Adding to the conflict is the fact that the latter man is somewhat corrupt. As we view this conflict, we realize that it is only a matter of time before it is resolved or Squizzy goes too far or both. And both it proves to be as Brophy orchestrates a violent shootout that takes out both Taylor and Cutmore. We sense, long before Squizzy does, that his run will eventually end.

In some ways, Squizzy is reminiscent of Ned Kelly and Daniel Morgan. Kelly puts on his armor suit and defies the authorities, and Morgan marches toward the assembled police of Victoria. Pride contributes to both bushrangers' deaths. Similarly, Squizzy keeps pushing for greater glory. Ida begs him to quit, but he seems to need that glory, whether because competing and winning are in his blood or because he must compensate for his short stature is difficult to determine.

ROBBERY UNDER ARMS (DONALD CROMBIE AND KEN HANNAM, 1985)

This production is, of course, not the first rendering of the story of bushranger Captain Starlight. His story has been the subject of several works of fiction and four other films—so much so that Starlight's story, together with that of Ned Kelly, establishes in the Australian culture what a bushranger is. As a discussion of Crombie and Hannam's film and Tony Richardson's *Ned Kelly* show, the bushranger type could run the gamut from one social class extreme to another. Starlight (Sam Neill) is at the upper-class end of that spectrum. And he uses his upper-class upbringing to advantage during his crime spree. In the film's first scene, for example, he boards a train as a well-dressed gentleman. Then, after his compatriots stop the train using the trick of setting up a mirror in the train's path so the engineer will believe he is on the verge of a head-on collision, Starlight reveals his thieving purpose and escapes with the other gentlemen's valuables. In a late scene, he masquerades as Charles Lasalles, a member of the British nobility. In that role, Starlight hobnobs with the town elite, distracts the townspeople while his cronies rob the bank, and then wins the Falkland Cup aboard his beloved horse Rainbow.

Starlight's upper-class status and his money give him the freedom to move throughout Australian society. He can hobnob with the elite; he can also relate well with the Marston brothers Jim (Christopher Cummins) and Dick (Steven Vidler), their sister Aileen (Jane Menelaus), and aboriginal mate Warrigal (Tommy Lewis). In doing so, Starlight defies the class structure that exists in Australia—so much so that the police chief who is pursuing Starlight after Starlight wins the Falkland Cup and hurriedly flees town says he hates Starlight primarily because the bushranger has let his upper class down by befriending Australia's downtrodden.

Starlight defies authority at every turn. He also, despite the fact that he is British, acts irreverently toward the Queen, offering ironic toasts to her. But even he has to admit that the forces of authority are sufficiently strong in Australia to make total freedom there impossible. Thus, toward the film's end, Starlight joins Jim Marston and his wife Jeannie, Dick Marston and his wife Gracey, Aileen Marston (whom he will marry), and the Marston siblings' father in planning an escape to the greater freedom of the United States. The "Land of the Free" would offer Starlight a more congenial environment because the evils inherent in a strong social class structure have poisoned Australia.

Starlight never makes it to the United States, but he is willing to go. In being so, he seems not as attuned to the land as the typical traditional hero. Yes, he can handle himself in the wild just as well as in the parlor car or at a posh dance, but he does seem rather detached from the land he inhabits. Being British, not Australian, partially explains this detachment. So, to bring the idea of being attached to the land more strongly into the film, the directors stress aboriginal mate Warrigal's deep attachment to the land. When the Marstons and their various wives and husbands decide to leave Australia, Warrigal accusingly says they—and the white man in general—have no sense of the land. Warrigal says that his spirit will die if he leaves the land. Nonetheless, he does agree to leave with his mate Starlight. When he experiences inner pain when crossing from New South Wales to Queensland, he decides to thwart the Marstons' planned escape, and thereby his mate's departure, by informing the authorities as to Jim and Dick's planned crossing into Queensland. When Starlight finds out what Warrigal has done, he rushes to Jim and Dick's defense, which turns into an against-the-odds battle as the three of them take on the troops. The result is the death of Jim Marston and Captain Starlight and the capture and subsequent imprisonment of Dick Marston.

Mateship of course played a role in Warrigal's regretted decision to flee the country with Starlight. And Warrigal is a loyal mate until the end, as we see him crying over Starlight's dead body after the battle with the troops. Mateship shows up throughout the film. When Starlight is captured, Warrigal and Dick Marston rescue him; when Jim Marston is captured, Dick (the elder Marston) and Starlight rescue him. And, after the entourage has decided to go to the United States, Starlight and Dick decide to pull off one more "job," ostensibly to "raise" the money necessary for the voyage. Jim puts his mates ahead of his new wife and new baby and joins Starlight and Dick in a daring bank robbery.

Robbery under Arms was produced simultaneously for television and motion picture release. Doing so rarely produces both good television and good film. However, in this case, both are adequate, although the film has an episodic rhythm often characteristic of television drama (Stratton, *Avocado* 71–72). The fact that *Robbery under Arms* was produced for both media was probably why some of the characteristics of the Australian hero were toned down. There is not much emphasis on the hero's love of drink. We do see Jim and Dick pursuing two English girls they met in Adelaide. The brothers go as far as to masquerade as rich squatters during a sea journey from Adelaide to Sydney in order to seduce Jeannie and Kate. The brothers very much see the girls as prizes to be won, and, at least initially, the brothers are far more interested in talking the English girls into bed than in proposing marriage. The sexism implicit in this pursuit, however, is muted by other more positive male-female relationships depicted in the movie: the one that eventually develops between Jim and Jeannie, the one between Starlight and Aileen Marston, and the one between Dick and Gracey. I emphasize the last because it is the most fully developed relationship, it features the most fully developed female character, and it endures as Dick and Gracey marry after Dick is released from prison twelve years after the battle that killed Jim and Starlight.

If drunkenness and sexism are downplayed a bit, anti-British sentiments are not. Starlight has very little good to say about his native countrymen. He sings the praises of the land; but his dislike of English elitism is so deep that he hides—virtually renounces—his noble identity. Throughout the movie, small instances of anti-British sentiment pop up. When the heroes rescue Jim from jail, the very English-acting police condescendingly refer to the Marston clan as "colonials." The Australian audience would, of course, resent this condescension. When Dick is thought to be dead early in the movie after he falls off a cliff and into a body of water along with the fellow convict he was chained to, a priest assures Dick's mother that her son is in purgatory, not hell, for God will know that he was driven to his crimes by the detestable actions of the British Empire.

Those actions result in the Australians being underdogs in the movie. The audience feels that they are always fighting against forces that outnumber them. Perhaps the only thing that keeps them in the game is Starlight's refusal to accept that Australians were born to be good losers. He—perhaps because he is not Australian—will not accept the Australians' fatalism. He keeps pushing his Australians to win. However, in the end, even Starlight finds defeat and death when the numbers are overwhelmingly against the Marston brothers and himself in their battle at the border between New South Wales and Queensland.

Before Starlight joins the underdog Australians in this defeat, he joins them in competing. Each crime they embark on is an adventure. And each time, the level of bravado must increase: Starlight masquerades as a gentleman and uses a mirror to stop and rob a train; Starlight sells cattle that are not his to sell; the boys rescue him from jail using a hot-air balloon; and Starlight masquerades as a British earl while the boys use an elephant to pull down the back wall of a bank. Starlight and the boys seem intent on outdoing their previous criminal adventure as if competing for bigger and bigger headlines.

Starlight's being British and upper class mutes a few of the traits of the traditional Australian hero. So does the fact that *Robbery under Arms* was produced for both television and motion picture purposes. Nonetheless, Starlight and the Marston boys largely embody this hero. They show us what that hero looks like if a little bit of class and romance are added to it—the class being largely that of the dashing Starlight; the romance being that between the basically good Dick Marston and the very strong-willed Gracey.

Chapter 3

The Revised Hero

The eight heroes discussed in the preceding chapter evoke different reactions from audiences. There are traits to admire in them, even in an ocker like "Bazza" McKenzie. However, there are also reasons to reject them all as suitable models for a twentieth-century culture that is trying, via film, to discover and then present its idea of heroism. After all, these heroes of old are criminals. Or they exhibit a heroism that is passe. Or their heroism is either too comic or too coarse to be taken seriously.

So, the task of the filmmakers becomes to extract from these heroes those elements that are noble and, then, smooth away the rough edges that keep us from embracing them fully. The many films that are discussed in this chapter do just that and thereby present a hero suitable for late twentieth-century Australia. This hero will not prove to be identical in all of these films. In fact, there will be a good bit of variation as we move from Tony Petersen in Tim Burstall's *Petersen* (1974) and the scapegoated Aussie soldiers in Bruce Beresford's *Breaker Morant* (1980) to Albert Einstein in Yahoo Serious' *Young Einstein* (1988) and Darryl Kerrigan in Rob Sitch's *The Castle* (1997). Each hero, however, has certain core characteristics in common with the others, characteristics based on the traits identified at the beginning of Chapter 1. In fact, each listed trait could be repeated here but qualified so as to be sanitized.

Before I look at fourteen films that exhibit this revised heroism, I want to examine a small set of five films. These films go where the movies surveyed in Chapter 1 could not. They do not imply that there is something problematic with the heroism of old. Through nightmare and farce, these films clearly illustrate why the hero and the heroism of old need to be updated.

There is a strong suggestion in much film and literature that true Australian heroism is to be found in the outback. There are two problems with the suggestion: first, "outback" is a slippery term, meaning different things to different people and different things at different times; second, at least some elements of the outback myth, especially those chronicled in Russel Ward's classic study, may be much more an urban dream than a rural reality. Poorly defined and contested, the suggestion is nonetheless "out there." And, of the movies discussed in Chapter 1, only *The Adventures of Barry McKenzie* (1972) and *Squizzy Taylor* (1982) seem removed from this outback myth. None of the six other films confront the myth head-on. In fact, they all imply that at least there was something heroic out there, before it became corrupted or times changed. *Walkabout*, which is discussed in Chapter 5, even goes so far as to portray the outback in Edenic terms (Rattigan 307–8).

WAKE IN FRIGHT (A.K.A. *OUTBACK*) (TED KOTCHEFF, DIRECTOR, 1971)

Canadian Ted Kotcheff's *Wake in Fright* addresses this outback myth head-on. Kotcheff's outback is hell, and nothing heroic seems to grow out of life there. In fact, what emerges is perverse, not heroic at all.

The central character in *Wake in Fright* is schoolteacher John Grant (Gary Bond). He teaches in an outback town named Tiboonda. As a 360-degree camera pan reveals at the film's beginning, there is nothing but bleak desert near this town. Because of the terms of the educational loan Grant took out to finance his tertiary education, he is virtually trapped in Tiboonda. Thus, come vacation, he flees—for Sydney and his beautiful girlfriend. However, he never makes it to Sydney. He stops overnight in Bundandybee in the Yabba before catching a flight eastward. The film chronicles the descent into hell he experiences in this outback town.

Upon arriving in the town by train, he takes a taxi to his hotel. The cab driver tells him that the Yabba is "the best place in Australia." We find the evaluation comically incorrect, given what we have seen of Bundandybee; however, we will not realize how ironic the comment is until John Grant's story unfolds. The "Imperial Hotel" proves seedy, but its huge pub has hundreds of sweaty Australian males in it, "shouting drinks" (buying drinks for oneself and his mates). A police officer named Jock befriends John Grant and gets him fed and gets him drunk. Then, he is lured into an illegal two-up game. Initially, Grant wins—almost enough to pay off his loan and get him out of Tiboonda. So, he keeps gambling and ends up losing all that he had won and all that he had brought with him to pay for his vacation in Sydney.

John Grant (Gary Bond) waiting to leave Tiboonda on holiday in *Wake in Fright* (1971). Photo courtesy of National Film and Sound Archives. Permission granted by Anthony Buckley.

The next day, at the pub, he meets Tim Heinz, who orders Grant to drink and then takes Grant home. There, Grant meets Heinz' daughter Janette and a growing group of Tim Heinz' mates. Grant drinks and drinks—after all this is the "true" Australia. He ends up cozying up to Janette. The mates wonder why he would prefer to talk with a woman than with the men. When they hear he is a schoolteacher, they understand: evidently effeminacy is an undesirable but understandable consequence of higher education. When Grant goes outside with Janette, she propositions him, but in the midst of sex, he vomits—surfeited on beer and, perhaps, her body.

The next day, he wakes up in the house of an alcoholic doctor (Donald Pleasence), who tells him that Janette has had "a go" with most of the men in the town. He then goes kangaroo hunting with Doc Tydon and two of his mates. During a daylight sequence, they drive maniacally, sic a violently aggressive dog on a kangaroo, and then ritualistically eat the kangaroo's testicles. During an even scarier nightime sequence, they shoot many animals and then one of the ockers and Grant kill kangaroos in hand-to-hand combat, finally slitting the poor animals' throats. The sequence ends with a shot of dead kangaroo carcasses left lying in the dirt. The night ends with the mates' breaking into a pub (for more to drink) and John being raped by the doctor.

The next day, in a stupor, John tries to escape Bundandybee. He ends up in Silverton in New South Wales. There, he trades the shotgun his outback mates had given him as a present for a ride to "the city" with a truck driver, who orders John to have a drink with him before they depart. Unfortunately, the city the driver had in mind was Bundandybee, not Sydney. John is so desperate at that point that he attempts suicide; he does not succeed. Compelling John to sign a statement that covers up the suicide attempt, the police officer and the alcoholic doctor put him on the train headed back to Tiboonda. On the way out of Tiboonda, several ocker types on the train had invited John to join them in a drink. He had declined. Now, on the way back, what looks like the same group invites him and he assents. The suggestion is that he has surrendered himself to the outback.

And what kind of place is this outback that John Grant has surrendered himself to? It is a place where the consumption of alcohol and competition, as seen in the gambling and kangaroo-hunting episodes, are both manias. It is a place where sex is sickening and violent. It is a place where mateship is a deranged fraternity. It is a place that entraps rather than offers freedom. It is a place that replaces traditional authority with people who command you to drink. The land is desolate, not a land to love; and instead of noble horses, we have slaughtered kangaroos. And John, rather than being an underdog who finally gives way to stronger forces, is a helpless victim trapped in a hell from the moment the film begins. In sum, this place is not the breeding ground of heroes.

SURRENDER IN PARADISE (PETER COX, DIRECTOR, 1976)

Less nightmarish is Peter Cox's curious, very low-budget ($30,000) *Surrender in Paradise* (Pike and Cooper 305). I say "curious" because the film is a bizarre rewriting of the bushranger story we saw in movies such as *Ned Kelly* (1970), *Mad Dog Morgan* (1977), and *Robbery under Arms* (1985). It is bizarre because it is parodic but one is never sure of precisely what.

The bushranger hero in *Surrender in Paradise* is Rusty Swan (Ross Gilbert). Much as Ned Kelly was attached to his mother, so is Swan. And the journey the film takes him on is to see his mother, whose health is reported to be failing. The troops who have been mounted against Swan are so comically incompetent that we have very little doubt that he and his mates will find their way to his mother's side.

En route, curious things happen. The road turns from dirt to paved to paved with double white lines to paved with four lanes and entrance and exit ramps. The gang's mode of transportation also changes—from horses to a late 1940s Hudson to an early 1960s Plymouth Valiant to a late 1960s Pontiac Bonneville to a more recent Holden wagon. As they progress eastward, they play "I Spy" and have a contest to see how many different model cars they can spot and name. When they finally get to Rusty's mother's place, it turns out to be a high-rise condominium somewhere on Queensland's "Gold Coast." Once there, Dulcie, whom the gang left whining behind, arrives to join them in a 1970s-vintage jet.

The police follow, experiencing similar disorienting changes. As they speed down the expressway, with their stereotypical aboriginal tracker now in the backseat, a reggae band plays "Follow." Earlier, Rusty's gang was rallied by the Monkees' song (written by Neil Diamond) "I'm a Believer." Once at the Gold Coast, the police stay at the "Siesta Motel" and steel themselves for their confrontation the next day by watching *Dirty Harry* on television.

Rusty's mother is dying. She tells her son to surrender and, in keeping with the Christmas season, start his life anew: so he does. The police, however, are prepared to hang Rusty on the spot—so much for any rebirth. Then, the film dissolves in confusion. A character named "Raw Meat" (Don McAlpine; a noted cinematographer who was the cinematographer for this film) rescues Rusty, but a shoot-out, during which tourists come and go oblivious to the danger, ensues, leaving all the characters from former times dead—literally—in the water.

Surrender in Paradise is obviously a parody of some sort. The incongruity between the characters and their new surroundings is handled comically—for example, when gang member Valda is told she cannot drive the Holden wagon because she does not have a license, as if the rest do. But one senses that the film is not just a series of jokes. A country song played about halfway through the film offers a clue. Its lyrics contrast the way things used to be and the way they are now. They note that we have forgotten how good everything once was and are not adequately aware of how everything today is but a cheap facade of what it used to be. Taking that song as a clue, we might interpret the film as not rejecting the heroism of old but as showing how it is no longer viable. Today, we have, at best, a superficial version of that old heroism. The problem with this reading of the film is that Rusty Swan, even in the film's earliest frames, never seems noble. So, the song leads us to bemoan—as country songs often do—the heroism lost, whereas the film's images lead us to reject even that heroism. We are then left with an idea that is as dead as all the bodies floating in the Pacific Ocean at the film's conclusion.

DON'S PARTY (BRUCE BERESFORD, DIRECTOR, 1976)

Neither *Wake in Fright* nor *Surrender in Paradise* is particularly realistic. The former exaggerates in a nightmarish direction; the latter in a parodic. Bruce Beresford's *Don's Party*, however, is very realistic—as realistic as the David Williamson play on which the film is based. Nonetheless, the film, like the other two, undermines the bases of the heroism of old, although audiences—at least in Australia—tended to interpret the movie as celebrating a kind of heroism, not satirizing it (Rattigan 115).

Don's Party targets neither the outback nor the bushranger hero; rather, its target is the ocker. If nothing else, the film shows that not all ockers are as poorly educated as Barry McKenzie. Some have university degrees and even postgraduate degrees: the males who attend Don's party include an accountant, a psychologist, a dentist, and a lawyer.

The party is being held to celebrate what Don Henderson (John Hargreaves) imagines will be the victory of the Labor Party over the Liberal (what Americans would term "Conservative") Party in the 1969 election. Just as the election turns sour over the party's several hours, so does the party itself.

Sexism surfaces early when Mack shows up, newly separated from his wife and flaunting poster-size nude pictures of her. Then, the men huddle to tell off-color jokes, speculate about who among them will score that night with Kerry, and declare repeatedly what the Liberal Jody needs in the bedroom so that she will embrace the Labor cause. Then Cooley arrives with his latest girlfriend, the free-spirited, nineteen- or twenty-year-old Susan. It is not too long before the men strip her naked, throw her into Don's pool, and jump in after her.

As the gathered men turn sexual predators, they drink more and more. This drinking culminates in a scene not very far removed from one in *The Adventures of Barry McKenzie* with the men publicly urinating on Don's grapevines or tomato plants. The women, meanwhile, talk. Their conversation becomes increasingly sexually frank. The free-spirited Susan ultimately declares that all men are pigs, and their conversation turns to lesbian lovemaking before the men interrupt it. There is no real suggestion in the film that the women's conversation would have led any of them down the lesbian path; rather, there is the suggestion that the men's sexism and crude behavior almost leave women no other choice.

In the course of *Don's Party*, sex becomes a wicked game as drinking drives the men deeper and deeper into the depths of ockerism. In these depths, the Australian competitive spirit and the sacred institution of mateship are both revealed as shallow. The men, while relatively sober, compete: they one-up each other with stories about sexual and business exploits. Once drunk, the truth comes out: they are all, as Don terms it, "bullshit artists"; they are all failures who have not achieved their ambitions the same way the Labor Party is not achieving its goals that night. The men, while relatively sober, act as mates. But as the night wears on, mateship first becomes a transparent facade and then falls away completely. Even Don and Mal, mates since university days, end up fighting about the money Mal and Jenny have borrowed from Don and Kath and the borrowing couple's extravagance. In the midst of this argument, Don and Mal propose that they swap wives for the night—evidently a long-cherished fantasy of theirs. This suggestion reveals what has been rather apparent from very early in the film: that the marital relationships in the film are just as flimsy as the mateship relationships. Kath ends up accusing Don of, paradoxically, requiring her maternal care while regulating her life and behavior like an overly stern father.

The film ends the morning after with Don, beer cans still in hand, surveying the damage. Just as his garden is literally wrecked, so are marriages and mateships. The film, like Williamson's play, functions as a satire of Australian suburban lifestyles and mores in the supposedly liberated late 1960s. But the film and play go deeper and undermine some of the elements that the Australian culture and traditional Australian heroism are based on. Sexism and drinking come across as ugly; competition as empty; mateship as an easily pierced facade.

RAZORBACK (NICHOLAS MULCAHY, DIRECTOR, 1984)

Nicholas Mulcahy moved from directing music videos to directing feature films with *Razorback*. The film is in many ways an Australian rendition of *Jaws* (Rattigan 261). Perhaps *Razorback* even is a send-up of the entire horror genre (Helen Barlow in Murray, *Australian Film* 151; O'Regan, *Australian* 173). But rather than having a great white shark terrorizing a Long Island beach community, *Razorback* has a giant boar terrorizing an outback town. The creature has claimed at least two victims: a small boy and an American journalist. The boy's grandfather (Bill Kerr), whom the town still blames for the boy's disappearance, and the journalist's husband (played by popular American actor Gregory Harrison) lead the charge against the larger-than-life boar. Joining them is scientist Sarah Cameron (Arkie Whiteley). Some will draw parallels between the older man, Jake Cullen, and Quint in *Jaws* and between the duo formed by husband Carl and Sarah and the duo formed by sheriff (Roy Schneider) and scientist (Richard Dreyfuss) in *Jaws*. Following through on these structural parallels, Jack dies at the razorback's jaws, while Carl and Sarah desperately battle the giant boar and ultimately win.

This account of Mulcahy's film certainly does the plot justice as well as highlighting the extent to which Hollywood formulas are having their effect on Australian movies. But the *Jaws*-like story line is really not what is most interesting about *Razorback*.

One interesting dimension, perhaps more relevant to the next chapter, is the portrayal of Sarah Cameron. Australian films have created an environment in which viewers are predisposed to see the leading male figure as the hero and the female figures primarily as sex objects. *Razorback* seems to follow this pattern. Once the American Carl Winters arrives on the scene to investigate (and perhaps avenge) his wife's death, viewers assign him the heroic role. When Sarah is introduced to viewers, we see her very much through Carl's eyes. And we see her nude in an outdoor shower. Thus, we assign her the sex object role and fully expect that she and Carl will at some point in the film become lovers. The film, however, after having set up these expectations, undermines them. Sarah, once dressed, reveals herself to be a highly technologically literate biological researcher; and she and Carl very much together play the heroic role. One might even argue that she plays the role more fully insofar as she has the brains to track the boar and the spirit to rally the town's rather lackadaisical men to the cause. Furthermore, her role, as it pertains to Carl is very much friend and comforter. She recognizes the pain he is experiencing, because his wife's murder—and, as it turns out, near rape—that has brought him halfway around the world.

The other interesting dimension is very relevant to this chapter. To grasp it, we need to shift our focus from the film's plot to its scene: the outback town. That town is presented in terms not that different from the ones we saw in *Wake in Fright*. Bundandybee is much larger than Gamulla in *Razorback*, but both places are hellish. The major occupation of the (male) residents seems to be hanging around the hotel/pub and drinking. Despite the sexist welcome Beth Winters receives from them, these men seem relatively benign, too much in an alcohol-induced stupor to be much of a threat to her or anyone. More like the mates we meet in Kotcheff's film—right down to the nighttime kangaroo hunting—are the Baker brothers: Benny and Dicko. They drink as do the men at the hotel/pub, but the drink and the isolation and the whatever else of outback life have driven both of them over the edge to the point at which they are as much of a menace as the giant boar. In fact, Beth Winters was both their victim and the boar's. They forced her car off the road, they stripped her, and they began raping her; then, they were interrupted by the boar's appearance. The boar finished what they had begun, goaring Beth to death with its phallic-like tusks.

Benny (Chris Haywood) and Dicko (David Argue), grotesque outback ockers, are in fact implicated throughout the film's *Jaws*-like plot. One of them is beating Jake before the boar appears. Carl and Sarah must defeat them at the same time that they are battling against the giant razorback. Outback as menace and boar as menace very much coalesce in the film—so much so that one might even argue that the razorback symbolizes the evils the outback can create. Here, *Razorback* and *Jaws* part company because it seems quite a stretch to suggest that the great white shark in the American movie symbolizes any evil from within the culture that can threaten the nation's people or psyche. Thus, *Razorback*, although not as well-done a film as *Jaws*, may actually be a far more profound movie.

Both films end on "happy" notes. The menaces are dead; the heroes return to town scarred from battle but safe. However, as we all know, it was not quite yet safe to go back in the water because a sequel to *Jaws* was in the offing. No sequel was made to *Razorback*. However, there is a similar sense of unease at its end. The particular razorback was a freak of nature, but one that might reoccur. More important, Benny and Dicko were menaces that the outback might produce again. Sarah's ability to rally the town's men to join in the attempt to defeat the boar should not be viewed as her having overcome permanently the outback's stultifying effect on these men. The next day, one envisions them back in the pub. And from their midst might well soon spring the next Benny or the next Dicko.

RECKLESS KELLY (YAHOO SERIOUS, DIRECTOR, 1993)

The films discussed thus far in this chapter have different tones. As a result, the indictments they offer of the bases of traditional Australian heroism come across differently. *Wake in Fright* and *Razorback* are somewhat similar, although the former's nightmarish quality is unrelieved by any uplifting victory. *Don's Party* is satiric, not nightmarish, but the satire is vicious. *Surrender in Paradise*, on the other hand, is more jocular in its satirical parody of the bushranger hero and its commentary on how times have changed in Australia for the worse. There are many gags in *Surrender in Paradise* that help lighten its tone. Somewhat similar to *Surrender in Paradise* is Yahoo Serious' 1993 film *Reckless Kelly*.

Like Tony Richardson's *Ned Kelly*, *Reckless Kelly* deals with the legendary bushranger hero; like *Surrender in Paradise*, *Reckless Kelly* is set in the present day, not in the nineteenth century. We do not, however, travel forward to the present in Serious' film; rather, we are in the present day from the motion picture's very beginning.

We meet Ned and the rest of the Kelly Gang as they are robbing ATM machines, not banks per se. They are doing so because it is less likely that innocent people will get hurt if they hold up the machines. And they are still giving their loot to the poor. Therefore, as in the earlier century, they are very much national heroes based on their philanthropy and on their defiance of the establishment.

The banks strike back in Serious' film. Discovering the semitropical island where the Kelly gang lives, the banks sell it out from underneath the Kellys to an Asian country. The Kellys retaliate by declaring the island to be aboriginal land (and themselves, Irish although they might be, to have aboriginal roots) and thereby stopping the sale. Serious is, of course, offering a comic glance at the aboriginal land rights controversies of the 1980s, the irreverence of which might not please progressive thinkers in Australia. But such is Serious' humor, and the irreverence cuts in all directions, as we shall see.

The Kellys' move proves only to be a stopgap measure. To secure their island, they need money. And since they cannot, by creed, steal Australian money to help themselves, they sent Ned off to the United States to earn the necessary cash. The scenes of the film that feature Ned Kelly in the United States play off of moments in the 1986 *Crocodile Dundee*. Here Serious is indebted to Peter Faiman's and Paul Hogan's work, but, rather curiously, Serious anticipated the Dundee films by several years and takes Ned Kelly to Los Angeles—more specifically, Hollywood—years before Paul Hogan's character ends up there in the second sequel to the 1986 hit.

Once in L.A., the Ned Kelly character becomes the focal point for satire that targets both the United States and Australia. The United States is depicted as a gun-crazed nation overrun by members of the Christian Right. Australians, on the other hand, are depicted as beer-swilling ockers, and Ned Kelly is presented as being as comically out of place in 1993 Los Angeles as Rusty Swan was in the 1976 Queensland Gold Coast.

As is true of many satirical films, sometimes the satire is more effective than at others. Furthermore, the satire, because it is so very topical, runs the risk of hitting the mark in the year the film is produced but not in later years. As a result, viewers today will probably find *Reckless Kelly* uneven in much the same way that Beresford's *The Adventures of Barry McKenzie* seems very uneven when seen now, thirty years after it was produced. One then needs to ask about the overall effect such works have. Whereas *Surrender in Paradise* leaves us with dead bodies floating on the ocean and the suggestion that old notions of heroism are not viable today (if they ever were), both *The Adventures of Barry McKenzie* and *Reckless Kelly* hit their targets, move on, and eventually move back to Australia where all proves to be well. In Beresford's film, we assume that, returned to ockerdom, Barry will thrive. In Serious' film, we witness the Kelly gang's defeat of the evil banks—a defeat partially brought about by the gang's catapulting cans of Australian beer at the invading "suits."

So, given this "happy" ending, we need to ask what Serious is saying, if anything, about Australian heroism. Given the film's very frivolous tone, one is reluctant to conclude that Serious has anything especially profound to offer in *Reckless Kelly*. However, it is rather difficult to take the character of Ned Kelly—or any bushranger character, for that matter—seriously after viewing Yahoo Serious' take on the legendary figure in this film.

Taken together, the five films I have just discussed suggest why the traditional bases for heroism in Australian film may no longer be viable. As a group, they suggest what may no longer work or work well in Australian film. However, there are still elements in the heroism of old worth revising and therefore saving. Sometimes, their redemption will entail relocation—to the arena of war, for example. But sometimes, a new arena seems unnecessary.

PETERSEN (A.K.A. *JOCK PETERSEN*) (TIM BURSTALL, DIRECTOR, 1974)

Tim Burstall's *Petersen* offers an arena only slightly different from what we have seen before. Its central character is an ocker named Tony Petersen (Jack Thompson). We oftentimes see him in ockerdom, but we also see him in the rather unlikely scene of the university. We see Petersen there because this ocker is intent on self-improvement.

Tony seems very happily married: the film begins with rather sexy domestic scenes between Tony and his wife (Jacki Weaver). However, we also learn that

Tony has had numerous extramarital affairs. Much like the more comic Alvin Purple in other Burstall films, Tony proves irresistible to the women he meets on his rounds as an electrician.

Given Tony's ockerlike sexism and infidelity, one might think he would be anything but an appealing character. However, Jack Thompson brings so much charm to the role that we actually like Petersen. Furthermore, we admire his desire to improve himself by attending university. We admire his genuine openness to new ideas, whether they be Dostoyevsky's on life or radical feminism's on sexual equality (which leads Petersen to participate in public sex with a beautiful coed). We also find ourselves very much on Petersen's side when he, like the hero of old, challenges authority. Late in the movie he will tell off librarians and police officers, but the authority figure who is at odds with Tony throughout most of the film is his rather stiffly proper English professor. This man feels threatened by Petersen's rather unorthodox ideas about literature; more important, this man feels threatened because he suspects that Tony is having an affair with his wife Trish. Trish, also in the university English department, is Tony's tutor, and, yes, they are having an affair.

Tony Petersen has entered a world that he only partially understands when he enters the university. At times, his naïveté is refreshing, although it will, we sense, eventually lead him into trouble. At a birthday party for one of his wealthy fellow students, he saves the day when a motorcycle gang crashes the party and theatens the friend, Annie, with rape. Later, he goes to Annie's side when, pregnant by her fiancé, she struggles with his request (or demand) that she have an abortion. So, Tony demonstrates that he knows how to deal with bikes and unwanted babies. However, there are other situations he cannot deal with.

His affair with Trish Kent and his final examination in his English class, which of course are entangled, are good examples. Trish likes Tony, but she tends to see their affair in purely sexual terms. Perhaps she feels too much his intellectual superior to define the relationship in any other way. Tony, on the hand, loves not so much Trish but the higher social status that she represents. When Trish proposes having Petersen's baby after she leaves her husband and then raising the child on her own, Tony cannot grasp what she proposes. She says he would not be in any way obligated, but he cannot see how he could not be obligated to help with his child. This conversation between Tony and Trish evokes tension, so does her decision to leave Australia and accept a position at Oxford. It's a "dream" position, and she suggests that she will only hold the position for a few years (although it is a potentially permanent one) and then return to Australia and the idea of having a child fathered by Tony. He simply does not grasp her reasoning. His way of thinking puts family first, hers puts family later—and that family need not include a father.

The failed examination causes the tension to explode. Husband Charles Kent fails him—perhaps out of revenge. Although university rules require that such examinations have multiple readers, Petersen finds out that that particular rule is rarely observed—although students are not privy to that secret. So, Charles can clearly get away with failing Tony. Tony wants Trish to come to his defense. When he coerces her into reading his examination, she tells him it is on the borderline between a D and an F. Thus, her assessment is of no help to Tony in his fight against what he perceives as injustice. In fact, he now feels as if Trish has closed ranks with Charles (and the establishment) against him. In response, he violently rapes her on the office floor where they had previously made love. Later, he gets obnoxiously drunk—like the stereotypical ocker—and is beaten badly by the police whose arrest he resists.

Even before these climactic moments, we have glimpses of Tony's drifting back to his former life—more positive examples than the ockerism shown in the sexual assault and the drunkenness. When his daughter falls violently ill, he harangues the doctor for his tardiness and, then, sits up with her until the medicine begins to take effect. Meanwhile, he lets his weary wife Susie sleep. However, what stands in the way of his reconciliation with Susie is, as he tells his minister father-in-law, that he feels she is intellectually beneath him. The father-in-law's comment that perhaps Tony is "no Einstein himself" proves ultimately true as Petersen begins to realize that he is probably not university material.

So, Tony goes back to the life we saw him living at the beginning of the film. Sexy moments with Susie alternate with quickies with the sex-starved women whose plugs and light fixtures he repairs. The only difference now is that he can charm, and excite, these women even more than before by eloquently reciting (more as actor Jack Thompson than character Tony Petersen) some Shakespeare to them.

Petersen is a difficult film to assess. Some have panned it; some have termed it a key film in the Australian revival (McFarlane 91; Rattigan 215; Stratton, *Last* 115). Burstall's direction is good, as is David Williamson's screenplay. The cast is strong with Jack Thompson as Petersen, Jacki Weaver as Susie, Wendy Hughes as Trish, Arthur Dignam as Charles, and Helen Morse as coed Jane. These are the stars of the cinema that will develop over the next several years. Even Peter Best's score is good, and his scores can sometimes be heavy-handed. Because of the film's quality and because there are likable qualities in Thompson's Petersen, viewers may see his competitive spirit, demonstrations of friendship, and irreverence toward authority as positive features. Add to those, if you will, his commitment to children and his openness to new ideas and experiences. With these traits, we are close to a picture of a hero perhaps suitable for the present day. However, Petersen's sexual exploits, which are at least partially premised on seeing a woman's body as an object to be "won," and his violent rape of Trish give one considerable pause. The rape is especially troubling. Because it is rape, we are repelled by it. And, like rape in general, it has everything to do with power. Tony is attempting to disempower Trish. But the troubling dimension of this rape is why he is disempowering her. He is doing it because—as Tony sees things at that moment—she, perhaps in collusion with her authoritarian husband, had disempowered Tony using their social and educational status to do so. The class conflict incipient in the film is made tangible at this moment (Pike and Cooper 280). One quickly rejects the very idea of excusing any act of sexual violence. However, in this case, one must at least grant that Tony's anger is somewhat justified. One only wishes he had reported their behavior to authorities rather than assaulting Trish. But, then, why would one turn to authorities for justice when it was the authorities who, in Tony's view, had conspired to destroy his aspirations?

One last disturbing dimension of *Petersen* is how graphically the rape was presented. That Wendy Hughes had already appeared fully nude in other scenes in the movie is no excuse for the explicitness of this rape scene. Another film discussed in this book, Steve Jodrell's 1987 *Shame*, is also very much about rape. Much of the commentary on that film, in particular Stephen Crofts' book-length study of it, *Identification, Gender, and Genre in Film*, notes how the film avoids the exploitative tendencies of rape–revenge movies by never depicting a rape on the screen. Crofts cites reviews of the film as well as viewers' comments on the film. One such comment comes to mind in conjunction with *Petersen*. Male teens were overheard commenting negatively on *Shame* that they did not even get to see her (a character named Lizzie) get raped (Crofts, *Identification*, 76). These male teens would have been much happier with Burstall's *Petersen*, and that is the problem with the movie and the idea of Tony Petersen being anything more than just potentially heroic.

The next several films I discuss take the Australian hero much further afield from "the norm" than the university campus Tony Petersen goes to. In order, we will go to war-torn South Africa, to war-torn Gallipoli, to war-torn Malaysia to a war-torn Pacific island, to war-torn Indonesia, and to a war-torn Southeast Asian nation. Two elements are common to all six of these films—and one is not Mel Gibson because he is only in three of them. First, the arenas are foreign to Australia; second, they all involve war. There seems then in this sequence of films to be a suggestion that a heroism appropriate for Australia today will only clearly emerge outside the constraints imposed by the culture on the proving ground provided by warfare.

BREAKER MORANT (BRUCE BERESFORD, DIRECTOR, 1980)

Bruce Beresford's *Breaker Morant* is one of the three without Mel Gibson. And it is also one of the best motion pictures ever made in Australia. Bruce Beresford's directorial skills have matured, although he may still be, as Robin Wood has claimed, an auteur without a clear defining characteristic; as usual Don McAlpine's photography is superb; and Edward Woodward, Bryan Brown, and Jack Thompson all give excellent performances. Furthermore, each actor brings a character to life before us who represents, in slightly different ways from the other two, an Australian heroism one might salute in this century. In fact, as Tom O'Regan has argued, the four represent different "takes" on the Australian character, the point being to distinguish them from the British and to reveal the heroic potential (*Australian* 313).

Breaker Morant, beautifully filmed in Australia, is set in South Africa during the Boer War. The Boers were defending the Orange Free State and the Transvaal against the British, who wanted to add those colonial states to their holdings in southern Africa. The attractiveness of these two Boer states was the huge deposits of diamonds and gold that had been uncovered in them. The Boers, primarily a farming people, fought a guerrilla campaign against the British. Thus, to win the war, the British had to bring in troops from all over the empire, including Australia. The Australians in Beresford's film were part of a special group trained to counter the Boers' guerrilla tactics. Partially because they were fighting "a new kind of war" and partially because they were following British orders, the particular Australians execute Boer prisoners in the field and murder a German missionary thought to be a Boer spy. These and other actions have given Germany the excuse she needs to enter the war on the Boer side. Thus, the British decide to put three members of the Australian troop on trial to appease the Germans. The trial is staged with its conclusion already decided by the British command. To ensure that the trial ends as it is supposed to, the British appoint an inexperienced Australian country solicitor to serve as defense attorney.

The film alternates between courtroom scenes and flashbacks, interrupting the flow with some nighttime scenes between the three accused men and their amateur attorney and one daytime scene when the accused help the others at the British fort defeat a daring attack by Boer guerrillas. As the film proceeds, the lawyer's skill visibly increases so that, by the end, he is mounting a surprisingly strong defense. Also as the film proceeds, it raises numerous issues about the morality of war in general and each soldier's personal moral responsibility for his actions. These issues had just come to the fore in Vietnam, a conflict Australia was involved in alongside its American allies.

The three soldiers—Morant (Edward Woodward), Handcock (Bryan Brown), and Witton—(Lewis Fits-Gerald) are very clearly underdogs in their battle against the British authorities who have decided that these three must be found guilty. Despite their lawyer's strong defense, the audience feels that the three men are doomed to die. That fatalism affects them as well, although they and the audience have faint glimmers of hope toward the film's end. In the end, they are acquitted of murdering the missionary—based on Handcock's perjury. But all three are convicted of murdering the prisoners. Morant and Handcock are sentenced to death; the younger and lower-ranking Witton to life imprisonment. So, the lawyer Thomas' defense does not win the day. But in the course of his fight, he does reveal how duplicitous the British are being in the whole matter. A pronounced anti-British message comes across in the film, so much so that the patriotic British music and songs played periodically throughout the movie acquire increasing degrees of irony as the movie moves forward. Several have suggested that the anti-British attitude is overdone (McFarlane 59; O'Regan, Rattigan 65; *Australian* 236). This attitude may have been so pronounced to signal the emergence of an Australian cinema separate from that of the rest of the English-speaking world.

These Australian heroes then are underdogs and are fatalistic; the fatalism, as Rattigan suggests, is stressed to differentiate the film from American cinema (66). The lawyer is joined by the others during the trial in exhibiting a competitive spirit despite the Australians' "inferior" position. The lawyer, brilliantly played by Jack Thompson, also does not hesitate to take on the British "authorities" at or behind the scenes of the trial. He thereby constructs the British versus Australian dialectic that defines the film, to the unfortunate exclusion of the Boer perspective (Crofts, "*Breaker*"). Initially, the British look down on the solicitor Major Thomas as "a colonial." Toward the trial's end, at least the opposing attorney views him as a worthy adversary. He manages to earn this respect in a style that is at times folksy, at times straightforward, and at times eloquent.

Initially, lawyer Thomas is aloof from the accused men. He hardly knows them. In addition, he clearly feels out of his league defending them and, of course, does not want them to know this. The men are also uncomfortable with him, partially because they justifiably feel he is an amateur. Gradually, the lawyer Thomas and the three accused men become mates. They share defeats and victories, as well as the liquor he smuggles into the prison for them. And, if the mateship among the four is strong, the mateship between Morant and Handcock is even stronger. The lawyer is not accused, and Witton is much younger and much less involved in the events that landed them all in the courtroom. Morant and Handcock had been through a great deal together, and, in the end, they will go off to face the firing squad hand in hand, as mates.

Morant and Handcock are, however, very different men. Morant is English, but he long ago came to Australia where he earned his living and fame breaking horses. He loves horses. In fact, at one point in the film, when the mates toast freedom, he adds "and horses" to the toast. Morant might well have added his mate Hunt and Hunt's beautiful sister to the list because it was Hunt's murder and mutilation by Boers that led Morant to order the immediate execution of a Boer caught wearing part of Hunt's uniform and it was the presence of Hunt's sister, Morant's betrothed, who Morant will miss the most should the trial go as he thinks it will. He is devoted to her, just as he is devoted to the poetry he reads and the Byronic poetry he writes.

Morant's recitation of Byron one evening inspires Handcock to recite what he thinks is poetry. What he recites is a vulgar limerick because Handcock is much more the larrikin. There has never been much of a place in his life for books. He loves the land he farms; he loves the wife and family he has left—because of their dire financial traits—to join the military. But he still finds a place in his heart, and elsewhere, for other women, even in South Africa where he has been consorting with Boer women while their husbands were away at the war. When the toast is raised, Handcock adds "women" to "freedom and horses."

All four of the central male characters offer a heroism of note. Whether it be Thomas, the underdog battler; Morant, the fiercely loyal lover of beauty; Handcock, the land-loving, fun-loving, sex-loving almost stereotypical Aussie; or Witton, the idealist who came to South Africa to fight for the empire he believed in, there is something heroic to be seen. Combine them, toss in the irreverence (especially against the British) and the fatalism that permeate the film, and add a drink or two or three, and you have a formula for the revised hero.

GALLIPOLI (PETER WEIR, DIRECTOR, 1981)

With *Gallipoli*, the work of a few important names in Australian film is considered for the first time in this study: director Peter Weir; cinematographer Russell Boyd; music director Brian May; and, of course, actor Mel Gibson. This talented group collaborated to create another masterpiece of Australian cinema, although some—for example, Graeme Turner—think Weir's work, especially the "period pieces," are overrated ("Art"; "Mixing"). Like *Breaker Morant*, we are taken to the arena of war; however, unlike in Beresford's film, we do not witness the fully developed heroism of soldiers but, rather, the emerging heroism of two boys who decide for different reasons to go to war.

Gallipoli is perhaps the movie that someone in Australia had to make because the legends of the Anzac troops in World War I, especially their brutal defeat at Gallipoli, are an important part of the nation's history and culture. The nation's awareness of the war story per se gave screenwriter David Williamson (with a bit of collaboration with Weir) a problem and an opportunity. The problem was knowing that the Gallipoli story could not give him much "new" material for a feature film; the opportunity was being able to merge some other story with the Gallipoli story, thereby giving that new story, almost automatically, the aura of legend. It is no wonder then that the script took Williamson years to write (Stratton, *Avocado* 22–23).

The new story, largely Weir's idea, was that of mates Archie Hamilton (Mark Lee) and Frank Dunne (Mel Gibson). The first part of the film has the two boys meeting during a sprinting competition in Western Australia and then forming a fast friendship as they travel across the desert together to Perth where they both plan to join the prestigious lighthorsemen. It ends with their departure across the Indian Ocean, but, since Frank, a city boy, cannot ride a horse, he ends up with some other mates in the infantry. The second part of the film takes place in Cairo, Egypt, where the Anzac troops are being prepared for combat. There, Archie and Frank meet up again and spend time together in Cairo, cementing their mateship. The tone of these first two parts is fairly light: the first is very much a boys' adventure; the second a comic look at Aussie irreverence in mock battles as well as in the streets of Cairo. Throughout these parts, Weir may be trying to blend two facets of the Australian character into one by having Frank be Irish, urban, and larrikin-like and Archie be English, rural, and bushmanlike (O'Regan, *Australian* 313; Rattigan 147). The tone changes abruptly when we make a shocking transition from waltzing with confetti falling at a dance the Anzac nurses are hosting to the men's somber, moonlit journey across the Mediterranean to the narrow beach and high cliffs of Turkey.

The third and final part of the film has its frivolous moments (including another male nude swimming scene), but, gradually, the focus becomes increasingly focused on the battle ahead. That battle the Aussie troops feinting an attempt to go up the escarpment and inland to distract the Turkish forces from a British invasion elsewhere. British artillery will open fire on the plateau above the cliffs, driving the Turkish machine gunners out of their nests and making the Aussie charge relatively safe. Tragically, the British artillery ceases firing prematurely, giving the machine gunners the opportunity to reoccupy their nests before the charge begins. The British commanders do not want to hear that something has not gone according to plan, and they repeatedly order the Australians to charge, even though the British are being told repeatedly that the Australians are being slaughtered by the machine-gun fire seconds after they "go over the top." As a result, the Australian losses at Gallipoli were staggering.

As the Australian troops prepare to "go over," the fatalism is palpable. It mutes all other heroic notes that the film sounds except for mateship. The men who survive—because they were not called on to charge—tend lovingly to their dying mates. Those not called heed the last wishes of those about to die. Archie Hamilton, chosen to stay behind and serve as a runner (because of his speed) between the Australian commanders on the cliff face and the Australian command station at its base, asks that Frank take his place. Archie does so knowing that switching will probably save Frank's life while ending his. The mateship that Archie and Frank cemented when they raced to the top of a pyramid, to carve their names there into the stone face, ends in this noble self-sacrifice.

Mateship is rarely this somber. Back in Cairo, we see Australian mates carouse together, drinking a bit, whoring a little, and brawling just once. We see Frank and his mates mock the British officers by trailing a horseback group of pommie (disrespectful slang for British) officers on donkeyback while mocking the British officers' affectations. "Crude colonials," the British officers call Frank and his mates. At Gallipoli, we see the noble side of mateship; in Cairo, the frivolous—mixed with antiauthority, anti-British irreverence. The larger anti-British message of the film—that the British sent the Australians charging to their death while they, the British, sat comfortably on the long-since-taken beachhead, drinking their tea—is also delivered. This message may have been miscommunicated to audiences. Both McFarlane and O'Regan cite this ending in explaining the film's anti-British message, but Stratton argues that an Australian officer with a somewhat English accent has been misunderstood by viewers and critics alike to be British (McFarlane 57; O'Regan, *Australian* 313; Stratton, *Avocado* 26).

The Aussie troops are presented as a rambunctious lot in the film—much to the dismay of the British authorities. However, it is worth noting that the drinking, whoring, and brawling are restrained. This Australian hero is not a young ocker; he is simply a normal young man who loves a good time and has not yet been smothered in spirit by the horrors of war. As such, he very much represents the nation of Australia, which, at that point in time, was young, fun-loving, and not yet tragically touched by war. Weir and Williamson steer the rowdy portrayal away from any ockerlike excesses. The rowdiness in *Gallipoli* reveals itself in sport—a footy game between Western Australia and Victoria—and in the men's refusal to take a mock battle, infantry versus lighthorsemen, seriously, turning it into a comic brawl with much melodramatic dying. The rowdiness shows up in competition and in exuberant irreverence.

Much in this portrait may be oversimplified and oversanitized, as Amanda Lohrey has argued, totally overlooking the hell the Anzac troops really raised in Egypt. Perhaps Sam Rohdie is right in blaming the "distortion" on the film's need to follow an internationally recognized commercial formula to cover its costs ("*Gallipoli* as world"; "*Gallipoli*, Peter Weir"). The film then may be more myth—commercially viable myth—than reality with some unseemly reality ignored. If so, the myth is a powerful one and a defining one, as it does speak to both Australian and non-Australian audiences.

A TOWN LIKE ALICE (DAVID STEVENS, DIRECTOR, 1981)

Robbery under Arms, discussed in Chapter 2, was made for both television and motion picture release—a difficult feat given the differences between the two media. As we move well into the 1980s, an increasing number of projects, which would have been made as motion pictures in the previous ten or fifteen years, were being made as television miniseries. Among these were the period pieces that graced the screens between 1975 and 1982. *Robbery under Arms*, because it was made for both media, is often treated as a film. Television miniseries, regardless of how well made, are usually treated as non-films and ignored in books such as this one. However, here I make an exception to that "rule" and discuss *A Town Like Alice* because of the production's quality—contributed to greatly by Russell Boyd's photography—its popularity, and its relevance to the topic of heroism.

A Town Like Alice, based on Nevil Shute's 1950 novel, featured two heroes, Jean Paget and Joe Harmon. Jean (played by Australian Helen Morse) is an Englishwoman. In Malaysia at the time of the Japanese takeover during World

War II, she becomes a prisoner of war. The Japanese, however, did not know what to do with female prisoners because no prison camp, it seems, was prepared to accept them. So, the Japanese kept marching them from place to place. Gradually, the old and feeble, as well as the very young, began to fall sick and die. Jean, one of the healthier ones on the "death march," plays a heroic role in which she helps the suffering women and children.

Along the way, she meets Joe Harman (Bryan Brown). He is an Australian soldier captured by the Japanese. He and other Australian prisoners in Malaysia are given a great deal of freedom because they provide heavy labor on many projects for their captors. Thus, he is able to visit Jean. He even brings her, and the other women, a plump chicken so they can make a stew that will bolster their health. Unfortunately, the chicken was the property of the Japanese commander. Joe confesses to the crime rather than allow the women to be punished for it. And he, in sight of the women, is crucified for his theft.

Years later, Jean is back in England. She has inherited a sum of money. She decides to travel to Australia—to the town of Alice Springs that Joe had always talked so fondly of before he died. After she arrives, she discovers evidence that Joe had not died after all, that he is alive and back in Australia although not in Alice. Then begins Jean's quest to find Joe. From that point on, the novel and miniseries both are rather romantic tales. Although it is worth noting how persistent Jean is in seeking out and finding Joe, I want to focus on the heroism they both displayed during the war.

They are strikingly alike beneath the surface. On the surface, Jean is proper; Joe the larrikin. However, beneath that surface they both have a passionate desire for freedom that keeps them going despite the odds. They are both underdogs in the battles they are fighting to survive their capture, and, in their darker moments, they both wonder if they will ever see their homes again. They do not, however, let this fatalism affect the way they live day to day. Jean, for the sake of her mates, and Joe, for the sake of Jean, keep fighting.

Joe is, of course, the more Australian type. One can imagine the irreverent man he would be if he had greater freedom because he is irreverent enough already. He defies authority at every turn. In fact, it is that defiance of authority (e.g., stealing the commander's chicken) that seems to be the reason Joe was put to death. But even though he is crucified on a barn door, he fights on and survives. One can also imagine the beers he would drink down if he had them; one does not, however, need to imagine his love for his homeland, because he talks with Jean about Australia and especially his little town of Alice Springs.

Jean and Joe both give greatly to others: Jean to her fellow prisoners; Joe to Jean and the other women. Joe's generosity extends so far that he sacrifices his life (or so it seems) for Jean and the women. He did not know, when he confessed, how severe the penalty would be, so we cannot say Joe chose to give his life. Nonetheless, he was willing to suffer greatly rather than see them suffer. This generosity softens the character of Joe. He seems more noble than the normal larrikin. He also, in both the novel and the miniseries, seems to be less sexist and more sentimental. Many of the traits of the typical Australian hero are present in Joe; however, there is a definite softening of them. Ned Kelly and Daniel Morgan robbed from the rich and gave to the poor; therefore, they might have stolen the commander's chicken if they had been in Joe's shoes, but these bushrangers would not have offered quite as strong a romantic lead to match with Jean Paget.

ATTACK FORCE Z (TIM BURSTALL, DIRECTOR, 1982)

Tim Burstall's directorial career perhaps had an "up" with *Petersen*, but then it clearly had a "down" with *Attack Force Z*. The parallel between the two very different films is apt, because in both cases Burstall was working with star-studded casts. As already noted, in *Peterson*, he had Jack Thompson, Wendy Hughes, Arthur Dignam, and Helen Morse. In *Attack Force Z*, he had John Phillip Law, Chris Haywood, John Waters, Sam Neill, and Mel Gibson. In fact, it is the presence of these stars—perhaps Gibson more than the others—that has brought audiences to view *Attack Force Z*. Perhaps in Burstall's defense is the fact that he took over the job from Phillip Noyce rather late in the process after Noyce's repeated disagreements with the producers made it impossible for him to continue with the project (Stratton, *Avocado* 43).

The film deals with an operation launched by an elite allied force under Australian command during World war II. This elite force's fame is for slipping in, quietly doing its job, and then slipping out. The film is clearly not intended to be a parody, but, if presented just slightly differently, it could be because this group of men do everything wrong in attempting to evacuate a defecting Japanese official from an island somewhere in the Pacific. In fact, of the six men who go in, only one, Paul Kelly (Mel Gibson), survives. Furthermore, the Japanese dignitary is accidentally shot and killed during the evacuation attempt.

Yet, the movie presents these men as heroes. But in what sense? They seem to enjoy the freedom to operate outside the lines that their elite status provides them. They are competitive, fighting on and on against superior numbers and, therefore, against the odds. They are, numerically at least, underdogs, but we never sense that they truly are. They have been introduced with such hype that we expect them to prove victorious. And it is in this hype that the film's problem may lie, because the hype just does not fit an Australian military unit. The hype is much more appropriate for an American unit, or at least for the kind of units one finds in conventional Hollywood war movies (Rattigan 54). The hype is misapplied to a group that we should see—if we are to see them as Australian—as underdogs doomed eventually to lose. They do indeed end up enacting this very Australian role; however, because they have been introduced in other terms, we interpret them as surprising failures, not as typical Australian underdog heroes.

The group also does not exhibit much in the way of Australian mateship. As several have noted, the film's departure from mateship is signaled early when a wounded Ted King (John Waters) is killed by his supposed mate Danny Costello (Sam Neill) to ensure that the group's operation remains secret. Mates simply do not act this way toward each other: something is amiss (Rattigan 55; Stratton, *Avocado* 44). Sometimes, these mates stick together, but, quite frequently, each is off doing his own separate thing. One, a Dutchman who grew up in New Guinea, even falls in love with a heroic Chinese girl and decides to stay behind with her and her townspeople. There is also squabbling among them, primarily because the Australian leading the operation has less experience than some of the men he is commanding. To the extent each man seems intent on carving his own heroic path, the film again seems more American than Australian. Its focus is on the individual, not the group of mates.

Attack Force Z, then, deserves the lack of attention and applause it has received: it is a flawed film, wasting a very strong cast (McFarlane 177). It does indeed contribute to the portrait of heroism I am attempting to sketch. There are some ways in which the men in Burtstall's movie are Australian heroes—for example, their competitiveness and their underdog status. However, the film seems to have received, at some point in its troubled history, a pronounced American stamp. The problem then is that the American and the Australian do not work well together. Some commentators suggest that the differences between the Australian culture and the American culture are negligible. The incongruities in *Attack Force Z* suggest that, at least as far as heroism is concerned, there are some crucial differences

THE YEAR OF LIVING DANGEROUSLY (PETER WEIR, DIRECTOR, 1982)

The Year of Living Dangerously brings together much of the group that worked on *Gallipoli*. Weir directs; Weir and David Williamson join novelist C. J. Koch in writing the script, although not entirely harmoniously; Russell Boyd directs the photography; and, of course, Mel Gibson stars (Stratton, *Avocado* 166). Joining him in starring roles are Sigourney Weaver as an official at the British embassy in Jakarta and Linda Hunt as dwarfish Indonesian photographer Billy Kwan, a role for which she won an Academy Award.

Gibson plays Guy Hamilton, a rather inexperienced Australian journalist thrown into a deteriorating political situation he barely grasps. Feeling that his career is perhaps on the line, he is determined to get on top of the story in Jakarta. His fellow Australian journalists are not as enthusiastic about the job before them: wary of the costs of too much involvement at this point, they prefer to sit back and drink their beers. Hamilton then might seem more ambitious than the typical Australian and, therefore, perhaps more American. But that ambition is really just a reflection of his Australian competitiveness. He is just more naïve than his more jaded compatriots, who have put their competitive spirit largely on hold. Any journalist, they sense, will be an underdog, fighting a losing battle. They let their fatalism cow them; Guy Hamilton charges forth, much like Archie Hamilton in *Gallipoli*, despite the pervasive feeling that the situation is clearly a no-win one.

The film offers us several glimpses inside the British embassy at the time. It is a locus of formality, of stuffiness. An anti-British attitude is apparent in *The Year of Living Dangerously* as in *Gallipoli* and many other Australian films. We get the sense that Sigourney Weaver's character, Jill Bryant, finds Guy so appealing because, as Australian, he lacks the formality and stuffiness of her current lover, the older Colonel Henderson (Bill Kerr). There is more life in Guy. Billy Kwan, who is hopelessly in love with Jillie (as he calls her), also detects something special in Guy. Thus, he very much orchestrates the love affair that blooms between Jill and Guy, a love affair Weir chooses to emphasize more than Koch had (McFarlane 118–19). He also helps Guy's career along because he senses in Guy's innocence a willingness to tell the truth about Indonesia.

Billy is driven by political passion; Jill by passion—both dangerous courses. Guy joins them in tempting danger. His motives are, however, more complex because he is drawn by both passion for Jill and passion to win at the journalist's game. When the two passions conflict, he initially chooses the game, exposing Jill to greater danger and losing Billy's admiration and support. Guy does, however, redeem himself from this mistake and, against the steadily increasing odds, gets safely out of an exploding Indonesia with Jill. He does not, however, decipher the ambiguities of the political situation in Indonesia. The ending then is not as optimistic as it seems because Guy ultimately surrenders (as do many Peter Weir heroes), to a force that is beyond his comprehension (Rattigan 324–25).

There is much that is Australian in Guy's portrayal, just as there is in the presentation *en masse* of the soldiers in *Attack Force Z*: his free-spiritedness, his defiance of authorities, his contempt for the British "attitude," his competitive urge, his camaraderie with his beer-swigging Australian mates, and his underdog position in a quest for "the story" that he seems fated ultimately to fail in. However, his career orientation, his fidelity to Jill, and his relative success in the end mark him as more in line with American heroes and, thus, American movie heroes. Thus, *The Year of Living Dangerously* and *Attack Force Z*, although very different films as to quality, do conflate the two cultures and, as a result, offer us heroes for Australia who are not as "pure" examples as the soldiers in *Breaker Morant*, the mates in *Gallipoli*, and even Tony Petersen in *Petersen*. What is happening in these films probably has a great deal to do with money. Entering the 1980s, Australian films began having larger and larger budgets. They needed these budgets to buy the performers and stage the special effects necessary to win a large audience. Having spent more money, however, the films needed an even larger audience. Australia alone simply did not offer an audience large enough to pay the films' bills. Therefore, producers and directors began pitching their films, at least partially, at the much larger American audience. The incongruities in Burstall's *Attack Force Z* and the

American dimensions of the Mel Gibson character in *The Year of Living Dangerously* reflect the fact that Australian motion pictures were now being made for both Australia and the United States.

FAR EAST (JOHN DUIGAN, DIRECTOR, 1982)

The setting in *The Year of Living Dangerously* is identifiable; not so in John Duigan's *Far East*. It is somewhere in Southeast Asia, but not in Vietnam. We know this because the two lead characters, Morgan Keefe (Bryan Brown) and Jo Reeves (Helen Morse) had met in Vietnam twenty years earlier. David Stratton identifies the country as the Philippines, but he cites no evidence (*Avocado* 221).

Morgan and Jo meet again in the "Koala Klub," a bar Keefe runs in this country. Although we are not sure where we are, we do know that much is amiss politically and economically in this country. We see the contrasts between the living conditions of the bulk of the population and those enjoyed by Westerners there. We learn that multinational corporations are hand-in-glove with government authorities to profit at the expense of the nation's resources and people. The presentation of the Far East in both this film and in *The Year of Living Dangerously* has been criticized as "orientalist" (to use Edward Said's concept); however, both presentations, especially Duigan's, do seem sensitive to the economic and political realities of the region and the West's complicity in creating them (O'Regan, *Australian* 184, 282). We see and learn these facts primarily because Jo's husband Peter is a journalist who is in the country investigating the economic conditions there. His probing brings him into contact with Rosita Constanza and others who are actively opposing the government. This contact gets Peter into more and more trouble, bringing him, close to the film's climax, to a "safe house," where a division of the country's military can interrogate elements thought to be a threat to the government with impunity. There Peter is beaten, while Rosita is tortured and gang-raped.

While Peter is pursuing his story and getting into serious trouble, his wife Jo is reigniting her love affair with Morgan, who has been eyeing her in a very sexist manner since she first appeared in his bar. His sexist leer, however, belies much deeper feelings. Because of his love for her, Morgan gets involved in the politics of the country, something he has stayed out of in his safe Koala Klub for many years.

Morgan was an Australian soldier in Vietnam. He was wounded there. For reasons that are never fully explained, he chose not to return to Australia after the war ended. Like many Australians who were involved in the war, he may have become embittered by the experience and cynical about relationships among nations as well as those among people. This cynicism enhanced an already "free" spirit and put him in what one might describe as a permanently disengaged state in the unnamed Asian country. There he has created a little bit of Australia—complete with daily news from Down Under posted on a blackboard at the bar. But this little bit of Australia features no real connections: the bar is populated by transient Westerners, bar girls who dance and in some cases prostitute themselves, and Morgan and his mistress–business partner Nene. There is gambling in the backroom, booze and sex all around.

Morgan is certainly an unlikely hero, but, for the love of Jo, he springs into action. Spending his own money freely, he finds out where Peter and Rosita are being held. He then masterminds and executes a daring rescue attempt. He delivers the two to a cargo ship about to leave the port and pays for their passage, as well as Jo's.

Jo had very freely entered into a revival of her affair with Morgan; however, when she realized that she and Morgan had been making love while Peter and Rosita were being seized by "authorities" and beaten, she feels guilty and, then, sincerely becomes concerned about Peter's welfare. She might have more passion in her soul for Morgan, the twenty-year-old surfer from Australia who had won her heart back in Vietnam, than for her husband Peter; nonetheless, it is clear she does love Peter. Her guilt is further exacerbated when she discovers that part of the price Morgan had to pay for the information about Peter's whereabouts was forcing into prostitution a virgin girl from the countryside who was dancing in the bar. In the end, Jo has the opportunity to make a choice between Morgan and Peter. Saying that she does not think a relationship with Morgan would work, she chooses to go back to Australia with Peter. We detect that her guilt has a great deal to do with her decision.

Morgan's rescue effort was indeed heroic. It was also very much against the odds, because the "safe house" was well-guarded. In addition, once that house was attacked, government forces would be mobilized against him, the rescued Peter and Rosita, and Jo. There was just enough of a window to get them on their way out of the country. Peter and Jo escape through that window. Rosita refuses to abandon her people and goes back to the Koala Klub. Then, the authorities arrive. To protect Rosita and Nene, Morgan opens fire on the "police"; they take him down in a machine-gun barrage. That his life would end this way should not have surprised him. When he made his decision to help Jo, he knew he would henceforth be a marked man and unable to live any longer in his safe Koala Klub enclave.

There is a Casablanca-like sadness at the end of *Far East*: Morgan and Jo, having found each other, lose each other (Debi Enker in Murray, *Australian Film* 98). Much of the ending is oddly upbeat given the concluding scenes of corpses lying where the bar girls once danced. The "innocents"—Peter and Jo—escape; the true crusader—Rosita—survives. Morgan, one might argue, deserves his fate given how complicitous he was in the exploitation of young girls at the Koala Klub, an exploitation that, of course, mirrored the larger exploitation throughout the country (Debi Enker in Murray, *Australian Film* 98). However, Morgan was not a bad person. The girls at the Klub performed with surprising modesty, and no one, except the unfortunate virgin from the countryside, was coerced into prostitution. He tried to behaved as decently as possible as he drifted along in his disengaged state. Therefore, we are sad that Morgan loses Jo and then suffers the fate that he probably chose when he decided to rescue Peter for his love of Jo. We are also sad that there wasn't a "right" way for Morgan and Jo to be together. The film's fatalistic note, however, just adds to the way in which it presents a fairly good example of an Australian hero in Morgan Keefe, even though his Australia is only the confines of the Koala Klub

THE MAN FROM SNOWY RIVER (GEORGE MILLER, DIRECTOR, 1982)

Director George Miller denies that he cast Kirk Douglas in a dual role in *The Man from Snowy River* to appeal to an American audience (Hamilton and Mathews 116). Although his giving Douglas such prominence and noted Australian actor Jack Thompson a relatively minor role (as the legendary bushman Clancy) does seem peculiar, let us assume that Miller was simply putting the best people in the appropriate roles. And his casting of unknown actor Tom Burlinson as young hero Jim Craig and relatively unknown actress Sigrid Thornton as Craig's beloved Jessica does seem to support Miller's claim. So, the casting is not the reason the film has struck many as having an American "feel," despite the producer's insistence that "the film is intrinsically Australian—it is socially and culturally specific to Australia" (Tosi 211). What is behind it is the way the hero Jim Craig is presented.

Throughout most of the film, Jim is the underdog. When his father dies accidentally early in the story, the mountain men send Jim away, into the valley. Perhaps blaming the boy for the accident, the mountain men tell Jim he must earn the title "a man from Snowy River." So, with some advice from the aging gold miner Spur, Jim begins his quest. His boss in the valley, an arrogant American named Harrison, does not like Jim and neither do the Australian mates in Harrison's bunkhouse. So, when he is accused of deliberately setting Harrison's prized colt free to join the brumbies (wild horses), everyone seems to believe he did free the horse to spite Harrison, who had detected the developing romance between his daughter Jessica and Jim. When Jim tries to vindicate himself by joining the men who are going after the colt, only the legendary Clancy believes him. And so, disliked by almost all he sets out to prove his true worth to all of them.

He is the underdog; he is also youthfully naïve. Both seem to be emerging as characteristic of the revised Australian hero. The former was present in the hero of old; the latter was present but was more often than not negatively portrayed, whereas with heroes such as Archie Hamilton in *Galipoli*, Guy Hamilton in *The Year of Living Dangerously*, and Jim Craig in this movie, the naïveté is a positive trait. He is also competitive: we see this as he tries, earlier in the film, to tame the prized colt and to win (one might say "tame") Jessica; we see this as he rides off with the men to prove his worth. Craig also loves the freedom of living in the Snowy Mountains and the horses there and in the valley. All of these traits make him an Australian hero.

He departs a bit from the hero of old by keeping his sexism at bay. He is not a womanizer. And, unlike other hands who often send lurid messages to Jessica, he treats her very much as an equal, as a mate. In fact, while living on Harrison's property, he seems to reject the company of his bunkhouse mates as crude in favor of that of his true mate Jessica. He thus seems at least a sanitized (perhaps for family viewing) Australian hero if not some other kind of hero—no condescending sexism; no crude, alcohol-fueled bunkhouse camaraderie. Given how Jim comes across in these early dealings with Jessica, it is then quite surprising how, at the movie's end, he seems to lump her in with the "brood mares" he will, the next morning, return to collect (Rose Lucas in Murray, *Australian Film* 103). Jessica's wild spirit has been tamed by her frightening experiences, on her own, in the mountains; Jim has won her admiration by saving her from the edge of a precipice and, then, single-handedly roundingup the escaped colt and numerous other valuable horses. She is no longer the fiery, independent girl who refuses to be controlled by her domineering father. Rather than turn to her as his mate, as he had when they were breaking the prized colt together earlier in the film, Jim now turns to her as property he has won.

Jim falls back into the sexism of the Australian hero just after doing something very atypical of that hero: he captures the renegade colt alone. The other men, his mates on the quest, pull back when the horses begin running along mountain paths that strike them as too treacherous. But Jim, who is from the Snowy Mountains, charges on after them. As an individual, he overcomes the odds and wins in spectacular terms. This ending, because of Jim's sole pursuit and because of his glorious victory, gives the movie and its hero something of an American "feel." Of course, one needs to keep in mind that the ending was not something Miller or scriptwriters John Dixon and Fred Cullen had anything to do with because the ending was in the Banjo Patterson poem the film is based on. In fact, the ending is the only true thing in the movie to be found in Patterson's "The Man from Snowy River" (O'Regan, "*Man*").

So, despite touches that may seem American, Jim Craig is rather Australian in his heroism, although we do seem to be seeing some of the rough edges of that heroism being sanded away as we move through the films of the 1980s. At least in this film, another edge that is lacking is the anti-British one. What replaces it here—and in several other films we will discuss—is opposition to an attitude that overvalues and, with nose in air, flaunts material wealth. This attitude, which seems to run contrary to the Australian culture's belief in simpler things and in social equality, could be British, but it also could be American. In *The Man from Snowy River*, the attitude is clearly exhibited by the American Harrison.

The attitude is countered by Jim Craig, who plans to go with Jessica to the mountains and build (one senses) a different kind of house and ranch and life.

The mountains, in a mythic way, seem to make the difference. Harrison's attitude is also countered by Spur. Here, the movie becomes diagrammatically symbolic. Since Harrison and Spur are brothers, they can be viewed as the two courses open to the nation. Harrison's way is carefully measured, as is the land in the valley; he is controlled, focused on material wealth, and successful in those terms but perhaps not in emotional terms. Spur's way is a wilder and freer one, much as the land and paths in the Snowy Mountains are; it is focused on one's mates; and it is a failure *if* the measure of success and failure is the accumulation of wealth. Spur's way seems more true to Australia; Harrison's is foreign. And the symbolic question is which path Australia should take. It is arguably symbolic that Harrison and Spur fight over a young girl named Matilda (the name of the unofficial Australian national anthem). She makes a frivolous choice—of the one who first becomes a rich man—and she lives to regret that choice. The film is perhaps suggesting that Australia at some point chose as Matilda did. However, the land now has another chance because Matilda's daughter Jessica has chosen not a man of worldly wealth but "The Man from Snowy River."

Miller's film appealed to audiences in both Australia and the United States. And maybe he did do some things to tweak the motion picture to attract the latter audience he needed to please investors. Nonetheless, on both the literal level and the symbolic level, the movie speaks to Australia. It tries to tell Australia what it should be and what its heroism should be. As producer Geoff Burrowes put it, "We sought to make a film that was about Australia, as Australians would perceive it. . . . [W]e tried to provide a literally classic view of Australia and of an Australian hero" (qtd. in Hamilton and Mathews 117). The public loved their work; in general, however, critics hated it (Stratton, *Avocado* 66). McFarlane went as far as to call it a "foolish film," "a splendid film for deaf people," and "a witless extravaganza" (50, 83, 151). The explanation for these contradictory views may be found in how fully the film exploited popular culture elements that would appeal to the masses but not the more "cultured" critics (O'Regan, *Australian* 131, "*Man*" 242–52). It is, however, worth noting that in using these elements *The Man from Snowy River* also used mythical elements right out of Arthurian legends (Rattigan 199–200). The popular, then, may not be as objectionably Hollywoodish and objectionably pop culture as the "high culture" critics suggested (Rose Lucas in Murray, *Australian Film* 103).

PHAR LAP (SIMON WINCER, DIRECTOR, 1983)

The Australian audience would have known of "The Man from Snowy River" because Banjo Paterson's poem is known well by just about everyone. But "The Man" probably would not have made their list of heroes—not because of anything he did or did not do but, rather, because so little of his story is in the poem. There just is not enough substance to lift "The Man" to the sta-

Tommy Woodcock (Tom Burlinson) and Phar Lap in *Phar Lap* (1983). Photo courtesy of National Film and Sound Archives. "Phar Lap" © 1983 Twentieth Century Fox Film Corporation. All rights reserved. Permission also granted by Sexton Films.

tus of Australian hero in Paterson's thirty-some lines of verse. The same cannot be said of the racehorse Phar Lap (modified Thai for "lightning"). His full story was extremely well-known, so much so that the Australian version of the film could begin with the horse's tragic death and flashback. Phar Lap would also have made any Australian's list of heroes, a list that, as Rattigan notes, would include bushrangers, athletes, and not much else (247).

Therefore, he was an inevitable subject for a film. With the aid of David Williamson's screenplay and Russell Boyd's cinematography, Simon Wincer turns the story of the ill-fated racehorse into a beautiful motion picture. The only problem Wincer had to deal with was the absence of suspense because the Australian audience already knew the story. He compensated by turning the film into a visual tribute to the horse and by shifting some attention onto the less well-known stories of the horse's trainer Harry Telford and the horse's strapper (then trainer) Tommy Woodcock (Tom Burlinson).

Before dealing with their stories, we need to focus on Phar Lap's. As his story will reveal, he may well be the quintessential revised Australian hero. After his arrival by ship from New Zealand, the horse neither looked nor acted the winner. His trainer Telford believed in him, but very few others did. He lazily resisted the hard work necessary to be a winner. If he had been entered in any races, he would probably have been favored—to finish last. Phar Lap was very much the underdog; his name is ironic.

Then, the competitive urge flashed within him, and he began winning race after race. He, and his trainer and strapper, defied what the racing authorities had said. Perhaps it was this defiance of authorities that made Phar Lap the common person's favorite horse. In much the same manner that people admired bushranger heroes such as Ned Kelly, they admired—loved—Phar Lap.

Unfortunately, the horse's constant winning was not "playing" well with the elite of the Australian racing world. The horse did not look the part of a champion, he was owned by a brash American—Dave Davis—and his constant winning was reducing gambling revenue. Then, these authorities, played in a rather British manner so as to rally Australian anti-British sentiment, handicapped Phar Lap, loading the horse down with progressively heavier and heavier weights. They weighted him to an extent that was unprecedented, to an extent that had many fearing for the life of the horse.

Seedier Melbourne gambling "interests" were also distressed by Phar Lap's constant success because they needed other horses besides this at-one-time underdog to win if they were to make money. These interests were also a threat to the horse. In fact, they were undoubtedly behind an attempt to assassinate the horse. The Australian audience, of course, knows from the outset when and how Phar Lap will die. But even the American audience, watching the film without the initial flashback, senses that the horse's death is inevitable. This hero may win and win, but, eventually, as a typical Australian hero, he will lose. Under very suspicious circumstances, Phar Lap dies in the United States, where he has gone to race when the heavy handicaps had made winning in Australia virtually impossible.

A free-spirited, somewhat lazy, and very competitive underdog, Phar Lap fits the bill as an Australian hero. His story, with its anti-British flavor and its fatalistic feeling, like that of the Australian soldiers in *Breaker Morant* or Archie Hamilton in *Gallipoli,* is very Australian. So, in rather different ways, are the stories of Harry Telford and Tommy Woodcock.

Telford himself was an underdog. He had been in the business for many years but had never made it to the top. He kept looking for the horse through which he could achieve fame, but his fellow trainers had pretty much written him off. He defies what those with more authority in racing circles say about Phar Lap as he works and works the horse, trying to ready him for competition. Harry is determined to win, even if the horse is not. But Harry's drive has a dark side. His methods are, perhaps, too brutal to be successful. Arguably, it is the special bond that develops between Phar Lap and Tommy Woodcock that inspires the horse, not Telford's methods. Furthermore, Telford just lacks the skills and the charms necessary to achieve his rather grand dreams as a famous trainer and breeder. Nonetheless, he keeps throwing whatever money he makes, thanks to Phar Lap, into this dream. Viewers have a sense throughout the movie that Harry will inevitably fail.

Casting Tom Burlinson as Tommy Woodcock was perhaps risky, since many viewers would inevitably see Jim Craig not Tommy Woodcock on the screen.

Wincer accepted the risk, and, perhaps, the fact that viewers already associated Burlinson with the heroic worked to Wincer's advantage. To that initial advantage, Wincer and Burlinson quickly added other dimensions. They portrayed Tommy as free-spirited, to the point of questioning Telford's harsh methods; they suggested that he was from a poor background and determined to compete and succeed; and, of course, they made him a lover of horses. There is a real Tommy Woodcock, beloved in Australian racing circles, so Wincer and Burlinson did not have an empty canvas on which to paint their portrait. Nonetheless, they tried to present in young Woodcock many of the heroic qualities found in the horse.

Wincer and Burlinson also strove to present Tommy and Phar Lap as mates. Their loyalty to each other is as strong as that of Archie to Frank and Frank to Archie in *Gallipoli*. Their closeness is commented on several times in the course of the film. Toward the film's end, one man even wonders if they sleep together. He meant nothing sexual by the remark. However, Tommy does seem more strongly attached to Phar Lap than to his girlfriend and then-wife Emma. That attachment is evident in Tommy's leaving Emma behind as he crosses the Pacific with the horse on his fatal tour of North America; it is even more evident when Tommy's buddies jokingly tell Tommy, on the steps of the church right after his wedding, that the horse is ill. Tommy is ready to leave Emma standing there and run to the side of his beloved Phar Lap.

If Tommy's relationship with Emma plays second fiddle to that with Phar Lap, at least the relationship seems a fairly equal one. Sexism does not enter it, just as it does not enter the movie at large except, maybe, in the somewhat abusive relationship between Telford and his long-suffering wife Vi. Drinking also does not have much of a place in the film's portrayal of heroism. The trend toward sanitizing the traditional Australian hero seems to be continuing with *Phar Lap*, helped along perhaps by the fact that the primary Australian hero in the film is equine. In such a case, shouting a round for one's mates just is not relevant.

EMOH RUO (DENNY LAWRENCE, DIRECTOR, 1985)

Phar Lap, in a way, is a film out of time. The time for period pieces was the late 1970s and very early 1980s, 1983 was just a bit late. Most Australian movies had shifted to portraying present-day Australia. Heroism, then, had to be depicted in the sprawling cities. And if an Australian hero were to be found there, he or she would probably be challenged not by British-acting horse racing officials but by someone or something else. *Emoh Ruo*, a rather lighthearted film that offers, according to critic Bruce Sandow, "no pretensions to social comment," offers us in Des and Terri Tunkley just such heroes (qtd. in Murray, *Australian Film* 167).

The comparison will strike many as odd, but *Emoh Ruo* is reminiscient of *The Man from Snowy River*. In both films, the "enemy" is a kind of materialism. In the period piece, it is the materialism of large landowners such as the American Harrison; in Denny Lawrence's film, it is the Australian–American dream of one's own home in the suburbs. Terri is much more taken by this dream than is her husband. Thus, she convinces her loving husband Des to leave their shoreside caravan park behind and move to a new suburban home in the far western suburbs of Sydney.

Several dimensions of this move should be noted because they are culturally important. The fact that they lived in a caravan park in and of itself suggests mobility and the freedom it provides. Further suggesting freedom is Des' boat, which he evidently works on lovingly. He dreams of traveling the open waters in that boat, freely sailing from port to port. He gives the boat and the dream up as they move to the suburbs because the money he gets from selling both the caravan and the boat its barely enough for the down payment on their dream home in the suburbs.

The caravan park is also on the beach. The beach plays an important role in the Australian psyche. It is a place of relaxation and recreation, but, beyond that, it is a state of mind. Des very clearly does not want to abandon this state of mind. His son Jack serves as a mirror for Des: just as Jack is upset at leaving the beach, so very much is Des. Note also that the Tunkleys are moving to the *far* western suburbs of Sydney—as remote from the ocean as possible within the sprawling metropolitan area.

The caravan park is also very much a community. The people living there are far from wealthy, but they seem to enjoy each others' company. This camaraderie is evident at the party Des and Terri throw. Everybody seems happy, even if they do not have the Australian–American dream of their own suburban home on their own quarter acre of land. The name of the caravan park—"Happy Daze"—seems apt, although the "daze" leaves us wondering if there is not a life "out there" that is better than that at this park.

There are forces, soon to be revealed as exploitative if not downright corrupt, ready to exploit those who are looking for something better. In this case, those forces are Austral Finance, which gives home loans when it probably should not, and Tregado Homes, which builds a shoddy product and then refuses to stand behind it. Des and Terri are very much the victims of Austral and Tregado, but, long before they are struggling to make their mortgage payments and witnessing their home's deterioration, there are signs that they have made the wrong choice. The drive to their new home is presented as insufferably long; their only neighbors prove to be anything but hospitable; and they must wake up each morning at four to commute to their city jobs.

Emoh Ruo, which by the way is "Our Home" backwards, is a comedy. Therefore, the Tunkley's defeat by Austral and Tregado is presented somewhat lightheartedly. Furthermore, they do not give up. Terri decides to take these "authorities" on. She confronts the builder; she confronts Margaret York, spokesperson for Austral. Fortunately, York, fearing bad publicity, turns on Tregado. Des, having been accused of never finishing anything he starts, goes on a barbie-building binge, creating in the Tunkley's backyard a monstrosity of a barbecue made from construction scraps Des has collected.

The film climaxes at an ironic housewarming party. The Tunkleys' friends are so impressed by Des' barbie that they all want one. Their desire, as grotesque as it is, inspires Des' entreprenuerial brother Les to add custom-designed barbecues to his line of "Tunkley Tyres." Des suddenly has good financial prospects, and, as the house literally starts collapsing, Margaret York arrives with good news for the Tunkleys from Austral Finance.

Des and Terri, however, do not accept Austral's offer of another new suburban home. They take the money from Des' custom-designed grotesque barbies, buy a new caravan, and hit the road. This ending is very lighthearted and, thus, not to be taken too seriously. It does, however, relate to the theme of heroism in two ways: First, we see the forces that threaten this heroism very clearly depicted in their modern guise, and second, we see, in both Des and Terri, the love of freedom, the willingness to challenge authorities, the underdog status, and the desire for camaraderie and community that typify the revised hero. We do not, however, see the fatalism, for, after all, *Emoh Ruo* is a comedy, although it is one that, through satire, does indeed offer a social comment.

COOL CHANGE (GEORGE MILLER, DIRECTOR, 1986)

The Man from Snowy River does have a sequel: *The Man from Snowy River II* (1988), however, like many, it suffers from repetition. It offers story lines so similar to the original that it becomes too predictable. In some ways, the better sequel to George Miller's hit movie is his *Cool Change* (Greg Kerr in Murray, *Australian Film* 185).

Like *Emoh Ruo*—but unlike most of the films I have discussed thus far—*Cool Change* focuses fairly equally on the male and the female leads. The male lead, Steve Mitchell (Jon Blake), grew up in the Snowy Mountains and had left his hometown, but his work as a park ranger brings him back. His job, however, is not a pleasant one: he must oversee the transformation of the cattle-raising country into a national park. Thus, he is pitted against many of those whom he grew up with. Among them is the female lead, Joanna Regan (Lisa Armytage), a former lover, who has inherited her father's ranch. In the face of sexist suggestions that she ought to sell because she could not possibly manage the ranch because she is a woman, she is doing a reasonably good job running the place.

The title *Cool Change* draws our attention to Steve. In Australian meteorological slang, cool change refers to a dramatic dropping of the temperature brought on, usually, by a wind shift. Melbourne is notorious for its cool changes, as are the mountains (including the Snowy Mountains) to its northeast. Once in those mountains, Steve will experience a comparable dramatic change. And, as one might expect, Joanna plays a major role in bringing about this cool change.

Miller believes in directing films that are primarily entertaining. He does not worry a great deal about a film's "message." This lack of worry is at times evident in the film. For example, Miller and scriptwriter Patrick Edgeworth make the forces who want a national park "the heavies." They do this by suggesting that the political aspirations of corrupt government officials are behind the move instead of noble conservation motives. Furthermore, they make the battle lines stark by depicting greenies (environmental actvists) stereotypically as hippies a decade or two too late, something David Stratton describes as a right-wing political attempt to discredit the environmental movement in Australia (*Avocado* 224). To increase the dramatic tension, they create a social class tension rich in Australian history between the English-descended Mitchell family and the Irish-descended Regans, taking us back to the time of settlers and squatters. They also create an ockerlike rival for Joanna's affection, thereby positioning her between Steve's sanitized heroism and this ocker–cowboy's crudeness. Perhaps too much is going on in the film, without any of these elements—and still some others—being developed with any great depth. But, as I said, the film was intended as entertainment, not social or political comment.

We can, however, extract from *Cool Change* two interesting heroic portraits: Steve's and Joanna's. Steve's desire for independence had led him away from the Snowy Mountains. Once back, his attraction to all that the mountains stand for is suggested by his immediate attraction to Joanna. The film depicts Steve overcoming one obstacle after another until he can finally re-embrace the mountain's ethos. He must overcome the perspective he brings and again see the land as the people who live there do, not as a resource to be preserved for weekend hikers but as beloved land to make one's living from. He must overcome the lustful temptation offered by his city boss Lee, who comes to the mountains, doffs her duds, goes for a swim, and invites Steve to join her for a dip. He must overcome his revulsion when he believes that the father of Joanna's child is the ocker–cowboy type. Joanna helps him see and love the land as she does, and his growing true love of Joanna helps him overcome the of temptation of Lee. Steve's mother plays a major role in helping Steve overcome the obstacle posed by the ocker–cowboy. Jo finally confesses to Mrs. Mitchell that her son's father is Steve. Mrs. Mitchell uses this knowledge not only to put an end to the antipathy between the Mitchells and the Regans but also to unite Steve and Joanna. Then, he and Joanna, together with others from the mountains, will fight against the "evil" government forces.

Steve is a freedom-loving, land-loving, authority-defying man who will fight. No sexism; little alcohol: the heroism is again sanitized, and anti-British feelings have been generalized into antipolitical feelings, with "political" almost automatically pejorative. He fits the heroic mold except, as seems typical of Miller's films, he wins. Fatalism is replaced—for the sake of entertainment and, maybe, the American audience—by "happily ever after."

Joanna does not change as noticeably as the film progresses. Like Steve, she is freedom-loving. She is defying the male mountain "authorities" by running her deceased father's ranch, and she will defy the government authorities as well. In both fights, she seems the underdog. Steeled by her need to provide for her young son and encouraged by Mrs. Mitchell to reject the sexism all around her, she fights on for the child she loves and, also, for the land she loves. One feels that Joanna, ultimately will not be able to win: the forces aligned against her are too strong. She is even on the verge of accepting this fate when Steve appears at the film's climax. He has quit the rangers and rallied the men to her cause. With a few notes of comedy thrown in, Joanna and Steve and the forces he has rallied defeat the government. As noted earlier, the Steve who leads this defense has changed dramatically. Joanna has let some of the walls she built up around her fall because her trust of Steve has increased. So, in the end, she is less steeled. However, she has also acceded to her need for male help, although the film does allow us to see it as community help. All of her mountain mates come through for her, although it took Steve to orchestrate the display of Snowy Mountain solidarity that ends the film.

CROCODILE DUNDEE (PETER FAIMAN, DIRECTOR, 1986)

Crocodile Dundee is the most successful Australian film ever made (O'Regan, *Australian* 83). It may not be the best, but, its blatantly commercial dimensions aside, it is a well made motion picture (Rattigan 101). Some in Australia saw in Mick Dundee (Paul Hogan) some foreign (i.e., American) characteristics (Turner, *Making* 204). But others saw in Mick Dundee a too-stereotypical Australian, one as seen by tourists and marketed by tourism concerns (O'Regan, *Australian* 224–25). Yes, the film stereotypes Australians, just as it stereotypes Americans, and, rather evenhandedly, the film satirizes and salutes both. It is a film one should not take too seriously: after all, Paul Hogan and company, like the George Miller of *Snowy River* fame, were primarily interested in making an entertaining film. On the other hand, one should not neglect how the character Mick Dundee embodies a heroism that blends elements of the old—both ocker and bushman, according to Rattigan—with refinements of the new and, thereby, offers a quintessential revised Australian hero (102). Australian audiences certainly saw in Mick Dundee a send-up of several Australian traits (Abbey and Crawford). However, you cannot send up something that is not there. So, taken with a strong dose of whatever, Mick Dundee comes very close to being *the* revised Australian hero I have been pointing to in this chapter.

We first meet Mick on his turf, the tropical outback of the northern Northern Territory. During this stretch of the film, several of Mick's traits become set. He lives freely there, enjoying the company of his mates in the pub but also enjoying quiet time alone. He thus has a bit of the ocker in him, but is far more solitary and far more pensive than the typical pub-loving ocker. We can see, in the pub scenes very early in the film, how Mick fits in but also how he does not.

He seems to have a certain measure of (for lack of a better word) class that most of the men gathered there lack. We can already see how Faiman and Hogan are sanding the rough edges off the traditional hero. It is also worth noting that he counts the aboriginal Neville (David Gulpilil again) among his mates. So, the rough edge of racism is also sanded off.

Mick does not have much use for the authorities in "the Never, Never." He defies their rule against hunting for crocodiles, but seems otherwise unaffected by the "authorities." He is not flamboyantly against them, but neither is he with them. If he is against anything, it is urban life. But his opposition to the city is not prompted by its commercial or materialistic values; rather, it is because he cannot imagine the population density of the city as being especially enjoyable. He even imagines that the others who reside in the city must are unlike him insofar as they are friendlier. They must be friendlier, he conjectures, if they want to live that close together.

The way Mick thinks, as just exemplified, is certainly anti-intellectual insofar as it relies (rightly or wrongly) on common sense, not research or reading. Mick does not make a point of being anti-intellectual; he simply reasons the way he reasons and asserts that that is good enough for Mick Dundee. His comments on aboriginal land rights, for example, have prompted a good bit of negative commentary. First, his statement that aboriginals do not "own" the land has been criticized as a dangerous oversimplification of aboriginal beliefs; second, his comparing the court battles between the descendants of settlers and aboriginals to fleas fighting over who owns the dog has been criticized as disrespectfully reductive (Morris, *Pirate's* 138). These critiques, however, strike me as taking the film far too seriously and Mick's statements as if they represent those of the filmmakers. These comments are in the film—I would suggest—not as Paul Hogan's foray into serious political issues, but as, first, satirical comedy and, second, a suggestion of how Mick Dundee (rightly or wrongly) thinks without bogging himself down in matters he (and others) might dismiss as intellectual niceties. It is indeed difficult for academic scholars, of film or anything else, to tolerate anti-intellectualism. Mick Dundee makes it tolerable, I would argue, by making it disarmingly charming.

While on his own turf in the Never, Never, we do not see much in Mick's character that would strike one right away as competitive. Do, however, note that he hunts—a competition in itself, and one can imagine that Mick would not be especially happy if some of his mates were to intrude upon his hunting grounds. Also note that he is very much competing for journalist Sue Charlton's journalistic attention because that attention means publicity and publicity means more business for Dundee and his mate Wally. Thus, he shows her his wrecked "fishing" boat and plays up the "outback man" role by pretending to tell time by looking at the sky and shaving with his hunting knife. We see still more of Mick's competitive streak when the story shifts to New York City and he competes with city slicker Richard Mason for Sue's non-journalistic attention.

Dundee's sexism provides a good bridge between Walkabout Creek and Manhattan. When Mick and Sue are in the outback together, Mick very clearly views her as a sheila. She rebels at the characterization and insists on going off on her own. Mick lets her, but he trails behind—carefully guarding her—and then saves her life when she is attacked by a crocodile. After being saved, Sue seems much more tolerant of Mick's paternal sexism, laughing at his remark about eating her up and almost kissing him before Wally rudely appears on the scene and interrupts. Mick's sexism, however, has lost its edge a bit. When Wally, with a leer on his face, wants to know what happened "in the woods," Mick brushes him aside in a manner suggesting that Mick sees Sue as much more than a potential sexual conquest.

In New York City, Mick fights and competes. He stands up to a pimp and to a knife-wielding punk. Unlike Barry McKenzie, who was abused by the British in Beresford's 1972 film, Mick Dundee proves able to handle himself quite well initially: the pimp and the punk, however are easy compared to Richard Mason who has the big city charm and the money that Mick assumes Sue delights in. Mick and Richard are, of course, competing for Sue. In this battle, Mick feels he is the underdog. Winning Sue will not be as easy as pulling out his Bowie knife and saying to the punk, "You call that a knife?" When Mick surreptitiously slugs an intoxicated Richard in a posh restaurant, Mick perhaps thinks he is winning the battle. However, when Richard announces their engagement at a dinner party at Sue's family home, Mick despairs. Accepting his fate—his loss—he goes off to get drunk. Note that he chooses liquor this time, not beer: he is not engaging in the social drinking that beer connotes; rather he is engaging in solitary drinking designed to numb him as he ponders his loss.

If *Crocodile Dundee* ended at this point, Mick would offer us an excellent example of revised heroism. He embodies what we find admirable in the hero of old. He also embodies some of the less admirable qualities with the roughness at least partially smoothed away. Thus, he is a freedom-loving, authority-defying, land-loving, mate-loving, competitive underdog. He is anti-intellectual, but not oafishly; he is sexist, but not offensively. The film, however, ends instead with the crowd-pleasing scene of Sue chasing Mick onto a crowded subway platform, where they exchange words of love, surrounded by many New York City "mates." So, Mick wins. Like Jim Craig in *The Man from Snowy River* and like both Steve Mitchell and Joanna Regan in *Cool Change*, he triumphs. In all of these cases, I would suggest the filmmakers' desire for a popular movie won out over offering a distinctly Australian hero.

However, one should not discount an alternative explanation: that the filmmakers made the film with such obvious "popular" touches to offer a parodic statement about the "pompous high cultural (bourgeois) aesthetic proclamations" that has elevated films such as *Breaker Morant* and *Gallipoli* to the pinnacle of Australian filmmaking while denigrating all other modes (Laseur 371). If one knows just a bit about the Paul Hogan television team that wrote, directed, and produced the film, one knows that an anti–high culture "statement" is not at all out of the question. In any event, after *Crocodile Dundee*'s phenomenal success, it would prove difficult to denigrate films that contained "popular" elements designed to enhance their mass audience appeal.

GROUND ZERO (MICHAEL PATTINSON AND BRUCE MYLES, DIRECTOR, 1987)

Ground Zero ought to have been a much better movie. It has a strong cast, and it deals with a very controversial subject, U. S. nuclear tests near Maralinga in the Australian desert in the early 1950s, tests that allegedly killed large numbers of aborigines. It also deals quite responsibly with its subject matter, basing itself on solid research (Stratton, *Avocado* 249). It is admittedly an old subject, but the subject of American "use" of Australia's emptiness in this manner is not dated. As all the legends about the *real* work at Pine Gap, a secret U.S. military installation near Alice Springs suggest, there remains a feeling in Australia that the United States is "using" its Australian ally in a manner that is both objectionable and dangerous.

The central character in *Ground Zero* is a cameraman named Harvey (Colin Friels). He is drawn into a quest for the truth about the tests when his apartment is broken into and some of his films are stolen. He obviously wonders what whoever broke in is looking for. The answer to the question of who is never clearly answered in the film because it seems as if everyone is involved in wrongfully covering up what happened in the early 1950s—perhaps partially because some fear how this example of abuse of the nation's indigenous people will exacerbate the current controversy surrounding aboriginal land rights. The answer to the question of what are films Harvey's father took of the testing and its devastating results.

Harvey, as far as he knows, does not have any such films, but he feels the need to reconnect with his deceased father by finding out what his father knew. So, he journeys into the nation's interior. There, in the middle of the desert, he meets a reclusive former soldier named Prosper (Donald Pleasence). Now an artist, Prosper (whose name perhaps alludes to Shakespeare's *The Tempest*) is carried from place to place on the back of a blind aboriginal man, a victim of the blasts. In a box in a cave, Harvey finds the photographic evidence of what happened back in the early 1950s. His estranged wife Pat, a television reporter, helps him get this evidence before a government hearing. The government officials, however, after viewing the films, declare that they were blank. Having ourselves seen them, we know this declaration to be false. Harvey's quest and crusade then seem to have been for nought, sabotaged by a government that wants to continue the cover-up.

We are then asked to recall a telephone conversation early in the film. Harvey's sister had asked him to copy (in order to preserve) several of their father's films that she had. She had put them in the mail. When Harvey's apartment was searched and when her home was searched, these films were in transit. As *Ground Zero* ends, these films arrive. They contain the incriminating footage. We are left to believe he now might be able to expose those who have been covering up the tests and their effects on the aborigines.

Harvey's portrait does not have the richness of other Australian film heroes. We do know enough to know that he is like many others because he cherishes his freedom from responsibility to the point that his wife Pat has left him, declaring him to be no more mature than a child. If we assume that her evaluation is at least partially accurate, then the film's quest is Harvey's maturation. Very much the underdog, he defies authorities at every turn to find out the truth about the nuclear tests. Never before in his life having been engaged in a quest like this one, he suddenly turns competitive, fighting the forces that oppose him no matter whether they come after him by jeep or by helicopter. At some point, the movie changed from political exposé to thriller, and, perhaps, never regains its political edge sufficiently (Geoff Gardner in Murray, *Australian Film* 220).

Prosper's presence in the film is, if nothing else, designed to suggest the futility of the quest. He knows the truth; Prosper has in the films and in his aboriginal companion the evidence to prove what the government did. He also knows how difficult it will be to communicate that message. Thus, he has receded into his desert cave, numbed by what he knows and by his awareness that he will not likely ever be allowed to share it. Harvey, however, will not accept that attempting to expose the truth is futile. His experience before the commission established to study the matter causes him to realize that Prosper had been right. But then the package his sister sent arrives.

Ground Zero ends ambiguously. How one chooses to read the ending will determine how fatalistic one thinks the film is. Does the ending suggest that Harvey will now be able to win the day? Or does it suggest that he will try again but probably suffer the same fate as before? Or does it suggest that Harvey, like Chicken Little, will never be believed even though he now possesses photographic evidence again? This latter possibility could then leave us with a Harvey very much like the character Prosper.

THE LIGHTHORSEMEN (SIMON WINCER, DIRECTOR, 1987)

Simon Wincer eventually comes to the United States to direct the television miniseries adapted from Larry McMurtry's novel *Lonesome Dove*. As suggested by Wincer's trip, he loves horses and he is not averse to the television medium. Those two observations are relevant to his *The Lighthorsemen* because it is a film that offers the viewer beautiful images of horses in motion and because it is a film with a television miniseries "feel" to it.

Like *Gallipoli*, Wincer's film is a World War I story. It takes place in what was then Palestine, about two years after Gallipoli. On one level, it is a movie about military strategy. We are told at the very beginning, by a Nazi officer, that the British simply do not know how to use the Australian Lighthorsemen effectively in battle. This Nazi is quite glad the British are so inept. As the film climaxes, the Australian commander of the Lighthorsemen is given sufficient freedom over an attack on Beersheba that he is finally able to show the British how these mounted infantry might be effectively used.

Up to that point in the Palestinian campaign, the Australians were not particularly underdogs as much as they were benchwarmers. By the time they were sent on their dramatic charge to seize Beersheba, they were underdogs, however, because the time was running out that day and that day was the only day the allies had because they would run out of water at sunset. They also, on that charge, faced artillery fire and, then, machine-gun fire. It is no wonder then that the Anzac–led victory at Beersheba is celebrated in Australia. (The surprise is that this victory has never captured the Australian imagination as much as the catastrophic defeat at Gallipoli, a failure that, perhaps, suggests the culture's pronounced fatalism [Stratton, *Avocado* 27]).

The more important story in the film is not that of the battle but, rather, that of young Dave. We first meet him in Australia where he joins the Lighthorsemen. We next see him joining Tas, Chiller, and Scotty, who will become his wartime mates. Initially, they do not want to accept him as a mate. Their rejection is partially because they find him young and untested, partially because he is from Melbourne not the bush, and partially because their fourth mate had just died and they could not accept Dave (or anyone) as a substitute for this man. When a surprise Turkish air attack startles their horses and city boy Dave manages to calm them and keep them from running off, the men finally embrace Dave; henceforth, they are mates. They eat together, they recreate together (another male nude swimming scene), and they drink together, although the drinking in this film is different from others because the men reject the pub where the British enthusiastically welcome them and instead head to the shore where they sip and talk melancholically of home. They also talk about the war. They reflect on how the first wave of Australians who enlisted all naïvely thought the war would be over in months, on how these enlistees, including Dave's older brother, had seen action and, in most cases, death at Gallipoli. They, on the other hand, are not naïve; they are resigned to a war that would drag on. Being caught up in it was their unfortunate fate.

Dave's story will take two important turns. First, he gradually discovers that he cannot bring himself to kill another man. He hides this discovery as best he can. But mates look after mates, as well as "number one," so his mates, a bit worried about the "weak link," confront him and suggest he transfer to a noncombat unit. When Dave transfers, they see him off as a mate, not as a liability in combat they are glad to be rid of. Second, Dave falls in love with a nurse Anne (Sigrid Thornton). Somewhat to Dave's surprise, his switch from combatant to medic does not alter her feelings in the slightest because she is in love with him, not a heroic soldier.

Wincer's film shows us heroes who are very much mates as well as lovers of horses, but the film tones down the antiauthoritarian and heavy drinking streaks. There are a few sexist remarks offered now and again among the soldiers, but, in general, they are loyal to their women at home or, in Dave's case, at the Palestinian hospital. The mates Tas, Chiller, and Scotty, in fact, all recall how it was the infidelity of their previous mate's girlfriend back in Australia that caused him to lose his fighting spirit and die. The relationship between Dave and Anne is the only male–female relationship we actually see, but, based on that, we might conclude that relationships in the world of this film feature a fair degree of equality.

So Dave and his fellow Australian soldiers are heroes but with much that makes the hero of old seem coarse smoothed away. And on the day of the fateful battle, it was these men, three as combatants and Dave as medic, who charge upon Beersheba—800 Aussies trying to accomplish in an hour what 60,000 British troops had failed to do all day. The Australians are underdogs, but they throw themselves into the charge with a competitive spirit and a fatalistic acceptance of what the cost might be. The Australians succeed, but not all of the members of the quartet the film focuses on survive. Seeing one die, Dave abandons his role as medic and throws himself into the fighting. Dave, showing much the same depth of mateship that Archie shows in *Gallipoli*, then saves another mate's life by throwing his own body between his mate's and a grenade. This display is perhaps why Rattigan termed *The Lighthorsemen* "Gallipoli II."

Dave does survive. The film has its several melodramatic moments (thus, giving it a television rhythm). Anne's search for and the discovery of Dave among the wounded are probably the most melodramatic. As words on the screen tell us at the film's end, they return to Australia and marry. So, we have the happy ending of films such as *The Man from Snowy River*, *Cool Change*, and *Crocodile Dundee*. However, we also have characters whose fates are not as happy as that of Dave and Anne. So Wincer manages to combine in this film the Australian fatalism with the American optimism, creating a film that ought to have fared better than it did commercially, especially given its $10.5 million price tag as compared to *Gallipoli*'s $3 million (Stratton, *Avocado* 28). Perhaps, its commercial failure is due to period films really having had their day long before 1987. Critical consensus suggests that they were fading in popularity years earlier than this.

YOUNG EINSTEIN (YAHOO SERIOUS, DIRECTOR, 1988)

With Yahoo Serious' campy, rock-scored *Young Einstein*, we certainly come a long distance from such period films. The conception of heroism found in Serious' film, however, is not that different from that in a film such as *The Man from Snowy River* or even *The Lighthorsemen*, although Serious' film is not the paean to mateship that Wincer's film is.

The central character, young Albert Einstein, usually works alone, although the focus on this character alone in this film has more to do with the film being a vehicle to display Serious' comic genius than the film reflecting Australian culture. As we all come to know, Einstein grew up on a farm in Tasmania. And, as we also all come to know, he discovered the principle of relativity when trying to find a way to add bubbles to beer. In fact, young Einstein nonchalantly stumbles into discovery after discovery as the film proceeds. Most of them involve very little intellectual effort on his part. The discoveries may well be part of the intellectual heritage of the twentieth century, but, if you accept this film's fictitious account of them, very few of them required much intellectual input.

Young Einstein, however, becomes convinced of his genius and decides to go to Sydney—to share his ideas and to patent some of his discoveries. Once there, away from the safe, beautiful Tasmanian countryside he loves (which is actually the New South Wales Hunter Valley), Albert finds himself in danger. Many people who meet him realize what these various ideas are worth, and they plot to steal the credit for them from Albert. He does not take this thievery lying down. He determines to fight. Not knowing the ins and outs in Australian (or global) scientific circles and not yet having a reputation for anything, he is very much the underdog in this competition against those who are trying to profit from his ideas.

Since these nefarious others are part of the establishment, young Albert Einstein must defy the establishment to defeat them. To some extent, the Australian scientific establishment comes across as having a British flavor. The facade of fastidious politeness in addition to the preference for a more British (as opposed to Australian) accent would lead one to conclude so. As a result, Einstein's defiance of authorities has a rather anti-British ring to it.

Albert does receive some help along the way from beautiful, young Marie Curie, whom he meets on a train he catches from somewhere in the outback to Sydney. A romance develops between them. Young Einstein is both shy and polite in his interactions with women, exhibiting no sexism, even in his dealings with the prostitutes he ends up sharing a cheap hotel with. As a result of Albert's deferential behavior toward women, we really cannot tell if there is much passion in this romance. But passion or not, they do manage to combine wits and save the world from nuclear destruction. In the course of doing so, Einstein discovers rock and roll music. Then, he and Marie return to the family farm in Tasmania.

There is, perhaps, a tendency to associate a concept such as heroism primarily with dramas focusing on serious subjects and secondarily with comedies containing at least some serious substance. *Young Einstein* falls into neither category. It is an irreverent look at twentieth-century science, not to satirize as much as just to have fun with such a weighty subject. Yahoo Serious is being outrageous with something usually revered (or treated very seriously) just for the sake of being outrageous. Nonetheless, he does offer a hero with traits similar to others treated in this chapter.

THE CASTLE (ROB SITCH, DIRECTOR, 1997)

The Castle is also far removed from the period films viewers perhaps first think of when thinking of the concept of heroism. Sitch's *The Castle* does, however, present in Darryl Kerrigan a very Australian hero. Initially, we tend to laugh at him because some of his behavior is stupidity masquerading as sincerity. After some time passes, we begin to admire Darryl. Yes, he still says outrageous things, but, as we become increasingly convinced of the man's basic decency, we find buried beneath the stupid behavior and outrageous words a heroism that has him taking on a major corporation and proving victorious.

The Castle has proven very popular in Australia—so much so that lines from the film have passed into popular culture. Phrases such as "straight to the poolroom" and "he must be dreamin'," although not identifiable in the United States, are derived from things Darryl Kerrigan says repeatedly. Gifts or souvenirs, no matter how tacky, go "straight to the poolroom" to be displayed in a place of honor. The asking price for used jousting equipment, for example, prompts a "he must be dreamin' " from Darryl if it is too high. The film's family and basic story line are also extremely well-known in Australia.

The Kerrigan family consists of Darryl, a tow-truck driver; his wife; his older son, who is in jail for armed robbery; his married daughter Tracy, who is contemplating giving up her career as a hairdresser to raise children; and his younger son. We see them eat dinner, at which the wife's rather ordinary food is praised lavishly by Darryl. We see them converse, usually about the same topic (for example, the superficial aspects of Tracy and husband Con's honeymoon trip to Thailand). We see them watch rather stupid television programs. We see Darryl and his younger son buying up junk, such as the jousting equipment or a pulpit. We see them all head up to their vacation cottage on "Lake Bonnie Doon," a seemingly shrinking body of water surrounded by scrub and passed over by high-voltage electric power lines.

The power lines are perhaps important to the Kerrigans because similar lines run near their home. Also near their home is the end of the Melbourne airport runway. This proximity leads to the film's plot because the airport needs to expand. Therefore, the Kerrigans and their very few neighbors have been served with notices telling them that their homes will be acquired—no choice in the matter—for $70,000. Darryl, however, does not want to sell his house and land. So, he rallies the other residents together; then, he asks the family's lawyer to take the case.

Such a case is clearly beyond this lawyer's ken. They lose before a federal administrative court, although Darryl thinks the lawyer was eloquent. He tries to dissuade Darryl from continuing, but Darryl will not give up the fight. They seek an injunction, prompting the airport authority to offer each property owner $25,000 more. They reject this offer and proceed to a higher court. The lawyer's performance is comically incompetent, but Darryl cannot see that. He thinks his attorney has done splendidly. After they lose, Darryl becomes despondent: he no longer compliments his wife's cooking; he no longer is interested in buying junk at bargain prices. Then, an older man Darryl had met in the courthouse hall asks Darryl if he can take over the case. Reluctant to offend his attorney, Darryl initially declines, but eventually he accepts. The older man proves to be Lawrence Hammill, a retired Queen's Councilor, who takes the case to the high court in Canberra, eloquently pleads it, and wins.

The basic story line is familiar: movie-goers have encountered it in movies such as *Erin Brockovich*. What gives the film its appeal is not the plot *per se* but the humor as the plot unfolds. What makes the story interesting to us are the qualities of character Darryl Kerrigan exhibits as he fights on. He defies the authorities in defense of his home, which is (he insists) his castle. Although others might not think much of it, it is his land and his house, and he loves them, just as he loves his rather ugly vacation land. He opposes their fancy language and smart lawyers' talk with emotion, common sense, and—when they do not work—working-class profanity. Most important, he will not give up. Although he knows he is very much the underdog, he keeps battling. And he rallies his neighbors—his mates, in a sense—whenever the going gets tough.

One other dimension of *The Castle* should be mentioned. In the background of the comic movie is the issue of aboriginal land rights. The precedent that Kerrigan's inept lawyer stumbles upon and the precedent that Hammill actually uses is *Mabo*, the landmark case that began unraveling all of the compulsory confiscations of aboriginal lands down through the centuries. At a couple of points in *The Castle*, Darryl Kerrigan says he now knows how the aborigines feel. It is perhaps ironic that a case that bestowed land rights of Australia's indigenous people can be used to "save the day" for a white Australian, who in some ways fits the stereotype of those who dispossessed the aborigines.

In this chapter, we have seen many heroes. In general, we can make two observations about them. First, they exhibit many of the traits of the hero of old. Loving their freedom, they challenge authority if authority attempts to squash their freedom. As underdogs, they fight, often with mates whom they love. Second, they often do not exhibit all of the coarse touches of the traditional hero. Drinking and sexism diminish, as do extremes of irreverence and boorishness. The rough edges have been smoothed away. The hero of old has become sanitized. There are, however, two categories into which we might place these revised heroes. In one category are those who are, or will inevitably be, defeated. This category may contain the more authentic Australian heroes. In the other category are those who succeed: the ones who face happy endings instead of an ominous fate. These heroes might be viewed as more American. In any event, they are more appealing than the fatalistic heroes to the viewing audience in the United States. Darryl Kerrigan clearly falls into this second group. He lives on next to the airport runway, and, even more improbably, he and Lawrence Hammill become fast friends and even vacation together at Lake Bonnie Doon. This improbability—as well as that of other films that fall into this second category—does make one wonder if the revised Australian heroes who live happily ever after are not the illusion and the ones who finally meet their sad fate, the reality.

Chapter 4

A Woman's Role

With just a few minor exceptions, all of the heroes we have talked about thus far have been men. The three exceptions can be easily pushed aside. In *Emoh Ruo*, (1985) Terri does stand up to Austral Finance. However, it is her desire for a suburban life that gets the Tunkley family into trouble, and it is Des' design and construction of monstrous barbies that get them back on the road in their caravan. In *A Town Like Alice* (1981), Jean Paget is indeed heroic in her fighting against the odds in Malaysia and in her generosity toward the women and children she is suffering with. However, she is British, not Australian. In *Cool Change* (1986), Joanna Regan does play a heroic role in managing her deceased father's ranch against the odds and in resisting the government's plan to turn the high country into a national park. However, she remains rather static throughout the movie, only softening a bit when she begins to trust Steve Mitchell. Furthermore, she ultimately needs to be saved by Steve and the Snowy Mountain men he rallies.

When one pictures the Australian hero, whether it be old or new, it is typically a male figure: Ned Kelly or Captain Starlight or an Anzac soldier or Michael J. "Crocodile" Dundee. However, there are many fine Australian films that focus on women, many of which were produced and/or directed by women. Andree Wright concludes her study of Australian women's involvement in film with a discussion of Gillian Armstrong: obviously, much precedes Armstrong's work. In addition, much of the work done contemporaneously with Armstrong was, as Adrian Martin notes, in non-feature-length films ("Double"). Still, the number of feature-length films has been strikingly high

(Pip, Marsh, and Cox; Robson and Zalcock; Ryan, Eliot, and Appleton; Sands).

In this chapter, I examine those films by women, as well as films about women produced and/or directed by men with an eye to determining how the women fit the concept of heroism we have developed thus far. We will find that some come close to being this very kind of hero. We will also find that there are dynamics of oppression and victimization that work against them and make the battle to be that kind of hero very difficult.

I need first to address the rather obvious question of whether that definition is one women should aspire to. Might it be, in other words, a male-derived definition they might do better to reject? I do not want to list, one through ten, what characterizes this hero because I do not want to reduce the issue to using a checklist. But what we have seen thus far leads us to a revised hero who loves freedom and does not accept the restraints or dictates of authority too willingly. The anti-British attitude has faded somewhat, perhaps replaced with an opposition to crass materialism when it subverts more communal values. In line with those very values, one's mates are still loved, as is the land and maybe horses or horse substitutes, such as automobiles. Some of the characteristics of old—anti-intellectualism, sexism, and even drinking have been suppressed, if not entirely put aside, in the formation of this revised hero. The underdog status and the competitive spirit have not: the revised hero is still a fighter against the odds. And sometimes the hero even wins; therefore, the fatalism of old does not cast quite the gloomy shadow across this hero as it once did. I would suggest that this definition fits women as well as men. Some of the women we will discuss, in fact, are quite in line with this definition. The only difference one might note between male and female revised heroism is that often the latter sets itself explicitly against the patriarchy as opposed to the rather vague "authorities" who seem resented and rebelled against by the men.

CADDIE (DONALD CROMBIE, DIRECTOR, 1976)

Crombie's film is set in Sydney in the 1930s. Thus, it appeared on the screen at the time period films were quite popular. The period *Caddie* chronicles is the Great Depression. The film tells the story of the Depression from the point of view of a young woman who eventually acquires the nickname Caddie because a bar patron thinks she has the class of a Cadillac. The film was based on the 1953 autobiography of a barmaid identified simply as Caddie.

Caddie (Helen Morse) leaves her unfaithful husband, taking their two young children along with her. Pawning her diamond ring for capital, she begins a life on her own just as hard times strike Australia. In this environment, she has to battle to earn the money she and her children need. She gets a job as a barmaid and prospers as the bar does. The bar seems more immune to the nation's economic problems than other institutions, and we see the bar take a marked upscale swing during Caddie's years there. However, the Depression deepens, the bar is sold, and Caddie finds herself out of work and living on welfare. In fact, if it were not for the kindness of two rabbit-selling brothers, who look after Caddie when she hits rock bottom, Caddie would probably not have survived the Depression. Viewers undoubtedly are waiting for romance to blossom between Caddie and either of these brothers, but it does not. Rather, they—all three of them—remain mates, helping each other through the very hard times. One's mates, regardless of gender, play an important role in Caddie's life. She is helped along by these brothers just as earlier she helped along her fellow barmaid Josie (Jacki Weaver) when, pregnant, Josie has an illegal abortion and falls quite ill as a result.

As she battles her way through hard times, Caddie is not just looking out for herself; she also has her children's welfare to consider. She moves out of one boardinghouse because she finds it disreputable; she is asked to leave another because the children are getting into too much trouble. Day care arrangements she makes are often not at all satisfactory. Once, for example, she found her daughter ill with diphtheria while the care provider entertained family and friends. She finally puts her children in a home. She does so because she cannot work and provide adequate supervision of them, but it breaks her heart to do so. After a while, she finds this arrangement too emotionally draining for her and brings the children back "home" with her. She eventually has at least the emotional support of a somewhat older Greek man named Peter who seems to truly love her. Throughout, she receives no support whatsoever from the children's father.

Given the era during which the events of *Caddie* took place, one would not expect much in the way of feminist commentary on them. But there is some. At one point, she complains about wage inequity based on gender; and at another, she becomes angry when it becomes clear to her that she cannot get credit without having a husband. She does not comment on the divorce proceedings she eventually goes through, but it is clear from her reluctance to initiate them that her husband's gender and higher social class advantage him in such matters. There then is a proto-feminist message in the film. Neil Rattigan may be right in arguing that the women's films of Australia are not as set against the patriarchy as in the United States; however, he is incorrect in arguing that Caddie's conflict is primarily with "the situation," not with the patriarchy because male privileges are very apparent in the film (73–74).

Economic circumstances, however, do seem to be the greater culprit in her suffering. Being alone with her children makes Caddie's life very difficult, but the Depression is what drives her close to the edge. With help, she fights on. Peter returns to Greece when his father dies; while there, he divorces his wife. Caddie divorces her husband. All seems set for a happy ending to Caddie's battling. However, Peter returns to Australia only to die in an accident before they could marry. So, we imagine that Caddie will keep on struggling, day by day, to provide for herself and her children.

Caddie is a period piece, but it lacks the stunning photography of other period pieces such as *Breaker Morant* (1980) and *Gallipoli* (1981) (discussed in Chapter 3) and *My Brilliant Career* (discussed in this chapter). The director's intent seems to be to depict a depressing time in Australia's history in appropriately muted tones. The overall effect of *Caddie*, then, is somber. Very different in tone is Tim Burstall's *Eliza Fraser*, which debuted in the same year.

ELIZA FRASER (TIM BURSTALL, DIRECTOR, 1976)

In the directing of *Eliza Fraser*, Tim Burstall seems somewhat influenced by Tony Richardson's award-wining *Tom Jones*. Just as the British director turned Henry Fielding's classic novel into a romp, Burstall had the prolific David Williamson turn the sensationalistic tale of an English sea captain's wife into a film that is, by turns, bedroom farce and satire against the puffed-up English. To gain an audience, Burstall cast Susannah York, who played Sophia Western in *Tom Jones*, as Eliza.

Eliza exhibits a sexual freedom certainly atypical of women of her stature in the 1830s. On one comic night in Sydney, for example, she makes love with a sailor named Bracefell (John Waters), who has fled Captain Foster Fyans' (Trevor Howard) homosexual advances. Then, with Bracefell beneath the bed, she tries to make love with the dashing Captain Rory McBryde (John Castle) but, alas, he falls into wine-inspired asleep atop her. And then her husband Captain Fraser (Noel Ferrier) arrives. Not all of Elisa's sexual exploits are this farcical, but, throughout the film, she freely reveals her frank desires.

Most of the men in the film come off poorly. Captain Fyans, who is in charge at the Moreton Bay penal colony, has his string of "bed boys"; and Captain Fraser proves inept at navigating, commanding the shipwrecked survivors, dealing with the aborigines, and—one imagines—quenching his young wife's appetite. These are the older British authority figures, but even the younger Captain McBryde proves not up to the task of satisfying Eliza: he falls into drunken sleep. In fact, making a satirical commentary on social class, the script has only the common sailor Bracefell prove sexually competent. Insofar as the only two competent characters are Bracefell and Eliza, the film may be making an interesting satirical comment on class and gender (Rattigan 121).

The plot has many comic twists, too many to cover here. The crucial point is that the free-spirited Eliza survives—shipwrecks, capture by the aborigines, and many sexual escapades. In the end, we meet her again in Sydney. She is telling her sensationalistic tale at a country fair to make the money necessary to "buy" back Johnnie, her son, who is living with Captain Fraser's brother in Parramatta. Bracefell reappears. They kidnap young Johnnie and head off to New Zealand. On board the ship, they make peace with McBryde, and, as the film ends, we discover that Eliza is making a fortune telling her tale at a sideshow in London "managed" by McBryde. British gullibility is being satirized, just as British leadership was throughout the bulk of the film (McFarlane 164).

Although the patriarchy is surely presented in unfavorable terms in *Eliza Fraser*, Eliza does not seem its victim. She has too much energy and too much resourcefulness to be a victim, especially given how pathetic the patriarchy is. So, her story is less a story of victimization and more a story of a freedom-loving, sex-loving, authority-flaunting battler who comically overcomes every adversity that comes her way to live, and love, the next day.

JOURNEY AMONG WOMEN (TOM COWAN, DIRECTOR, 1977)

Eliza Fraser takes us to the Moreton Bay penal colony (now Brisbane); *Journey among Women* takes us to the Port Jackson, or Sydney, colony. Whereas the former movie has a light tone and more than a few touches of farce, the latter has a disturbing tone and more than a few strong feminist notes. Brian McFarlane has termed it "one of the most provocative and intellectually ambitious films of recent years" (161).

In the low-budget (i.e., $150,000) *Journey among Women*, we learn what life was like for the female convicts in the early months of the Port Jackson penal colony. Too often that life featured sexual exploitation by the British soldiers: women were forced to exchange sexual favors for the food and wine they craved. Women unwilling to make such deals, as well as the very young and the very attractive, were simply raped. As a result of this treatment, the female convicts became a coarse, bitter lot.

Elizabeth Harrington, the refined daughter of a judge advocate there and the intended of one of the British officers, unfortunately sees more of the female convicts' life than she should. As a result, she helps the women take advantage of the celebration the soldiers are enjoying at the fleet's return to Sydney by escaping. She shoots one of the British officers during the escape, and she then chooses to flee with the convict women into the wilderness. Not long afterward, some convict women help Elizabeth remove her tight corset, an act that is clearly symbolic of her throwing off the restraints the patriarchy had placed on her.

The next part of the film—perhaps, ironically exploitative itself—presents the escaped women as they try to create some sort of community. This part, much like the initial prison scenes, featured a great deal of improvisation among the performers. Initially, having discovered a still in the woods, they get rowdily, raunchily drunk on the rum. Then, aided by an aboriginal woman who believes they, with their white skin, are angels, they focus on their day-to-day existence. Repeated attacks by the men cause the women to adopt a militaristic posture. This, in addition to their gradual embrace of nudity, makes the proper Elizabeth increasingly uncomfortable. She wants to return to the settlement. However, despite this discomfort, she is one of the first to experience a lesbian embrace.

The captain, to whom she was betrothed, manages to "rescue" her during one of the skirmishes between the soldiers and the war-paint covered women. She, somewhat reluctantly it seems, returns to "civilization." Meanwhile, the battle continues, with the men intent on winning it because the stories of the female convicts' free lives in the wild are causing some discontent among the other women in the penal colony.

The escaped women fight, as a tribe (as a group of mates), using weapons they have fashioned in the wilderness. They are naked, with the sounds of nature very much surrounding them. The fully uniformed men, on the other hand, roll in the cannons. After loading them with balls and much semen-white wadding, they fire these phallic weapons rather inexpertly in the women's general direction. Their heavy artillery proves useless. Then, spooked by all the strange sounds of Australian nature, the soldiers flee, only to be fired on by the captain. He accidentally sets the brush on fire, trapping himself. The clear indication as the film ends is that the women have triumphed. Elizabeth, back in "civilization," is presented walking along and singing. Although she is not among them, it is clear that she has shared in the joy of their triumph.

The women in Cowan's *Journey* yearn for freedom. They defy the authorities to secure whatever small measure of psychological freedom they might gain while in prison; then, they defy the authorities more dramatically in escaping and then defending their freedom. They are mates: when they defend the young against rape in prison, when they get drunk once outside of prison, and when they go into battle against the British troops. And, from the very beginning until the surprising end, they are underdogs who, despite the numbers and the technology directed against them, fight on. The women then very much fit the profile of the revised hero sketched in the preceding chapter.

What makes their story different from those that focus on men is the degree of oppression they suffer. Yes, the Australian male hero, particularly if he is from a lower social class, is arguably oppressed. His oppression, however, rarely comes near the horrors we see the jailed women suffering in this film's initial twenty minutes. There undoubtedly was such victimization back in the early days of the Sydney colony. However, those who produced this film were less interested in making a historical point than they were in using the veil of history to make a point about the status of women in 1977. They wished audiences to find common ground between the literally imprisoned women in the film and the figuratively imprisoned women of 1977; they wanted audiences to see in the suffering of women back then a mirror of the victimization of women now (O'Regan, *Australian* 197).

MY BRILLIANT CAREER (GILLIAN ARMSTRONG, DIRECTOR, 1979)

Given its low budget, *Journey among Women* is not a bad-looking film. It (and most other Australian films) pales by comparison with Gillian

Sybylla Melvyn (Judy Davis) sadly rejects a proposal of marriage from Harry Beecham (Sam Neill) in *My Brilliant Career* (1979). Photo courtesy of National Film and Sound Archives. Permission granted by Margaret Fink Films, c/o Property Group.

Armstrong's *My Brilliant Career*. The film, an adaptation of (Stella) Miles Franklin's turn-of-the-century novel, featured strong performances by Judy Davis as Sybylla Melvyn and Sam Neill as Harry Beecham, and others. Furthermore, it showcased the at-times impressionistic cinematography of Don

McAlpine. *My Brilliant Career* is one of the masterpieces of Australian cinema. It does, however, share one similarity with *Journey among Women:* although set in an earlier time, its message was directed at the 1970s audience. Although screenwriter Eleanor Whitcombe (with help from producer Margaret Fink) did not invent the proto-feminism in the film, she did take what was in Franklin's text and gave it, at times, a much more modern flavor. Critics do, however, disagree as to how modern (McFarlane in Murray, *Australian Film* 43; Rattigan 222).

When we first meet Sybylla, she is at her parents' sheep-raising farm, Possum Gully, in the near-outback. She is very discontent with her life there; she wants a life in the arts. Her parents, on the other hand, unable to continue paying for her keep, want her to take a servant's position elsewhere. Her refusal to even consider the idea causes her mother much grief. Fortunately, Sybylla's maternal grandmother comes to the rescue and arranges for Sybylla to spend some time living at Caddagat, her beautiful estate further east.

During her time at Caddagat, Sybylla continues to resist authority. She will not heed her grandmother's advice; although Sybylla becomes close to her Aunt Helen (Wendy Hughes), she will not heed her comments on how women need to be married to be thought respectable. Sybylla finds that notion offensive. Furthermore, she has no desire to marry. Thus, she repeatedly dismisses the attentions of Frank Hawden, an Englishman who will soon inherit a fair amount of money. The only person who seems to really lift Sybylla's spirits is her Uncle J. J., who finds her so entertaining that he thinks she ought to go on the stage. This suggestion delights Sybylla but appalls her very proper grandmother.

Sybylla's behavior can, at times, lack the dignity that her grandmother exudes. When picking apples and approached by a flirtatious young man, she puts on a cockney accent and pretends to be a new servant girl. When that young man, who proves to be Harry Beecham, comes to dinner, she ends up being the focal point of the after-dinner entertainment—playing the piano, dancing, and singing risque barroom songs she had learned in the pub back home. This supposed lack of dignity, although it appalls her grandmother, delights J. J., appeals to Harry's Aunt Augusta, and wins Harry's heart. They see it as spirit, and Sybylla's spirit seems indomitable.

Aunt Augusta invites Sybylla to spend a few days at the Beecham estate, "Five Bob Downs." There, Sybylla and Augusta, both artists, discover their common attitude toward life. More crucial to the plot, there, Sybylla and Harry become closer and closer friends. After they overcome a few misunderstandings, Harry proposes marriage to Sybylla. Although their "courtship" had exhibited all of the usual flirtation, jealousy, and heartache, she acts surprised at the fact that Harry wanted anything other than to be "mates" with her. She responds to his proposal by lashing him across the face with a bridle whip; later, more calmly, she responds by saying she is not ready yet. She needs first to develop her artistic abilities and, thereby, to find out who she is. She says she will marry Harry in a few years if he still needs her help at Five Bob Downs. She will then join her mate. She makes the matter sound so utterly unromantic. That is because she is still trying to deny her love for Harry and because she wants to play a role in the male institution of mateship just as she wants to play a role in many other male-dominated realms, such as literature.

Many young men, at this point, would have walked away and found someone else. Not Harry. Meanwhile, Sybylla's life changes. To repay one of her father's many debts, she has to go back into the outback and work as a live-in teacher to the unkempt McSwat children. Initially she holds herself so much higher than these uncouth settlers; then, she takes to the task, disciplines the children, and actually brings them to the point at which they are delighting in learning. Eventually, fearing that she has taken a liking to their elder boy Peter, the McSwats send her home. Once again in Possum Gully, she seems more mature and more content. She will try to pursue her literary dreams while helping her parents out with the farm. Her help is more necessary now because her younger sister Gertie has gone off for her time at Caddagat. She hears that Harry has been spending a great deal of time with Gertie.

One afternoon, while she is pulling a poor animal out of the mud it is stuck in, Harry rides up. Sybylla believes Harry has come to ask her parents' permission to marry Gertie. He tells Sybylla that it is she, not Gertie, whom he wants to marry. He hopes that she has found herself and is ready to begin a life with him in which they can be mates as well as spouses. But Sybylla has not given up on her artistic dreams; she has not allowed the everyday forces that have conspired against her to squelch those dreams. She feels that should she belong to someone else, even someone as nice as Harry, she would be destroyed and, then, in anger, she would destroy that someone else. Therefore, she once more turns down Harry's proposal. When he cites her pledge, she reminds Harry that she said she would marry him if he needed her. Well, he has put Five Bob Downs back on such a strong footing in the intervening years that he clearly does not "need" her help as he might have when he had originally proposed.

The film's last scene has Sybylla sending off the manuscript of her initial novel to the publishers. The novel *My Brilliant Career* was written by teenage Stella Franklin. It was largely, although not totally, autobiographical. When Stella sent it off, she used the male pseudonym Miles Franklin, thinking the male name would enhance its chances of being accepted by a publisher. As it turned out, Henry Lawson, as part of his crusade for a national literature, befriended the manuscript because he thought it to be so authentically Australian. Although he was not fooled by the pseudonym, he nonetheless recommended that *My Brilliant Career* by Miles Franklin be published. At the end of the movie, we are to imagine Sybylla to be in much the same position as Stella Franklin: young, female, previously unpublished, an underdog in the literary world but not giving up in the face of tough odds. To the extent that the character and her original creator conflate at this point in the film, the ending is a moment of incipient triumph.

Sybylla's personality, a very Australian one, plays a major role in this triumph. And, if we project the conflated Sybylla Melvyn–Stella Franklin forward a bit, we encounter the second book, *My Career Goes Bung*, which shows how, with the Australian hero, today's success is but tomorrow's failure. So, in addition to being a freedom-loving, defiant, mate-loving, and competitive underdog not entirely averse to downing several glasses of wine, Sybylla also is in the fatalistic shadow that seems to affect so many of her countrymen. She is also in a shadow that does not affect them: one created by those social forces—embodied by men and women alike—that try to constrain her as a woman to certain roles. Her triumph in *My Brilliant Career* is so much more important than just any hero's victory because it is also a triumph over these sexist forces.

HARD KNOCKS (DON McLENNAN, DIRECTOR, 1980)

Not every woman's story, however, is as triumphant as Sybylla Melvyn's. A much less successful story, that of a young woman named Samantha Naidu, is presented in Don McLennan's *Hard Knocks*.

In *Hard Knocks*, We first meet Sam (Tracy Mann) as a punk teenager. Arrested (rather brutally) for theft, she is sent to a juvenile detention facility. Next thing we know, it is years later. Sam has turned her life around and is pursuing a career as a model. She has earned enough money to have her own apartment. At this point, Deborah, a friend from the juvenile detention center, looks Sam up after being released. Sam gives Deborah a hard time about her lack of ambition. Sam might have exhibited more sensitivity, but her remarks do suggest the distance that Sam has traveled since we first met her as a teenager.

Sam wants to succeed, she wants her freedom, but she also wants friends to spend time with. Having recognized that her friends from the time before she was in detention are "bad news," she rejects them. However, she has a difficult time finding new friends.

Sam also runs into problems in the modeling business. She discovers its "sexploitative" side. When she resists the pressure being placed on her to reveal more of her body to the camera than she is comfortable doing, it is a woman at the agency who tries to coax her into nudity. Later, when a man assumes that women in the modeling business are readily available for sex and tries to force himself on her, she becomes angry with him. The result of her justifiable anger at him is her being dropped from the modeling agency's list. The agency, the vehicle Sam was counting on to take her to a better life, proves to be a sexist establishment that objectifies women as not much more than commodities. Women enforce this objectification, as do men, as does the neutral "agency."

Sam, lonely and frustrated, then turns to heavy drinking. Needing money for rent, she takes a job as a waitress. There, she confronts a holier-than-thou policeman with the fact that the woman he is with is not his wife. His hypocrisy, although it is not Sam's business, angers her: it is just another example of how the world preaches decency and hard work while practicing sexploitation and infidelity. The police officer's response is to arrest Sam, brutally beat her, and falsely charge her with drug possession. Brutalized by the adult world she had aspired to, Sam eventually returns to her apartment to find that it has been vandalized by her former friends. Thus, she ends up alone and rejected by both the adult and the young adult worlds.

Hard Knocks looks at how both gender and social class may end up functioning as barriers to heroism. Even if heroism does not mean always being victorious, the revised hero we have seen does succeed to a point. It is difficult to say that Sam has reached even that point. Her character traits, ones that might make her survive like Caddie in *Caddie* or win for the moment like Sybylla in *My Brilliant Career,* lead her face-first into a brick wall of oppression that seems largely rooted in sexism and classism.

THE KILLING OF ANGEL STREET (DONALD CROMBIE, DIRECTOR, 1981)

Urban development was all the craze in Sydney in the 1970s. As property in or close to downtown became increasingly valuable, techniques that were suspicious, if not criminal, were used by business interests to acquire the necessary real estate. An infamous case inspired both Donald Crombie's *The Killing of Angel Street* and Phillip Noyce's *Heatwave* (1982). In both cases, a central figure protesting the development is a woman.

In *The King of Angel Street,* Jessica Simmonds (Elizabeth Alexander) returns to Sydney from abroad to find her professor father leading the resistance. When he dies in a suspicious house fire, she becomes the leader of the Residents' Association. Her character is not as fully developed as those in other films discussed in this chapter; not surprising for an "action" film exposing corporate corruption. Crombie's emphasis is on the story, not on the people who live it. Thugs, corrupt businesspeople, and crusaders alike are sketched lightly. In addition, Jessica's figure-flattering, figure-revealing clothing draws attention to her sex appeal and away from her motivation.

Why, for example, is she drawn into the fight? Is it because she believes her father was murdered or because she believes that the cause of the Residents' Association is just, or both? Why is she so compelled while her brother is not? He was a professor, like their father, but abandoned academe for business, a switch that has given him the posh home and the fancy car. Is the film suggesting that commerce deadens sympathy, even for one's own father, as well as corrupts? Why have both children distanced themselves from their father—the son to the different culture of the corporation and the elite suburbs; Jessica to locales overseas? All of these questions go largely unanswered. We might conjecture that she needed her freedom; we might conjecture that both rebelled, in different ways, against their father's values. But we would be following hints, for the story rushes forward, only lightly sketching the major players.

Corruption proves to be widespread. Every place that Elizabeth turns, expecting honesty, she finds duplicity. She is very much the underdog and almost alone in that position. Only the self-confessed Communist union agitator Elliott (John Hargreaves) seems trustworthy, and a group of unidentified "thugs" murder him as they kidnap her and take her on a harrowing urban journey designed to intimidate her into dropping the matter. Whatever her motivation is, it is enough to keep her fighting, however. Even though her life is very clearly in danger, she goes on a television program, as she had planned, and calmly tells her story. The workers listen and withdraw from Angel Street, leaving the project there, at least, on hold.

We do not know, however, if Jessica was ultimately triumphant. We do know that the filmmakers were threatened during *The Killing of Angel Street*'s production (Stratton, *Avocado* 214). Perhaps the film's failure to proclaim Jessica victorious or clearly assign blame for the violence directed against the protesters reflects their fear (Rattigan 166). In any event, the shadow of the 1975 Juanita Nielson case, however, does hover over *The Killing of Angel Street*. In the real case, a woman led protests against redevelopment efforts in the King's Cross area of Sydney, redevelopment that would displace many lower-income residents. Nielson simply disappeared, and the redevelopment eventually proceeded. Many viewing Crombie's film may well wonder, fatalistically, if the same fate awaits Jessica Simmonds.

HEATWAVE (PHILLIP NOYCE, DIRECTOR, 1982)

Noyce's film deals with the Juanita Neilson story differently. In *Heatwave*, an activist named Mary Ford is playing a major role campaigning against the destruction of a row of downtown Sydney houses to create "Eden," a mixed-use development near Circular Quay that—like the Opera House—will make a strong architectural statement and thereby help define Sydney. In the course of the movie, she disappears under suspicious circumstances. However, the film does not focus on Mary Ford; rather, it focuses on another activist named Kate Dean, played by Judy Davis. Therefore, at least potentially, the central female character can triumph in her battle against development even if her female compatriot suffers the real Juanita Nielson's supposed fate.

Noyce also creates a meteorological backdrop that helps shape the film. Sydney is suffering from a scorching heat wave. The heat and the lack of rain parallel the tension created by the Eden development controversy. Controversy exists on several levels. As already indicated, activists are fighting it. They direct some of their efforts to maintain pressure on the developers, the rest to sustaining solidarity on the part of the residents. One holdout owner, an elderly man, in the initial row of houses to be demolished requires their special attention. On another level, the developer Peter Houseman is pressuring the architect to modify the plans in ways that will pacify the protesters. Steve West believes in his design, however. On yet another level, behind the scenes, Houseman is bailing out and quietly transferring property to Selcoe Nominees, an entity controlled by attorney Phillip Lawson. Lawson's plans for the property are less aesthetically appealing than Steve's: he only wants to make a quick profit and move on.

These are the tensions concerning the development, but there is also the tension between Kate and Steve. They are drawn together, but their differences on the project cause the relationship to suffer as many setbacks as moves forward. Kate is an impassioned activist, but there is a bit of the larrikin in her personality. It surfaces when she dresses up as a waitress at a fancy reception, staged to kick off the development, and assaults Peter Houseman with food. Steve West recognizes her before she launches her food attack but does not turn her in.

He is attracted to her, but things other than attraction per se cause Steve to drift in Kate's direction. The financial situation changes, resulting in pressure to change Eden's design to high-density. Steve begins to suspect that the aesthetic qualities and the mixed uses featured in his original design were simply bait designed to attract people, the intention being all along to scrap those elements and reap as much money as possible from the project. He is suspicious about Houseman's plans; Kate does not like Houseman's plans, whether they be Steve's or a revision. But opposition to Houseman does prove to be a starting point for their relationship. Steve had once been close friends with Mary Ford. Her disappearance adds to Steve's suspicions, just as it confirms Kate's. Then, the initial row of homes suspiciously goes up in flames, killing the sole squatter (the elderly man) in the process. The fire looks as if it were set by Houseman or, perhaps, set by some unidentified "others" who are trying to discredit Houseman. Standing together, Kate and Steve watch the fire, both convinced that there is something very wrong in the scenario being played out before their eyes. The fact that they do not see that scenario in quite the same way yet is less important than their shared recognition that something is wrong and that innocent people are dying as a result. There is clearly a villain in the piece, but, whereas *The Killing of Angel Street* treats the situation in black-and-white terms, *Heatwave* offers much gray (Rattigan 151). Kate and Steve are caught up in this gray area.

As Kate draws Steve into the battle, she faces threats against her life. Nonetheless, she continues fighting the development and trying to find out what has happened to Mary Ford. Someone plants explosives in her apartment, and she is arrested. Then, she breaks into Houseman's offices, and she is caught. Her credibility declines. Still, she fights on. She loses the union's support, but she fights on. She schedules a meeting of the residents to rally them against the development. The only person who shows up is Steve, who is now her lover.

The situation spins out of their control. After several of Houseman's other properties are blown up, he withdraws from the project, turning it all over to

Selcoe Nominees. Steve's wife Victoria leaves him. She is later found dead at Phillip Lawson's posh apartment. A thug attacks Kate, beating her badly. When Steve shows up, the thug runs off, and so does Kate—right into a New Year's Eve party in King's Cross being held to celebrate Selcoe Nominees' new design for the waterfront site. Steve chases Kate there. As they watch, the murdered elderly man's daughter (a King's Cross stripper) shoots Phillip Lawson, and his guards fire on and kill her. At that moment, the heat wave breaks as a stroke-of-midnight storm cools off and drenches Sydney. Stratton argues that this ending has gotten beyond Noyce's control (*Avocado* 215). To the contrary, I think the frantic pace parallels nicely the build up to a thunderstorm after days of searing heat. The meteorological backdrop then is used, beginning to end, to provide atmosphere.

This summary, as frantic as it was, does not even cover all of the twists in *Heatwave*'s plot: it is a very intriguing action movie. But unlike *The Killing of Angel Street*, Noyce's *Heatwave* does offer developed characters; thus, Rattigan is correct in finding less of a political comment than in *The Killing of Angel Street*, because Noyce's film is more about these characters than the politics of urban development (152). Steve, for example, is the dreamer who has let the desire for fame and fortune cloud important human values. His relationship with Kate helps him regain those values. Kate, on the other hand, is a complex character. She is the crusading activist, but she does not fit the stereotype. She lets herself be torn between fighting for the cause and finding the much-loved Mary Ford. Then, as events swirl around her, she lets herself get out of control and ends up losing vital support. In the end, she can only watch as it all explodes before her eyes.

Kate is a fighter, an underdog; She is loyal to her compatriots such as Mary Ford was. She defies authority left and right, but is not so serious that disrupting a gala by throwing food in the guest of honor's face is outside her repertoire. And there is very much the cloud of "lost causes" hanging over her effort to bring Eden to a halt, a cloud that delivers a somber last message when we see Mary Ford's body washing up from the construction project's initial pourings in the early New Year's Day storm. Despite the fatalistic aura, Kate battles on. This portrait is very much in line with that of the revised Australian heroes we discussed in Chapter 3. And for Kate, unlike many of the women discussed in this chapter, sexist oppression does not seem to be an issue. Any oppression she experiences is due to the cause she has embraced, not her gender.

WE OF THE NEVER NEVER (IGOR AUZINS, DIRECTOR, 1982)

Perhaps it is partially because we have gone back in time, but gender does play a major role in *We of the Never Never*. Based on the memoirs of a pioneer woman named Jeannie Gunn, the film quietly (perhaps too quietly) depicts a woman's struggle to gain respect for herself and then for oppressed others among the sexist, racist men of the Northern Territory outback near Katherine.

Jeannie (Angela Punch McGregor) has just married librarian Aeneas Gunn in Melbourne. He has decided to pursue a different course in his life and has accepted a position as a station manager in the northern part of the Northern Territory. Arthur Dignam portrays Aeneas with just the right blend of self-assuredness and self-consciousness. It is the latter that perhaps causes him to go overboard in proving to the men on the station that he is one of them, that he is their mate. Aeneas' need to prove himself, although understandable, causes him to leave Jeannie floundering without the full emotional support she needs. One facet of the story depicts their drifting apart and, then, their reuniting as full partners in the work at the station. Unfortunately, Aeneas and Jeannie find this strong, equal basis for their relationship shortly before Aeneas catches dengue fever from a passing itinerant worker and dies.

Jeannie's efforts have not, however, been solely focused on regaining solidarity with her husband. Her arrival is marked by station hands' gawking in amazement at the very idea of the new manager bringing his wife along and then announcing that they are going to quit because a woman has invaded their turf. Initially, she tries to win them over by joining them on roundups and the like. When she realizes that she shouldn't have to become a "man" to be respected by a man, she tries to win them over by asserting firm control over the household's management. The arrogant Chinese cook falls victim to Jeannie's attempt to gain control. The men tolerate her domestic management; however, when her Victorian furniture finally arrives from Melbourne, the men help fix up her now-shrunken domestic space, hoping that having her own furnishings will cause her to confine herself to that limited space (literally, a room of her own).

What finally wins the men over is not Jeannie's outback skills or her domestic skills; rather, it is her human warmth. One by one, she wins the men's admiration and, with that, a measure of respect. It would be going too far—and probably beyond what was possible at the time of the film's events—to say the men come to view her as their equal. Rather, they come to admire and respect the human qualities she brings to the station. Their admiration and respect show up best at the touching Christmas celebration the Gunns and the men have. Jeannie's human qualities show up best when she encourages the men to offer aid to the stricken itinerant worker, when she later tends to her sick husband, and, most notably, when she tends to the region's aborigines.

The latter requires some elaboration because Jeannie's heroic qualities are more evident in her dealing with the aborigines than in anything else in the film, including her indefatigable nursing of the dying Aeneas. Most at the station simply treat the aborigines as "there." They do not see the extent to which these people have been dispirited through years of white condescension and abuse. They joke about how the aborigines will work for just a bit of tobacco or liquor, not recognizing the extent to which the colonists have introduced these weakening addictions to the aborigines' lives. Jeannie also unearths the "dirty" secret that the men at the station do not want her to know: the extent to which the men at the station have turned to the aboriginal women for sexual recreation. Jeannie tries to get the men to recognize that such sex is immorally abusive. She also tries to get the men to realize what they have done to these people through tobacco, alcohol, and, more generally, thwarting their semi-nomadic life and the resulting culture.

Jeannie is also appalled at the sexism the aboriginal men display toward the aboriginal women, sexism that leads to physical abuse. She defends these women, berating the men for their treatment of them. One might say that Jeannie is interfering in their culture. Be that as it may, she is exhibiting the same human decency with regard to the aboriginal men's treatment of their women as she did with regard to the settlers' treatment of the aborigines. She personally displays this decency when she adopts an orphaned mixed-blood girl named Bett Bett.

She battles for these people, since they cannot battle for themselves. She defies the "authority" that has authorized certain modes of colonizing and settling as well as the patriarchal assumptions behind much of the behavior of their white men and the aboriginal men. She is clearly the underdog in these campaigns for decency and equality; nonetheless, she fights on. She perhaps realizes that she alone cannot change the ways people are acting toward other people throughout Australia; however, she is determined to change those ways to the extent that she can on her little piece of it.

To some extent Jeannie also tries to become mates with the aboriginal women. Initially, she treats them as servants, but gradually, she comes to see them as her compatriots. Perhaps she even comes to see them as fellow victims of sexist oppression. The scene in the film that symbolizes Jeannie's joining them is when she swims with them in the river. She puts aside most of the many Victorian layers of clothing that cover her body and jumps in. Her joining them is almost a baptismal scene, with Jeannie reborn as a woman who is not blinded by the assumptions about race and class that define white Australian society. I say "almost" because Jeannie does not remove all of her Victorian layers. Her swimming in the nude with them would have been historically improbable. That it was so, and that Jeannie conforms here to basic Victorian norms, suggests that even a woman who seeks to obliterate the differences that separate white and black because those differences lead to oppressive behavior cannot completely do so. Jeannie is, nonetheless, heroic to go as far as she does.

MONKEY GRIP (KEN CAMERON, DIRECTOR, 1982)

Sexism shows up very differently in Ken Cameron's adaptation of Helen Garner's semi-autobiographical novel *Monkey Grip*. Rather than a period piece with stunning landscape photography such as in *We of the Never Never*, *Monkey Grip* is a stark rendering of the Carlton district of Melbourne in the waning days of its counterculture ascendancy. There, we meet the young women and young men who are still living in a world of rock music, alcohol, and drugs. They are still dreaming of "making it big" as music-makers or writers or filmmakers. However, a sense pervades the film that most of these dreams are quite futile.

Men are not portrayed favorably in the film. The man who fathered Nora's (the central female character) daughter is gone, and the other men who play a role in Nora's life offer her sex but not much more. The man she devotes herself to throughout most of the film, Javo (Colin Friels), is simply too far gone on drugs to offer her the support she needs as a twenty-something woman and mother.

Nora, played by Noni Hazlehurst, is the film's focal point. Garner and Cameron succeed in bringing her thoughts, which in the novel are conveyed through her first person narration, into the script they coauthored. Therefore, we learn about not only her love life but her day-to-day life. She is still very attached to the club scene in Carlton; she still associates with the would-be artists because, like them, she is seeking to express herself artistically. Her medium is writing. But she also must earn money and tend to the daily needs of her child. As Nora lives the life we witness, she seems very torn by her artistic needs, her emotional needs, her sexual needs, and her maternal responsibilities. Being so torn is not easy for her, but we see her battle on. Whereas the men in the film might surrender to the alcohol and drugs that are very much a part of the Carlton environment, she cannot and will not.

Nora's battling on, despite the odds and without much male support, marks her as an Australian hero. And like the male versions of the hero we have examined, she values mateship. Her mates are the other young women living in the fading counterculture of this Melbourne neighborhood. She is frequently in conversation with them, showing her concern and offering her support. She also demonstrates her loyalty: she will not, for example, sleep with her friend Angela's man because Angela is her mate.

Nora's belief in mateship links her to the male heroes we have seen. The extent to which she has to deal with the "male world" she is in differentiates her from them. Nora's "male world" is not characterized by victimization or even oppression; rather, it is characterized by male indifference, an indifference toward life and the future that leads them to drugs and does not lead them to any kind of meaningful, committed relationship. The men talk about their dreams, but they do not actively pursue them. Unfortunately for Nora and other women of her generation, the world still expects that men and women will form adult couples and that these men and women will perform certain roles within that relationship toward each other and in society. Many of these roles are, of course, informed by sexism, but that sexism is really not the issue in *Monkey Grip*. What the issue is in Cameron's film—and Garner's novel—is that the men no longer seem willing or able to assume these relationships and play these roles. As Rattigan notes, in Australian films with urban settings, male weakness coupled with female strength is a recurring pattern, one he associates with the male's "belonging" to the outback (214). This male collapse puts additional burdens on the women, burdens they quite often cannot dismiss because the burdens are embodied by their young children. As a result, the heroism demonstrated by Nora, and others, has an extra hurdle to surmount.

Perhaps the situation will be different for the generation of Nora's children. However, the film ends with a scene in which two young (perhaps twelve years old) girls are seen flirting with two young boys. The suggestion in this scene is that the male–female dynamic will probably be no different for those who find themselves in Nora's shoes ten or fifteen years hence.

Geographically, Australia is the United States upside down. Thus, traveling north is the Australian equivalent of the American traveling south. Australians go north to retire, seeking the sun and all that the sun might symbolize. Toward the end of *Monkey Grip*, Nora and Javo travel north to Sydney to try to find "something" in their relationship. There is nothing: he is too far gone. So, Nora returns to Melbourne alone. And "alone" seems to be what the film suggests the fate of young women is and will be: alone despite their lovers, alone along with their mates, alone despite their loving children.

Monkey Grip is one of the most controversial films of the 1980s. Producer Patricia Lovell was hospitalized during its filming for nervous exhaustion. What drove her there were the obstacles that kept appearing in the film's path—put there by those who feared the social realism and the frank nudity (filmed by a nude crew) of the prospective film. The Australian government even put pressure on the Cannes Film Festival not to screen the motion picture (Stratton, *Avocado* 140–41). The film clearly depicted an Australia that some, who strongly favored the period pieces as exports, did not want the world to see. From our perspective, however, *Monkey Grip* reveals not a different picture but the same picture with the hero gendered female and the environment urban.

FRAN (GLENDA HAMBLY, DIRECTOR, 1985)

Fran, written and directed by Glenda Hambly, also stars Noni Hazlehurst. Therefore, one cannot help making a connection between *Monkey Grip* and *Fran*, especially since the latter film met some official resistance from the Australian Film Commission (Stratton, *Avocado* 371). Although the characters of Nora and Fran are not the same, there are some ways in which the later film does seem a sequel. Unfortunately, *Fran* seems to fulfill the forecasts offered about male–female relationships in the earlier film.

The first trait we learn about Fran is that men are very attracted to her; the second is that she is very attracted to men. An older male neighbor refers to her as "a slut." Most would not agree with this description. However, Fran certainly does tread the line between being open about her sexuality and sleeping around. She has an ockerlike attitude toward both sex and marital fidelity; however, the fact that she is female does cause viewers, imprisoned by a double standard, to dump on her when they might not on a male with an equivalent liking for sex.

What saves Fran in the eyes of viewers is a background that explains why she is the way she is and her being, at base, a good albeit irresponsible person. Fran never knew the man who fathered her, and she lost her mother to alcoholism when she was but five years old. She married at a young age to a man who seems as irresponsible as Fran's father was. Ray is rarely with her at their home; rather, he is up north—presumably in Queensland—with his mates doing seasonal labor. When he is home, he shows no interest in his three children. Furthermore, he gets drunk and physically abuses Fran while the children watch. She ought to divorce Ray. However, any hope for what direction she might take should she divorce Ray is dashed when we get to know Jeff, the bartender she has an extended affair with shortly after Ray leaves again. Jeff does not like having the kids around; he also fears the suffocation of commitment. Worse, he makes sexual advances toward Fran's thirteen-year-old daughter Lisa when Fran is not around.

The film makes it clear that Fran loves her children. She tries to provide for them both materially and emotionally. However, battle as she may, Fran finds the forces arrayed against her—bill collectors, social workers, neighbors—too much to handle. So, she leaves her children with her foster sister and goes off on a very long holiday with Jeff. When she finally returns home, she finds her children have been taken into custody by the authorities. Her foster sister, not wanting to be bothered with them after a while, has turned them over as neglected and turned Fran in as derelict. When she sees her children again, Lisa is eerily quiet, younger Tommy is rather distant, and the very young Cynthia is quite clingy. The experience has obviously had a telling effect on them. However, Fran is not allowed at this point to take them home because Lisa has revealed Jeff's sexual advances and the authorities claim the home is unacceptable as long as Jeff is in it.

Fran will not accept the truth of Lisa's accusation. She is so emotionally and physically dependent on men that she cannot see Jeff as the creep that he is. So, Fran fights against the authorities who will not give her her children back. We have seen Australian battlers before, male and female. Usually, the battler is presented in such a way that we are on his or her side in defying authority. Not so in this case. We are glad that social services are keeping Lisa in a foster care facility and sending Tommy and Cynthia to foster homes. We are also, however, sad—for them and for Fran. Having lost her children, she is eventually abandoned by Jeff. Then, she suffers a nervous breakdown. Anna Dzenis notes how audiences probably have mixed reactions to Fran—sympathetic and blaming (in Murray, *Australian Film* 170). O'Regan notes how Jan Kenny's use of midway camera distances helps produce this effect by keeping viewers complicit while also distancing them from Fran (*Australian* 205).

Fran offers us a glimpse of the modern-day Australian hero gone wrong. She battles against those who try to tell her what to do; she enjoys the pleasures of life; and she loves her mate Marge, who more than loves her in return. She is much like characters we have met in countless films already analyzed. But Fran, unlike these others, falls apart. Her own background partially explains her failure, but there is also a sense in *Fran*, as there was in *Monkey Grip*, of men's failure to do their part in relationships as a major contributing cause of Fran's failure. She then proves to be a false hero: she has some of the makings, but her weaknesses, as well as those of all the men she encounters, prevent her from achieving the lonely success of Caddie in *Caddie* or even the very empty success of Sam in *Hard Knocks*.

The last image of *Fran* takes us back to the last image of *Monkey Grip*. Whereas the latter film gives us very young teens and asks if they will be like Nora, the former gives us Lisa, in foster care, looking in a mirror and asking if she will be like Fran.

FOR LOVE ALONE (STEPHEN WALLACE, DIRECTOR, 1986)

We feel somewhat happier for Teresa Hawkins, the central character in Christina Stead's 1944 novel *For Love Alone*. For her time, the 1930s, she is a liberated woman. Thus, she is like Nora and Fran, although her sexuality is held more in check by the mores of her era. And like the two modern-day Australian women, Teresa (Helen Buday) goes through a string of men: Jonathan Crow (Hugo Weaving), James Quick (Sam Neill), and Harry Bentham (Huw Williams) before finding love with Harry and bittersweet marriage with James. Like Nora and Fran, Teresa is too defined by these relationships. She speaks as if she were very much her own person, independent and with her own ideas; however, she proves to be much more controlled by the men in her life than seems the case at first glance.

What is true of the film is also true of Stead's novel. In all likelihood, when Margaret Fink (also producer of *My Brilliant Career*), chose to transform Stead's novel into a feature film, she thought she would be doing what she had done earlier: taking a proto-feminist "classic" before motion picture audiences with, perhaps, the feminism updated a bit. Unfortunately, *For Love Alone* is not as proto-feminist or as classic as Miles Franklin's novel. Stead's feminism is found in Teresa's refusal to settle for less than love and her willingness to throw caution to the wind to have that love. This "feminism" liberates her from a potentially mundane life; however, it offers very little self-definition apart from that the men she might love would provide. Unlike Sybylla Melvyn, Teresa is not trying to find herself; rather, she is trying to find the "right" man. Stead's novel is also long and episodic, whereas Franklin's, despite her youth, has a tightness provided by its beginning and ending in Possum Gulley and by its first climax when Harry proposes and its reprise climax when he proposes again. The film version of *For Love Alone* follows the less-than-satisfying course of Stead's novel. Director Wallace admits that half of the film's problem was the same as the book's. The other half was, he says, because he would not push producer Margaret Fink toward the "bold" treatment he wanted. Instead, he settled for a naturalistic style that did nothing to overcome the book's tedium (Helen Barlow in Murray, *Australian Film* 195; Stratton, *Avocado* 180).

Having already minimized any heroism that Teresa might show, I need to reverse my course and point out what is heroic about her character and her story because, especially in the context of the 1930s, she is exceptional. The easiest way to discuss Teresa, however, is to proceed man by man. That this is the easiest way suggests the extent to which her story, and thus her life, is structured by the men in it.

The first man in her life is her father. He is very much a negative influence on her. A bitter widower, he makes fun of her belief in ideals such as honor and love, tells her she is a plain Jane, and predicts she'll be an old maid. In her father's home, she also learns about the fundamental inequality of the genders as she watches her brother Lance revel in the freedoms he is allowed and she is not.

At the university, she becomes infatuated with her Latin tutor Jonathan Crow. Crow espouses radical idea about sex and marriage. A lower-class background, of which he is ashamed, and strident Marxism also affect the way he sees life. Teresa does not agree with his radical ideas; rather, she demonstrates her independence of mind by espousing her own radical ideas. She wants pornography to feature male nudes as well as female; she wants there to be male brothels as well as female ones; and she does not want to be kept as mistress or a wife. Instead, she wants equality to be the hallmark of her, and all, male–female relationships. Crow seems attracted by her ideas but, rather oddly, uncomfortable with her physical presence.

When he goes off to London, Teresa writes him incessantly, sharing her ideas. Then, she saves up enough money to sail to London to join him. When she arrives, he seems only somewhat glad to see her. Gradually, he reveals his inner turmoil. Beset by what Freud termed the Madonna-and-whore complex, Crow cannot love the women he lusts after, and he cannot express himself physically with the women he loves. Perhaps frustrated with himself, Crow chooses lust over love. And, because the objects of his lust are the lower-class girls he, the Marxist, has long empathized with, he justifies abandoning love by asserting what we might see as a strange type of "political correctness" in his couplings. He tells Teresa he never loved her and that their long-distance relationship had only been a game for him. Whether he speaks the truth or what is necessary to drive Teresa away is not clear.

On board the ship from Sydney to London, Teresa had met an older businessman named James Quick, played dashingly by Sam Neill. Witty and charming, Quick loves literature and the arts, and he wants nothing more than a companion who shares those interests. Once Crow is out of the picture, the relationship between Teresa and Quick blossoms. She thinks she loves him. However, there are indications that a combination of their mutual interests and his attentiveness to her wins her over, not any deep feelings. That this is the case becomes evident when the proverbial sparks begin to fly between Teresa and Quick's poet friend Harry Bentham.

Confused but still throwing caution to the wind, Teresa becomes Quick's lover. Defying her sense of what true love is, he tells her afterward that she can take lovers once they are married if she wants, as long as she still loves him. She is shocked at the idea, but, shortly after, she and Harry become lovers. Quick becomes aware of her relationship with Harry and finds that he can no longer live with the idea of Teresa's taking lovers. So, when Harry will not cancel his planned trip to Spain for her, Teresa marries Quick—in essence, doing what she had rejected since her days in Sydney: marrying a man she really did not love. Their wedding is a civil ceremony on a quiet, rainy day. At its conclusion, she throws her bouquet to a crowd of no one. The absence of the sacred, of any applause, and of any audience, as well as the dreary rain, visually suggest how empty this relationship is.

As I proceeded from father to Crow to Quick, several things changed in the film's depiction of Teresa. The defiance and the battling as an underdog, both of which marked her as an Australian hero, diminished. She ceased being an actor and became someone acted upon. Furthermore, her ideas became more conventional, and her pursuit of love less enthusiastic. Maybe, we are dealing with a poor film, one that loses both its sense of its central character and its energy. But it is also possible that Teresa's diminishment is deliberate on the part of director and screenplay writer Wallace. Perhaps, he wanted to show how the men really control one's life—for good or for ill. In this light then, Teresa's early iconoclastic and romantic pronouncements are nothing but adolescent bravado. The real world, interestingly presented as the old European world, pushes aside such statements. The men, with the power to choose, dominate the action and turn a young woman possessed of quite a spirit into a possession.

THE UMBRELLA WOMAN (KEN CAMERON, DIRECTOR, 1987)

If Teresa's life is controlled in any sense at the end of *For Love Alone*, it is by James Quick, the character played by Sam Neill. Coincidentally, it is another character played by Neill, Neville Gifford, who exerts controlling, mesmerizing power in *The Umbrella Woman*, written by Peter Kenna and directed by Ken Cameron. Like *For Love Alone*, *The Umbrella Woman* takes place in an earlier era—specifically 1939; like Wallace's film, Cameron's deals with a woman who defies norms.

The woman in *The Umbrella Woman* is Marge Hills, played by Rachel Ward. She is married to Sonny Hills, played by Bryan Brown. Their marriage, however, lacks passion, probably because Sonny is a rather inept lover, a role the rather handsome Bryan Brown seems to have difficulty portraying convincingly (Stratton, *Avocado* 159). But the other side of the coin may be Marge's rather strong desires, something she seems to have inherited from her mother. So, when Sonny's naïve younger brother Sugar (Steve Vidler) bluntly propositions Marge, she lets Sonny decide if she can have sex with Sugar or not. Wanting to give Marge anything she wants, Sonny consents. Then, he either tries to stop or watch their lovemaking, but a locked door stops him from either action.

Word gets around the scandalized town that Marge is now being shared by Sonny and Sugar. Marge, however, is not satisfied with this arrangement. The fact that Sugar, although more attentive to her needs, is a premature ejaculator may have something to do with her dissatisfaction. So, along comes the new barman Neville Gifford. As he arrives in town, he propositions Marge. She feigns offense and resists. But shortly thereafter, she begins actively pursuing this very affable ladies' man. Neville, however, is no longer interested. She then becomes obsessed with him, virtually stalking him for sex. When Neville has to leave town (because of his sexual indiscretions), she boards the train too. He rejects her advances one more time and literally throws her off the train.

Marge might be seen as a crusader for sexual freedom. However, she might just be a frustrated wife. In either case, she defies all norms and fights for the sexual fulfillment she believes she will finally find in Gifford's arms. He, the suave man of the world, clearly has the upper hand in his "battle" with Marge. She is the underdog. So, in some ways, she is much like the Australian hero, male or female, we have seen in many films thus far. She certainly is, however, a rather bizarre version of this hero.

Marge's heroism makes some sense if we try to discern what the filmmakers wanted us to see as her situation. Is it simply a matter of her being in an unfulfilling marriage? No, there seems to be more to her story than just that. The story is indeed about her—and by extension other women's—sexuality, but the emphasis is supposed to be not as much on her libidinous nature as on how the patriarchy regulates that sexuality. Sonny regulates it when he chooses to make love with her and when he consents to Sugar's making love with her. Gifford regulates it by calling the shots: when he is interested, she is not; so, as if to prove who controls matters, when she is interested, he is not. It is her body, but its sexual fulfillment is not something she can choose. For that, she is totally dependent on the men who regulate her sexuality and do not seem at all concerned that the sexual relations she has leave her unfulfilled.

Especially if one keeps this reading in mind, the film ends bleakly. Marge's battered body is returned to Sonny's care—or regulation. Sonny has beaten Sugar and told his brother to leave the house. Sonny has regained control over his situation and Marge's body. The film ends with a shot of a train speeding away, suggesting where she wants to be, and then a shot of her looking out a blinded window that almost looks as if it is barred. She is imprisoned, as is her sexuality. The heroic impulse that was very much within her has been thwarted. One might conjecture that it has been so thoroughly thwarted because that impulse had been directed by Marge toward the one freedom, the pursuit of which may be most threatening to the patriarchy. Employment rights, political rights—these the patriarchy can give—but sexual rights go to the core of the male ego.

AUSTRALIAN DREAM (JACKI McKIMMIE, DIRECTOR, 1987)

Like Gillian Armstrong's *My Brilliant Career* and Glenda Hambly's *Fran*, *Australian Dream*, written and directed by Jacki McKimmie and produced by McKimmie and Sue Wild, is often touted as a film designed to sound a strong message on behalf of women. Lumping the three films together, however, obscures the fact that they take very different approaches. Armstrong's film retells a classic tale set at the turn of the century and offers a hero in Sybylla Melvyn who puts her artistry ahead of everything, even life with the dashing Harry Beecham. Hambly's film offers a contemporary portrait of a somewhat likable woman who is beaten down in large part because the men in her life all prove worthless. McKimmie's film presents a satirical picture of the "Australian dream," a dream that proves both silly for the men who follow it and unfulfilling for the women who do. This satire has been described as "cruel" by both Geoff Gardner (in Murray, *Australian Film* 212) and Tom O'Regan (*Australian* 248).

The central male character in McKimmie's film is Geoff Stubbs, a butcher who is running for public office backed by a rather right-wing political party, the Prosperity Party, which is Queensland's National Party thinly disguised. He is the caricature of a one-issue candidate, his one issue being "beef." He is also very afraid that his rather free-spirited wife's activities will embarrass him and cost him the election. The most embarrassing thing he knows about is her writing, which, unbeknownst to him, has taken a marked erotic turn of late. If he only knew that she attended erotic toy parties for girls featuring male strippers, then he would be mortified.

He suppresses her writing, and he suppresses her sexuality. The two are associated in the film as the ways the wife, Dotty Stubbs (Noni Hazlehurst), might be able to escape an environment that is characterized by its sameness and its sexism. Both notes are sounded early in the film by an opening shot of their Brisbane suburbia in which house after house are exactly the same, and an opening scene at an Australian university at which a female student's enlightened comment is responded to by the male professor with suggestive remarks and a leer.

Dotty, the central female character, plays her assigned role as best she can. She pretends to be the "wifie" Geoff needs to achieve his political goals; she does all the housewifely and motherly chores. Since she and Geoff are throwing the neighborhood's rotating party that Saturday evening, her chores are far more numerous on the weekend in question than usual. Nonetheless, she does all that she is supposed to do.

The party is the film's climax, and it is an absurd send-up of so many things that a summary cannot do its satire justice. So let me keep the focus on Dotty, who is getting ready to snap as the party begins. The party's theme is "come as your favorite fantasy." So, she initially dresses up as Geoff, complete with goofy tie and goofy hat. Her rendition of her husband is double-edged: he is, in a sense, her fantasy because he holds all the power, but he is also absurd. His absurdity suggests that those who hold power are all absurd and raises the question why all these absurd men have that power. Her dressing up as Geoff disturbs him, so she shifts from her fantasy to his, dressing up as a tart in revealing lingerie. Her costume embarrases him, and Dotty knows that, but she wants the world to know how Geoff sees her—and women generally—by parading as the fantasy that he wishes she (more privately) were. This costume is also double-edged, however, because, to the extent it implies sexual liberation, it does represent her fantasy as well.

As the party develops, it gets increasingly wilder and increasingly more absurd. The tone of the party bothers Geoff, especially when the rock musicians Dotty invited show up. Geoff is afraid the high officials of the Prosperity Party whom he invited will be offended by the tone and no longer support him for public office. He has nothing to worry about, however. Reflecting their hypocrisy, their stupidity, and their drunkenness, they find the party just wonderful. At this point, McKimmie is particularly satirizing Queensland politics in terms that American viewers might understand if they imagined that the scene was the United States and the Prosperity Party officials were representatives of the Christian Right.

Having made her political point, McKimmie returns to Dotty's story. The band Dotty invited was led by her daughter's new riding instructor who was also the stripper at the erotic toy party. In reality, he is a thief, and, while the band plays, his accomplices are going house to house in the neighborhood. Dotty distracts the band leader–riding instructor–stripper, Todd, by slipping off to the van with him for sex. Thus, she rebels against numbing suburban sameness, her oppression as a woman, and the right-wing politics that nods complacently at the sameness and the oppression. Geoff sees, her in the van, and, as the party gets even more out of control, he confronts her, telling her she is high, an unfit mother, and ruining his political career. He plans to take her to see a psychiatrist on Monday. Rather than accepting his accusation and his plans for her mental health care complacently, she leaves with Todd.

It seems that Dotty can only play the game so long. Iconoclastic at heart, she finally openly defies the leagued forces of patriarchy and suburban life that are oppressing her. Wanting freedom in general, she chooses to begin with sexual freedom. And she puts a lot of faith in Todd's being "the one" who will give her, sexually, what she has obviously been lacking in her relationship with Geoff. At the film's end, Dotty and Todd are at a beach and finally make love. He ejaculates prematurely, and she asks, "Is that it?" Clearly, her fighting for her self will either be not as easy as she had thought or futile. The possibility of her quest's futility gives her heroic story an Australian feel.

Back to the party for a second. The premise of a masquerade is both pretending to be someone else and not being yourself. A bunch of people walking around not being themselves is an interesting picture because it suggests that maybe these people, because of the world they inhabit, do not know themselves. They have all conformed to the norms of the suburban "Australian dream" and the norms of the patriarchy and, in the process of conforming, have lost touch with their true selves. Dotty's quest then may be as much for self-realization as for freedom. In this context, it is interesting to note that Todd's name and Dotty's name are almost palindromic, suggesting that he may be or may be seen by her to be a mirror image. If so, sex with him is a way of reconnecting with one's true self. Read this way, the film's ending not only suggests the difficulty or the futility of her quest for freedom, it also suggests the difficulty or the futility of her quest for self.

The ending can be read still another way. As rebellious as Dotty is, she still chooses to rebel through the male agency of Todd. Thus, the route she takes as she battles, at least partially, against the patriarchy is still dependent on a privileged member of that patriarchy. He fails to liberate her. This failure suggests both that the power of the patriarchy is sometimes unearned and that the better route to freedom for Dotty is not through a new lover but, rather, somehow through herself.

Thus far in this chapter, we have seen a dialectic emerge. The women who are central in these films do seem to embody some—sometimes even many—of the traits of the "revised" Australian hero. However, that heroism comes into conflict with not the usual authorities but the deeply ingrained sexist ones. This extra conflict often results in either a muting of the heroic or an altering of the heroic. What then results is oftentimes only implied: it does not come fully into the language of the film, perhaps because that doubly revised heroism is yet outside of any language, like many of women's experiences. It is even possible that the final revision means more than slightly altering the terms. It may mean rejecting the male-defined revised heroism and articulating something "other." This possibility is explored in one of the better films of the Australian cinema, Gillian Armstrong's *High Tide*.

HIGH TIDE (GILLIAN ARMSTRONG, DIRECTOR, 1987)

Armstrong's deft direction, Russell Boyd's beautiful but muted photography, and Judy Davis' stunning performance as Lilli make *High Tide* a pleasure to watch. Its rhythm is ever-changing, preventing the melodramatic potential of the story from becoming mawkish. The film masterfully understates. Very much the collaborative effort of Armstrong, producer Sandra Levy, scriptwriter Laura Jones, and gifted performer Davis, *High Tide* does much more than tell a single woman's story. It may tell the story of women in Australia who are conforming to a male code of behavior when something else—and something more difficult—is required of them.

We first meet Lilli as a chorus girl, backing up an Elvis impersonator who is touring the nightclubs at rather downscale resorts. We meet her at Eden, an actual beach resort in southeastern New South Wales. Lilli is discontent with her empty life, so she is being a troublemaker—so much so that Lester, the Elvis impersonator, lets her go. Unfortunately, she cannot go, at least right away, because her car has broken down and requires repairs she cannot afford. Lilli is very much the free spirit, but she is also very unhappy. We gather as much when we see her getting drunk out of a bottle of whiskey in the public restroom of the caravan park where she is staying in Eden. There, she meets a young adolescent girl named Ally, who helps her stumble back to her trailer.

The relationship between Lilli and Ally is at the core of the film, but the story is not as simple as that of a young girl helping a jaded thirty-something woman find herself or some meaning in life. It is not that simple because Lilli is Ally's mother. When Ally was but a baby, Lilli abandoned her. Lilli's husband (and Ally's father) John died. Distraught, Lilli came to hate the baby because she reminded her of the man she had lost to illness. After Lilli began her years of wandering freely from place to place and job to job, Ally's paternal grandmother took over and raised the child, telling her pleasant lies about her parents, who, according to the lies, had both died. The grandmother, Bet, very much hated Lilli, both because of her abandonment of Ally and because she had taken away Bet's beloved son John and, supposedly, shut others out as John died. The film then will be almost as much about the reconciliation of Lilli and Bet as the reconciliation of Lilli and Ally.

In many ways Lilli is a sad version of the Australian hero. She, for a dozen or so years, has seemingly loved her freedom. She has a pronounced antiauthoritarian streak as well as a penchant for alcohol. She seems to enjoy a night out with her mates, as well as no-commitment sex with the men who come along. She battles to get the money to get by. Even at Eden, she surrenders her dignity by stripping at two "bucks' nights" to earn the $600 she needs to repair her car. She will, it seems, fight to survive and move on and fight to survive and move on again. She does not talk in terms of getting ahead. Success does not seem a possibility for her, just getting by.

Sexism is present in the film. Bet's future is being defined for her by her country singer lover, who wants to leave Eden and go to Sydney. Ally's future is being somewhat defined for her by her boyfriend and her newly felt need to be sexually attractive to him, which reveals itself in the poignant scene in which she shaves her legs for the first time while Lilli surreptitiously watches. Lilli must strip, to the "bucks" hooting and hollering, to earn the money she needs; no other job is available to her. But these notes of sexism or, perhaps more accurately put, ways in which men define women's lives, are not unduly stressed. They are not stressed because the problem Lilli is dealing with is not something men have done to her. In fact, in the film, the men she encounters are all rather nonsexist. The garage mechanic, in a position to proposition her, does not and sympathizes with her plight. The club manager apologizes before mentioning the stripping job that is available. The man she meets and sleeps with in Eden wants a commitment and has his own sad story of being deserted by his wife, who took their son with her but left their daughter Fiona for him to raise alone.

Maybe, just maybe, the fact that the Lilli role was originally supposed to be a male role has something to do with the reduced importance of sexism in this film and the increased importance of the turmoil within (as opposed to imposed from without) the main character (Stratton, *Avocado* 366). I would rather think that the team of women behind *High Tide* saw in the film an opportunity to explore how a woman who embodied the traits of the typical male Australian hero or antihero would find life lived in line with that "code" unsatisfying, unhappy.

What brings happiness into Lilli's life is Ally. As the film progresses, the two drift more closely together. Lilli has no intention of revealing who she is to the girl. She wants to get to know Ally a bit, offer the young girl advice about being all that she can be, and then move on. Finally, Lilli's fisherman lover tells Ally that Lilli is her mother. Lilli denies it, but Bet confirms it. Tearful conversations between mother and child ensue. Lilli, whose real name is Julie, realizes that her free-spirited behavior has been cowardice, not anything adventurous and thereby heroic. She struggles with the idea of being a true hero, just as Ally wonders if her mother is capable of such or is selfishly ignoble. The striptease is, oddly enough, a pivotal moment. Taking her clothes off before an audience is not something Lilli is proud of, but she does see in the courage she musters to strip the potential for another kind of courage. Ally, who watches some of the performance (which is entirely offscreen) until forced to leave, reads it differently. She sees her mother as being willing to do anything, including something that demeaning, to get the money that will allow her to leave Eden and Ally behind.

Lilli does almost go, but at the last minute she acquires the courage to ask Ally to come with her. And together they head north. As noted previously, heading north has symbolic resonance in much Australian film, since it connotes heading toward the warmth of the tropics. So, the direction of their journey together offers hope. However, at a restaurant where they stop for food and fuel, Lilli almost abandons Ally once more. Lilli has courageously chosen a heroism that entails love and self-sacrifice and a reduction in her freedom, but she has not fully embraced it yet. We do not know if Lilli might not, at the next rest stop, take off in cowardice again. The film ends, then, with Lilli still having a battle within herself to fight and win. Perhaps a suggestion that the battle is not over is her not reclaiming her real name yet.

ECHOES OF PARADISE (PHILLIP NOYCE, DIRECTOR, 1988)

Echoes of Paradise ends in a manner that must cause feminists viewing it to cringe. The film is, on the surface, the story of a woman named Maria (Wendy Hughes) who leaves her unfaithful husband, her children, and the materialistic, politically corrupt world they inhabit for a long, liberating vacation in Thailand. That liberation includes a beautiful love affair with a Balinese dancer named Raka. In the end, however, she chooses to return to her husband and the kids. The ending feels almost like it would if Dotty in McKimmie's *Australian Dream* had chosen to go to the psychiatrist with her husband Geoff on the Monday after their "favorite fantasy" party.

High Tide may offer us another way to read *Echoes of Paradise*, however. Maria may play the role of the defiant Australian hero as she heads off to Thailand. However, through her relationship with Raka, she may come to realize that *both* the world she left *and* her flight to freedom are empty next to a kind of heroism that, like Lilli's, requires a courage that is difficult to muster.

Maria's husband George is involved in politics. For years, Maria has been living the posh lifestyle of a wife whose husband moves in the best and most powerful circles. Her father's death throws her for a loop, but what really sets her spinning is discovering her husband's many infidelities. Realizing that her marriage was a sham, she begins to wonder if her entire lifestyle was also empty and meaningless. Thus, she takes off on a holiday with a female friend to Thailand. After the female friend returns to Australia, Maria stays on, moving from a hotel room to a more "authentic" bungalow along the water. Her neighbor there is the Balinese dancer Raka.

The attraction between Maria and Raka is physical, but it really is more than that. As they explore each other's lives, they discover that they are both refugees. She has sought refuge from a lifestyle and family situation back in Australia that has proven untenable for her; he has sought refuge after an angry confrontation with his father back in Bali. They mirror each other in this way. They also mirror each other insofar as Raka's situation in Thailand has him trapped, almost like a tropical bird in a cage, on display but not able to fly (or dance). Paradoxically, the emotional ties that begin to develop between them only serve to increase his imprisonment there. So, Raka doubly mirrors Maria. His seeking refuge from a difficult situation in Bali mirrors her seeking refuge from a difficult situation in Australia; his entrapment at the Thailand resort mirrors her entrapment back in Australia. Raka's double mirroring, it should be noted, was an accident of production problems. The film was originally supposed to be shot in Bali. However, the dissatisfaction of the Indonesian government with an Australian newspaper's reporting on it led to the cancellation of all travel visas for Australians to Bali. So, at the last minute, the location was changed to Thailand and the script adjusted accordingly (Stratton, *Avocado* 113).

While in Thailand, Maria feels free. And her behavior while there certainly flaunts social norms. While there, she struggles to find something better in life. In feeling this way and in doing these things, she seems very Australian. However, what she finds is within herself, not in an exotic relationship. She finds that home for her is where she wants to be, others who might be there notwithstanding. She is perhaps pushed to discover this because Raka, like a mirror again, is making the same discovery about his true home.

This discovery requires explanation. She wants to be united with her children in Australia just as Raka wants to be reconciled with his family and to be dancing again in Bali. Neither is where they want to be because they have allowed others to define that desirable place for them. In Maria's case, her husband and the power-hungry, materialistic culture he is a part of have defined the place. That definition, however, need not be accepted. She can return, defy that definition, and make the place she wants to be what she wants it to be. She can do this if she has strength and if she has courage. She needs the strength because the others there will resist her attempts to define the place; she needs the courage because she will have to deal with her husband's duplicity and others' whispers.

Lilli in *High Tide* discovers that an alternative heroism may be necessary for women, one that requires strength within. Maria in *Echoes of Paradise* seems to make a similar discovery. Just as Armstrong leaves the ultimate resolution in *High Tide* unresolved, so does Noyce in *Echoes of Paradise*. Most would, however, grant that Armstrong is more skilled at suggesting the basis of this alternative heroism and its fragility than Noyce. Noyce's ending thus can be read as Maria's recapitulation rather than her return to claim her place on her terms. Noyce's film, then, is a much less successful work.

THE TALE OF RUBY ROSE (ROBERT SCHOLES, DIRECTOR, 1988)

Robert Scholes' film takes us to a landscape rarely seen in Australian film. We usually see Sydney or Melbourne or the outback near Broken Hill, New South Wales, the self-proclaimed "Film Capital of Australia." *Ruby Rose* takes us to the central highlands of Tasmania. And the photography of Steve Mason is "pictorially magnificent," so much so that the landscape plays a role in further isolating the film's central character, Ruby Rose, played by Melita Jurisic, because we are made to feel how remote from "civilization" she is, due to both geography and weather conditions (Stratton, *Avocado* 74).

Ruby has lived a life not only trapped by the landscape but also trapped or controlled by men. Her mother dies when she is very young, so she is brought up by her father. A broken man, he tells her virtually nothing about her mother. He is also there when Ruby acquires a pathological fear of the dark. We eventually are offered a literal explanation for this fear: one night, when Ruby was young, a forest creature burrowed into her room and into her bed. However, lurking beneath the surface of the film are hints that incestuous sexual abuse may be as much behind her night fears and nightmares as any literal forest creature.

Her father also kept Ruby illiterate. When she marries Henry (Chris Haywood) and leaves the valley for the mountains, he promises to teach her to read, and he does. Their life in the mountains, however, is shadowed by their rather desperate financial straits and, then, by her miscarrying their child. The former causes Henry to devise secret plans for the future of the farm; the latter causes them to adopt an orphan boy named Gem, who is rebelling against the killing of forest creatures that their winter lives as trappers depend on.

The secrecy and the tension in the mountain home cause Ruby's fear to increase and nightmares to return. So, she flees. She has practiced various magical ways of fighting off the dark during the past years. Her ostensible reason for returning to the valley is to find stronger magic.

Ruby meets a Mr. Bennett along the way. One night, he suddenly dies in a position that suggests that he was making sexual advances toward Ruby. She continues on with his corpse. It receives a bizarre funeral in a lumbering camp halfway down the mountain. The death and this funeral seem to exorcise demons—perhaps those dating back to earlier sexual abuse—from Ruby. Much concerning this journey, as well as the motion picture as a whole, is sketchy: the narration seems at times to have gaps in it (Stratton, *Avocado* 76). However, when she delivers the corpse to Mr. Bennett's wife's door, she seems freed of more than just the burden of the dead man's body.

Ruby has defied the regulating of her secret-keeping husband. She has battled the elements and survived the arduous journey to the valley. She has somehow been freed of some burden. She is now ready for both knowledge and community. Men, both her father and Henry, have kept her without both. Now, in the company of her grandmother, she learns about her mother and about herself. She discovers when her fear of the dark began: when she was ten years old and her grandmother gave her a book that told the story of the Earth's movement through light and darkness. She associated that movement into darkness with her mother's death. Because her father could not deal with that death, he did not allow Ruby to deal with it. Now, her grandmother helps her explore her mother's things and her mother's life so that Ruby will come to terms with the death and no longer be scared of the dark.

The extent to which this exploration helps is questionable because the grandmother's explanation deals neither with the creature in the dark nor the hints of incest. The communion with grandmother and mother that these explorations represent is, however, a kind of rebirth for Ruby. This is symbolized by the bath she and her grandmother take together (Ina Bertrand and Jan Chandler in Murray, *Australian Film* 259). After this symbolic rebirth from the womblike tub, Ruby must again live on her own. The grandmother quietly dies in the night, and Ruby then leaves for the mountains, carrying her mother's books and her grandmother's chair.

At this point, it might be useful to offer a bizarre comparison between Ruby and Maria in *Echoes of Paradise*. Maria was in some ways a typical Australian hero; however, that heroism had to yield to something other, the core of which was reclaiming her place on her own terms. Ruby also is in some ways a typical Australian hero. She even experiences mateship, although it is transformed from a very male Australian institution to a rather female, very communal, trans-generational bond. This heroism also has to yield to something "other." Like Maria, Ruby must reclaim her place on her own terms. Thus, she heads back into the mountains with the iconic books and grandmother's chair, suggesting what these terms might be.

We do not know if Maria succeeded, but Ruby did not—at least in the terms she envisioned as she began the dangerous trek back. She loses her balance in the snowy landscape, drops the chair into a ravine, and falls in after it. There, to postpone freezing to death, she burns the chair and the books. This ritualistic action seems less a rejection of them and more an embrace of the warmth they can provide. Then, she fades into death. When Henry and Gem find her, she is near death. She tells Henry that she will be home soon. "Home" for Maria was in Australia. That is the place she must reclaim. "Home" for Ruby Rose will prove to be the Heaven she believes in, a place where there is no darkness to scare her.

It took courage on Ruby's part to trek back to the mountains determined to bring her mother's and her grandmother's spirits to her home there. It also took courage on Ruby's part to face calmly her impending journey to another home. Perhaps whether one views the ending as positive or negative ultimately depends on one's personal views about Heaven. What, however, is less in doubt is the message that her quest to reclaim the earthly home, so regulated by Henry, was futile. She could not bring the spirit of her mother and grandmother to it; she could not get rid of the darkness there. Whatever is behind that darkness, whether a childhood delusion, a burrowing forest creature, or sexual abuse, is too strong in her.

SHAME (STEVE JODRELL, DIRECTOR, 1988)

Darkness does not envelop the Western Australia town of Ginborak as Asta Cadell rides into it on her motorcycle, but it might as well because the town has become a haven for rapists. The culture of the town has become such that, in the belief that boys will be boys, the gang rape of young girls has become tolerated by law enforcement and townspeople alike. Within this culture, victims find their reputations sullied, and should any of them dare to complain, they find themselves harassed by the perpetrators' parents and in more danger from the boys themselves.

Asta is an outsider. Just as Shane in the legendary American Western novel and film, she rides into town, not knowing what she will find and how involved she will become (Rose Lucas in Murray, *Australian Film* 257). Since Asta is quite attractive, the whistles and catcalls she receives along the town's main street might well have given her a clue about Ginborak's sexism. However, she undoubtedly dismisses that as small-town boorishness. Since her motorcycle has developed a mechanical problem, she is compelled to stay in the town. While there, she learns more.

Asta learns about the gang rape of young Lizzie Curtis. She learns about other victims. She even has to face down a gang of rather young teens who come after her in a dark dead-end street near the railroad station where she has gone to pick up a part she needs to repair her bike. When she injures one of the boys in the course of defending herself, the town's chief police officer threatens her with criminal charges. She then tells him what crimes he should be charging the boys with and what crimes he himself may be guilty of. He responds with a snide remark about "the little lady" and the law, which prompts her into confessing that she is a barrister in the city and does indeed know the law.

Since she has taken a room with the Curtises, she sees Lizzie's pain close up; she sees what the gang rape did to Lizzie. She also sees how, within the context of the town's sick culture, even Lizzie's father believes that his daughter was a slut who asked for what she got. She helps reconcile father and daughter, and she befriends Lizzie, becoming a surrogate big sister to the girl. Therefore, when her bike is fixed and she can leave, she does not—she stays. She teaches Lizzie self-defense, and she tries to rally the women of the community against the crimes that are being perpetrated against them. The culture of tolerance is so deeply ingrained in the town that she is only somewhat successful.

Asta plays the role of the Australian hero almost perfectly. She has a relationship back in Perth, but she is nonetheless a free spirit. Her riding through the countryside by herself on her holiday is evidence of that. She defies the male-defined authoritative culture of the town, as well as the authorities who, at best, go along with the rape culture. She loves, not horses, but a twentieth-century replacement: the motorcycle; and she is not averse to having a beer or two. She is fiercely competitive. One can only imagine what she is like as a barrister, but the impression she gives is that she is a battler. And perhaps she often battles on behalf of the underdog because she surely embraces the cause of the underdog in this Western Australia town.

She also believes in a kind of mateship. However, in the same key as the very different *The Tale of Ruby Rose*, she redefines mateship as female community. Her redefinition of mateship critiques traditional male mateship by implication. She also critiques the male-defined institution by depicting, as in *Wake in Fright* (1971), a solidarity that is so sexist as to condone gang rape (Stratton, *Avocado* 219). Her redefinition of mateship results in one important way in which *Shame* is not *Shane*. Whereas Shane would fight alone on behalf of those he befriended (his mates), Asta, the community developer, will fight along with her community members (her mates). Her heroism, then, is not that of the individual but, rather, that of the community of women she rallies.

What causes them to rally is a vengeful attack on the Curtis household. Asta manages to get Lizzie safely to the police station. But, by then, the boys have kidnapped the grandmother and taken her to a secluded area to rape her. Their lines make it absolutely clear that this potential rape, like all sexual assault, is all about power, not sex. They want to show her who is boss. The women of the community are so enraged at the idea of the grandmother being raped that they finally band together and counterattack the boys. This moment is Asta's triumph: she sees the community of women, no longer cowed or accepting, defending themselves.

The Australian hero will ultimately lose, however, and Asta is no exception because she is the best example of a female playing the role of hero even though its terms are arguably male-defined. Therefore, no sooner does Asta see this triumph than she faces defeat. Boys have seized Lizzie from the police station. En route to where they will rape her again—and probably worse—to teach her to keep her mouth shut, she bites one of the boys, and, in anger, he kicks her out of the speeding car onto the road. She will die of her injuries.

Much has been written about *Shame*, and, not surprisingly, much has been said about this ending (Crofts, *Identification*; Rose Lucas in Murray, *Australian Film* 257; Partridge). Some have even agreed with the policeman who tells Asta that this, Lizzie's death, is what you get by stirring up trouble. Disturbingly implicit in that message is that women, and men, should tolerate rape and other sexual crimes. Others see the ending differently. Its triumph is the fact that the women of the town have formed a community that will combat rape. Lizzie's death is a painful reminder of why such solidarity is so necessary. These commentators see Lizzie's death as neither Asta's fault nor her defeat; rather, they see the death as just another mark of shame upon the town. But, in this ending, the mark of shame is being worn by the town, not by the young girls who have been gang-raped.

We have, perhaps, seen in this chapter three different versions of the female Australian hero. The first is like the male, but has to battle sexism in addition to whatever else the plot involves. As a result, the heroism is muted or worse. The second is like the male, at least initially, but finds that heroic formula empty and that she must be a different kind of hero. We have a third in *Shame*, the woman who is like the male with, perhaps, a few redefining twists. Like the male hero, she fights; like the male hero, she wins; like the male hero, she loses too. The death of Lizzie sounds the fatalistic note. However, just as fatalism does not deter the male hero, it should not deter the female. The death of Lizzie, then, is not an indication that Asta and the town's women should surrender their fight; instead, it is an indication that winning is not as simple as many Hollywood movies make it seem, as well as an indication that their fighting and fighting on are so absolutely necessary in a world, not as bad as Ginborak, but nonetheless characterized by discrimination, abuse, and violence toward women.

This "feminist" reading of *Shame* seems to be what many would have made of the film when seeing it. Director Jodrell reports that many women have told him how cathartic and inspiring the motion picture was (Stratton, *Avocado* 220). This response puzzled Jodrell a bit because he felt the film was flawed. The flaw was rooted in the inconsistency between the writers' design and the director's. The writers wanted a heavily intertextual film that worked in several Hollywood genres and, perhaps, echoed both *Shane* and *Mad Max II* (1981). The director, on the other hand, wanted a piece of social realism (O'Regan, *Australian* 153; Stratton, *Avocado* 219–20). The result of this clash in vision is a film that might not bear the questions one would ask of social realism because so much is tied to generic formulations. Much to Jodrell's surprise, however, *Shame* does withstand the questioning fairly well.

THE LAST DAYS OF CHEZ NOUS (GILLIAN ARMSTRONG, DIRECTOR, 1992)

The Last Days of Chez Nous, scripted by Helen Garner and directed by Gillian Armstrong, is a sophisticated European-style film that seems on the surface to have very little to do with heroism (O'Regan, *Australian* 157). The reason, perhaps, is that there is no obvious force to fight against in the film. There are no gang-raping townspeople; there is no controlling husband; and there is no political asininity or corruption. But there is something very much the matter lurking in the film's background. It is not put into words, but it comes across as a spiritual emptiness that matches the geographical emptiness of the Australian continent and is figured in the gradual disappearance of the kangaroo (which is repeatedly noted) as well as in the fact that both Beth and Vicki have had abortions. As a result, the film has a quiet apocalyptic tone. The last days of the individual household most of the action takes place in may suggest the last days of something else.

A heroic stance is necessary to face this apocalypse. Sisters Beth and Vicki are the two possible heroes. The younger Vicki looks within their house, "Chez Nous". While Beth is busy, she becomes the lover of Beth's live-in lover J. P. The relationship may begin as just sexual, but, by the end of the film, Vicki and J. P. are in love and do choose to live together. Both, up until this point, seemed somewhat without roots: J. P. an expatriate Frenchman and Vicki a world wanderer. Perhaps Vicki should have respected her sister's "property," but we do feel that Beth's strong denunciation of Vicki toward the film's end is unfortunate.

The two sisters serve, at times, as mirrors to each other. For example, they are both writers. They are also both believers in personal freedom, and they both will, when necessary, defy authority. They both tend to fight, but, lately, ennui has set in. They both believe in community and loyalty to those in it, although this belief has faded, as the tension in the artsy community of "Chez

Nous" suggests. They are both, in other words, rather typical Australian heroes, revised so the edges are smooth. However, the era they are in does not seem a heroic one. Thus, the apocalyptic sense pervading the film only nudges them to do something. And what Vicki does is very inward-looking and very self-serving. She forms a bond that might, in some sense, save her but not others.

Beth looks more outward. Thus, she journeys with their father into the Australian outback on a spiritual pilgrimage of some sort. Their destination is vague, but it seems to be to Uluru or some place near Uluru. Given that site's sacredness to aborigines, its probably being their destination enhances the journey's spiritual quality. Along the way, however, they discuss God, and he denies God's very existence. Thus, the pilgrimage seems rather pointless. At the end of the film, however, Beth makes a second pilgrimage, and this one does not seem so pointless. In the Sydney neighborhood of "Chez Nous," there was a church spire that Beth always wanted to find the base of. As the film ends, she is finally walking off to find the church at the base of that often visible spire to heaven.

Beth's response to the pending collapse seems to offer something to others as well as to herself—at least potentially. Whereas Vicki and J. P. have each other to hold on to, Vicki may find beliefs that answer her needs and the era's needs. The spire is there; the church at its base is there; the walk to it is available to others.

The film's most optimistic note, however, may well have nothing to do with either Vicki or Beth. Throughout the film, Beth's daughter Annie is playing a piece on the piano. Initially, she makes many mistakes, but as the movie proceeds, her playing gets increasingly better. Even in the end, it is not without its wrong notes; still, it is better than the time before. Annie's piano playing may suggest that all is not declining in the world *The Last Days of Chez Nous* depicts. If one keeps battling, as Annie does as she practices and practices the piece, one can survive and, maybe, inspire those within earshot to survive.

THE PIANO (JANE CAMPION, DIRECTOR, 1993)

I feel I should begin this discussion by saying something like "speaking of piano playing" because playing to survive, an idea just implicit in Armstrong's film, is at the core of Jane Campion's *The Piano*. Its central character, Ada (Holly Hunter), is anything but free, trapped in a loveless arranged marriage with a very intense man, played by Sam Neill. But the piano frees her, and it also gives her voice, for she is a deaf–mute. She is, in general, willing to follow the dictates of authority and the norms of polite society—except when it comes to her piano. The piano brings out the defiance, and it brings out battling behavior. The piano also brings out the passion.

Some of these feelings are provoked when her new husband announces that there is no way he can transport the piano she has landed with in New Zealand to their home in the mountains. She tries to defy his order to leave the piano behind on the beach. The defiance really surfaces, however, after another man in the colony, Baines (Harvey Keitel), buys her piano from her husband. He wants her to give him lessons; but, in reality, he is sex-starved and wants to be with her and touch her and, ultimately, make love with her. So, Baines offers her a deal: she can buy back the piano piece by piece by trading her sexual favors. The very idea is appalling. It is appalling to us that he abuses his power over her in such a manner; it would have been appalling to anyone back at the time of the film's events that she might even think of betraying her husband in this manner. However, in defiance of her marriage vows and in defiance of what society would think, she agrees to the deal.

Baines eventually recognizes how he has forced Ada into prostitution. He apologizes and returns the complete piano to her. By this time, however, mutual passion, maybe love, has developed between them. Furthermore, by this time her husband has discovered and witnessed their liaisons. Initially, he tries to imprison Ada to keep her away from Baines. When she—still defiant—tries to flee to him, her husband captures her and bloodily amputates one of her fingers, thereby rendering her unable to play her piano and, thereby, unable to communicate.

He then realizes what a horrid thing he has done to Ada. So, he releases her and allows her to go with Baines. This eventuality may seem like a happy ending, but note how Ada is still very much controlled. It is perhaps this feeling of being regulated that leads to her last desperate act of rebellion. As she and Baines are leaving, her piano is causing the small boat to very nearly sink. She reluctantly consents to the dumping of the piano—the only means she has to make herself known—but then, loops a rope around her foot so that she will go overboard and under with the piano. Through her action she is, in essence, saying that if the piano is destroyed, her only means of self-expression will be destroyed. Furthermore, she is saying that she chooses to die rather than live without self-expression. She is also choosing, something she has been largely unable to do thus far in an environment in which the decisions have either been coerced or made for her.

Having chosen death, she then chooses life. Why? Perhaps she sees in the love that she and Baines are beginning to share the possibility of self-expression. Maybe she knows that he would not want her either muted or controlled. And, once the two are out of New Zealand and in Australia, he begins teaching Ada how to speak. Furthermore, he has her fitted for a silver finger, which allows her to communicate and express herself, once again through a piano. So her choice of life seems indeed fortuitous, but it is worth noting that, even in this happy ending, she is controlled by a man: her happiness and her self-realization depend on his actions (O'Regan, *Australian* 300).

Campion's film is a rich one. This sketch of it does not do it justice. Ada's relationship with her mirrorlike daughter is worth exploring, as is the influence of the Maori people on Baines. This sketch, however, does point to Ada's basic personality: she desires self-expression and communication beyond all things. This passion is perhaps so intense in her, a deaf–mute, because the basic abilities to hear and speak have not been given to her. As a corollary to this desire, she learns to desire the most intimate form of communication. She must, however, work past other definitions of such intimacy that are forced on her: sex as a price to pay and sex as an obligation to fulfill with the terms being set in either case by the man. She defiantly fights her way beyond these definitions. She embraces her sexual desire in what develops into a loving context.

Ada also wants freedom so she can express herself as she chooses. She lives as a piece of property, as purchased flesh and as regulated flesh. All along she wants her freedom—so much so that she almost kills herself rather than live on with her freedom to express herself denied. In her love of freedom and as she battles defiantly for it, she is very Australian. What makes Ada seem a bit odd (that is, unlike other Australian heroes, male and female, that we have encountered) is that she is deaf and dumb. One needs, however, to ask whether director and screenwriter Campion wants that to be a literal fact of the story or whether she wants it to be both fact and symbol. As symbol, the deafness and muteness, which together deny language and with that communication, can be interpreted as signifying her gender because women are, in various ways, kept out of language and thus out of full communication. If Ada's disability is read in such a manner, then she is really not that different from other female heroes examined in this chapter insofar as she has many of the traits of the Australian hero, but because of the gender-based oppression she experiences, she is not as able to fight or win as those not so encumbered. What then does the piano symbolize? It is her ability to speak of herself out of language, sharing that message with herself and with others. In so doing, she is doing something similar to the female heroes we have seen who are altering the male-defined norms and trying to put their revisions into words when, in some cases, words themselves resist or prove inadequate. Ada, then can be linked to Sybylla Melvyn in *My Brilliant Career*—a hero who encounters oppression and defies it—or, maybe, to Ruby Rose in *The Tale of Ruby Rose*—a hero who encounters oppression and deals with it by gathering resources from her mother and her grandmother that she can compose into her own sense of how she must be and how she must act to face and defeat the darkness.

MURIEL'S WEDDING (P. J. HOGAN, DIRECTOR, 1994)

Muriel Haslop, the central character in P. J. Hogan's film, may be as oppressed as Ada in Campion's *The Piano*, although one would be hard-pressed to think of two films more different in setting, mood, and music. Whereas *The Piano* takes us into the colonial past, *Muriel's Wedding* takes us to present-day Porpoise Spit, Queensland; whereas *The Piano* is poetic and somber, *Muriel's Wedding* is brashly prosaic and riotously funny; and whereas Campion's film features a largely classical score, Hogan's features the Swedish rock group

Muriel (Toni Collette) has her wedding day in *Muriel's Wedding* (1994). Photo courtesy of National Film and Sound Archives. Permission granted by House and Moorhouse Films.

ABBA. Ada and Muriel, however, are both oppressed: by the men who regulate their lives, by the society at large that embraces the "rules" the patriarchy sets up, and by their own low self-worth, Ada being plain and not virginal and

Muriel being overweight and not cool. Ada wants to play her piano; Muriel wants to play "Dancing Queen" and be "Dancing Queen."

Muriel (Toni Collette) is so put down by her peers and her overbearing father that she hardly has the chance to act in any even vaguely heroic manner—at least in the "real" world. So, she fantasizes about getting married. When her father's mistress helps her get a job selling cosmetics, she convinces her family that she is being successful and uses a blank check her mother gives her for necessary business supplies to take off on a resort holiday. There she meets another "loser" named Rhonda (Rachel Griffiths). Together, they carouse, tell the cool girls off, and win the resort's talent show by lip-synching to ABBA's "Waterloo." In just a few days, they are fast mates.

Unable to return home for more than just a few minutes, Muriel goes off to work in Sydney, where Rhonda works, and they become roommates. Life seems to be looking up for Muriel: she even acquires a boyfriend. However, her wedding fantasy is still very much alive. She spends her free time visiting wedding boutiques, trying on dresses, and having the salespeople take her picture so that her fictitiously ailing mother can see her so decked out. Back in the apartment, she is secretly compiling these photographs in a wedding album. Rhonda discovers this fantasy and thinks that it is bizarre. But, at about the same time, Rhonda discovers she has cancer. When the initial treatment fails, she faces a second procedure that will leave her forever in a wheelchair. It is at this point that Rhonda truly needs her mate.

Muriel, however, has been offered a deal. A South African swimmer who wants to compete at the Olympics needs to establish Australian citizenship because South Africa is still a banned nation. If Muriel marries him, she gets money up front and a lifestyle more comfortable than she ever knew back in Porpoise Spit. She also gets her wedding. She pretty much pushes Rhonda aside as she plans the gala event.

What Muriel has done (theft) and what she will soon do (fraud) are not admirable. We may well sympathize with her because she has, indeed, been called ugly and worthless too many times while growing up. However, it is difficult, at first glance, to see Muriel as a hero of any sort. But let us try to consider her a "misdirected" hero, exhibiting the traits but putting them all to either fantastic or wrong use. She wants the freedom a "dancing queen" would have, and she defies authority left and right. She competes for the wedding of her dreams and is clearly the underdog in that fight because she has no man really in sight—until the South African athlete swims into her life. She enjoys carousing; she is not into books but, instead, ABBA albums and bridal magazines; and she is devoted to her mate, although she does reject her in her true hour of need, when her mate and "the wedding" pull her in opposite directions.

One also needs to note that her background has not prepared her for truly heroic action. The Queensland that she grew up in is as absurd as that in McKimmie's *Australian Dream*, and her father is as much of a jerk as Dotty's husband Geoff in McKimmie's film. As is the case in many Australian daggy (comically dysfunctional) family films, her father has his wife and his children all convinced they are losers, so they look and act the part (O'Regan, *Australian* 39, 247). Oppressed as a human spirit in this home environment, Muriel knows only how to get by and how to escape into the dancing queen fantasy that had helped her survive.

Muriel's Wedding is a comedy; therefore, one should not expect intense drama leading up to a transformation in Muriel's character. Just a short time in a loveless marriage shows her how silly her wedding fantasy was. Just a short time away from her mate Rhonda shows her how much that relationship really meant to her. She competed and she rebelled, acting much like the male heroic norm. All of the energy had been misdirected. Now, she is going to defy all of the attitudes that so define the Porpoise Spit world and compete to win back her mate Rhonda.

Rhonda, not able to live on her own anymore, had moved back to the Queensland resort to live with her parents. Muriel goes there to offer to live with Rhonda in Sydney and take care of her. Rhonda's mother and two hypocritical girlfriends who are visiting are appalled at Muriel's nerve. How dare she, they ask, come for Rhonda after abandoning her in her hour of need? Rhonda, however, detects the genuineness of Muriel's offer. As the movie ends, the two are, in a carousing manner, leaving Porpoise Spit together as the credits begin to roll and ABBA sings "Dancing Queen."

The film's ending is happy and light. One should not, however, take too lightly what Muriel has done. She and Rhonda together will defy a world that tries to tell them how to be cool, a world that puts material goods and high status and good looks ahead of human decency. Together, they will battle a larger world that embraces these false gods as Porpoise Spit did, but not as absurdly. And together, they will carouse as mates do. But Muriel will have to help the crippled Rhonda along. Muriel will have to be truly devoted to her with an intensity that might make one suspect a lesbian attraction between them if it were not for the film's heterosexual love scenes (O'Regan, *Australian* 272, 301). It takes both love and courage to make such a commitment. Muriel demonstrates a heroism that is nobly directed in choosing to be Rhonda's true mate. Director Hogan said that he "wanted to make a film about the sort of girl you see everyday sitting in the Bourke Street mall eating her roll at lunchtime and tell a story of the heroism in her life" (Wignall 33). He did so, with that heroism concerning less her deeds than her true dedication to her mate.

LUCKY BREAK (A.K.A. *PAPERBACK ROMANCE*) (BEN LEWIN, DIRECTOR, 1994)

Ada, throughout most of her life, expressed herself through the piano. Sophie's mode of self-expression in Ben Lewin's *Lucky Break* (*Paperback Romance* in the United States) is the very erotic tale. She writes such stories, living very much vicariously through the adventures in them—until she meets Eddie. He overhears her composing one of her stories somewhat aloud in the public library and becomes fascinated with her. What might be just an ordinary romantic story of boy meets girl, and so forth, is complicated by their secrets: Eddie deals in stolen jewelry and has a beautiful fiancée Gloria; Sophie is a victim of childhood polio and walks with the aid of a brace and crutches.

Initially, Sophie is embarrassed by her disability and turns down Eddie's offers of a trip to Paris or a "small coffee." Then, she decides she is indeed interested in the man and begins her comic pursuit of him. Her disability, we are made to feel, makes her the underdog in the pursuit. Eddie lives a very active life; plus, he seems particularly drawn to the beautiful. Gloria plays racquetball with him and is superficially very beautiful. Sophie, on the other hand, struggles to get from place to place and is presented as a beauty but of a less flamboyant kind. Lewin here plays off stereotypes, making Gloria blond and glamorously made up and Sophie brunette and much more simply made up. Ironically, what gives Sophie a chance is when she has a comic accident while trying to escape Eddie and Gloria, on whom she's been spying, and breaks her leg. Disabled by a leg in a cast seems more acceptable (because it is temporary) than her true disability. Sophie is very much aware that her pursuit is probably futile once the cast comes off and Eddie becomes aware of what she sees as her physical imperfection.

As the film progresses, we see that Sophie has a great deal to recommend herself to Eddie or any man. She is sensitive, fun-loving, and quite erotic. She has, however, kept most of what she has to offer under wraps. She has lived a very independent life, not because she necessarily likes being independent but more because her disability has simultaneously made her too ashamed to connect with many others and very determined to conquer each day on her own, without help. Despite this fierce independence, she is also, as the plot will reveal, a very loyal mate.

Yuri, a Russian immigrant to Australia who is now a police officer, becomes interested in Sophie. They met when he interrogated Eddie about a stolen necklace. He is ostensibly interested in her because she might be able to provide information about Eddie's dealings. Later, especially after he discovers her disability, he becomes romantically interested. In fact, he and Eddie are both there at the hospital, as romantic rivals, when Sophie has her cast removed and must admit that she's a polio victim to Eddie. Eddie accuses her of lying to him and runs out. One would think that his rejection of her would cause her to not only rush into Yuri's arms but tell Yuri all that she knows about Eddie. She does neither. Under interrogation by Yuri and two other rather rude police officers, she remains true to Eddie. She is his very good mate.

Eddie has no knowledge of Sophie's loyalty when he walks out on his wedding to Gloria. He walks out because he knows that he has finally gotten beyond the superficialities of life with Sophie and that he loves her. Perhaps her sending him a copy of her *The Passion Anthology* as a wedding present helped, especially since Gloria responds to the book as if it were kinky smut, not poetic erotica. Sending the anthology also suggests that Sophie, despite being rejected by him at the hospital, is still battling for him. So, he runs from the wedding to her, and they hurry off to a somewhat seedy Melbourne motel to make love. The police are following—aided by an electronic device they surreptitiously placed in one of Sophie's crutches. Yuri, however, stops the police from making an arrest until the couple has consummated their love. They marry, and Eddie gets a light sentence, leaving the couple with several months of fantasizing before they are together again and can make the fantasies come true.

Lucky Break is a comedy, and one has to keep the genre in mind when interpreting it. It glosses over issues; and it ends in a very upbeat manner. Nonetheless, the film does offer in Sophie an Australian hero, one who ultimately defies the odds and wins. What has held some of the women we have examined in this chapter back has been the oppression they experience because of gender. Sophie's gender is not, however, an obstacle in this film—her physical disability is. One might conjecture that this physical disability is a way of presenting the obstacles facing women heroes without writing/directing another movie that points overtly at sexism. Or maybe Lewin is trying to broaden the discussion of those factors that might impede the heroic story, suggesting that gender and race and class are not the only barriers but that a range of physical disabilities might also be. If so, the most poignant point Lewin makes is that physical disabilities are a barrier as much because they inhibit the would-be hero as they prevent action or evoke negative reactions from others.

Chapter 5

The Aborigines' Role

I began Chapter 4 by noting how male-biased the preceding chapters had been. Let me begin Chapter 5 by noting how White-biased the preceding chapters, including the one on women heroes, have been. Australian cinema certainly has had, until recently, a "White face." There have, however, been some exceptions to this "rule." In this chapter, I consider some of these exceptions.

In the case of films focused on women, we found that the kind of heroism sketched in this study's earlier chapters was indeed present. The heroism might have been thwarted because of gendered oppression, or it might have been altered somewhat or even significantly, but it was there. In the case of films focused on Australia's indigenous people, the picture is not as clear. Most of these films are written and directed by Whites. Thus, the lives of aborigines are seen from the outside, a perspective that has unfortunately imprisoned all Australian arts (Jakubowicz). From that perspective, two interpretations of aborigines seem to obstruct one's view: aborigines as victims and aborigines as "other." Only one White director, Bruce Beresford in *The Fringe Dwellers* (1986) seems to overcome these blinding interpretations. He does so by simply presenting lives, without feeling obliged to make a statement of any sort about them. Recently, an increasing number of indigenous Australians have been making films. These directors offer us a view of aborigines that is authentic and quite surprisingly in line with the sense of heroism sketched in the earlier chapters of this book.

WALKABOUT (NICHOLAS ROEG, DIRECTOR, 1971)

Walkabout, a film by a British director working with American money, is a beautifully made motion picture based on James Vance Marshall's novel. The one element that might detract from it is its occasional heavy-handedness. For example, when the film cuts away from an aboriginal hunting to show us how the white man hunts, we may want to scream at Roeg that we get the film's point without such blatant contrasts. The film in so many ways sets up such contrasts that viewers are inclined to read the film in terms of dualities without being offered abrupt cutaways to scenes not relevant to the film's narrative.

The basic duality informing the film is that between white civilization and the aborigines' outback. The film begins in the city with frames that emphasize its congestion and regimentation. Then, it shifts to a desertlike outback that is, oddly, just a short drive from the big city. That Roeg's geography here is quite obviously wrong is an indication that we are to interpret the film's polarities as representations of two ways of life, not as two real places. A father has taken his two children to this outback. His plan is to murder them and then commit suicide. We never learn why. When the children run from him, he kills himself in his flaming Volkswagen, leaving the teenage girl and the younger boy to die in the outback. The outback does indeed prove to be a threatening place for the

Aboriginal boy (David Gulpilil) leads lost girl (Jenny Agutter) and boy (Lucien John) through outback to safety in *Walkabout* (1971). Photo courtesy of National Film and Sound Archives. Permission granted by EuroLondon Films.

two. The photography emphasizes the threat by offering vistas of great expanses of nothing and close-ups of menacing fauna. The film stresses their being out of their element by having them dressed in their school uniforms.

Just as this outback is about to take their lives, along comes an aboriginal boy (played by the ubiquitous David Gulpilil). We are to understand that he is an adolescent male on walkabout, which we are also to understand as a solitary period of reflection designed to prepare the young male for his adult role in tribal life. The boy, however, interrupts his sacred solitary time to befriend the White girl and boy. He shows them how to survive in the outback and he leads them back to "civilization." Along the way, the girl and boy are transformed. Initially, they were aliens, all too likely to succumb to nature. After the aboriginal boy's guidance, they are comfortable in nature. Roeg suggests their increasing comfort by gradually having them rid themselves of their uniforms. The scene, then, that epitomizes their new comfort is a nude swimming scene that, despite its full frontal male and female nudity, seems quite innocent. The scene's depiction suggests that the three have stumbled into if not a new Eden, then at least an idyllic moment that is so far removed from civilization that society's norms are totally irrelevant.

Unfortunately, this idyll ends as they near civilization. The uniforms come back on—gradually, piece by piece, as the girl and her brother (never named) prepare themselves to be transformed back to their civilized state. Their next step is to an abandoned mining town, whose ruins suggest the different way that the White man treats nature. Then, after that is the city and adulthood. It is from the girl's adulthood—married, living in a nice urban apartment—that we are then led to believe we have been seeing flashbacks. As she flashes back, it is clear that she longs for something she discovered in nature, that she regrets a moment back in nature when she chose civilization over nature without even knowing that there was a choice before her.

That moment comes at the end of their journey through the outback. Close to civilization, they stay in an abandoned house. Outside that civilized structure, the aboriginal boy (also unnamed) performs a dance. The girl is threatened by the dance, although she does not know why. The dance causes her to cover her body, although she does not stop to ask why the dance should have this precise effect on her. It is almost as if she, like Eve in Eden, has sinned and has then, for the first time, discovered her nakedness. But the aboriginal boy's dance is not sinful. Rather, it is a mating dance: he is, in essence, asking the teenage girl, with whom he swam unashamedly naked days earlier, to be his spouse. We are also led to believe that this proposal is a life-or-death matter for the boy. Having violated his walkabout by interacting with the girl and her brother, he is now no longer able to rejoin the tribe. So, for him, life will either be shared with the girl or spent alone.

The girl understands the boy's feelings but does not fully understand the dance. In any event, she does not respond. So, the aboriginal boy, not wanting to live his life alone, kills himself. The next morning, when the girl and her brother find the aboriginal boy's body, the little boy is baffled by the suicide, but the girl seems to know why he killed himself. Again, she understands at a deep level why the boy committed suicide, but either could not or would not articulate it. She either could not at that point articulate what was going on—in her and in him—or she was afraid to. To bring the idea into words would have given it a reality, so she keeps it unreal by never putting it into language.

She seems at that point to feel some guilt. Years later, she feels some longing, but the longing seems to be less for the boy as male and more for the boy as symbol. He symbolizes the natural and the innocent, and she seems to be longing for those qualities as she faces her day-to-day urban life. We can imagine what the aboriginal boy must have felt; however, we do not have much in the film to base that sense on because, as Michael Leigh and Sean Maynard both lament, Roeg is much less interested in portraying the boy as a person than in presenting him as a symbol. The boy is very much the "noble-savage" type. He lives in nature and in innocence. His nobility is rooted in his almost sacred closeness with the earth and its flora and fauna. He exhibits that nobility by befriending the girl and her brother, saving their lives, and leading them back to the world they could live in.

There are some ways in which the aboriginal boy is like the Australian heroes we have seen thus far in many films. He seems to love his freedom. He is willing to defy authorities by abandoning his walkabout and helping the two lost White children. He seems to love that land. And his quest—for the girl—proves futile. These Australian characteristics are, however, neither emphasized nor developed. Instead, his characterization is kept two-dimensional, at which level of development he is scarcely more than the noble savage type. Roeg seems to have been prevented from delving any deeper into the aboriginal boy's character because he was trying to present a story more symbolic than real, more defined by clear dualities than the nuances displayed by real people. One might also surmise that the notion of aborigine as noble savage held some sway at the time—so much that a director might even think that, in presenting the aborigine in such terms, he or she was offering viewers both "the truth" and a positive view of the nation's indigenous people to counter the nation's dominant racist view.

THE LAST WAVE (PETER WEIR, DIRECTOR, 1977)

We should not criticize Roeg too severely for presenting the aborigine so positively. Similarly, we should not criticize Peter Weir for presenting the aborigine in equally positive terms in his film *The Last Wave*. Weir's positive terms are, however, different: whereas Roeg presented the aborigine as the noble savage, Weir presents him as a mystic. Both, as Leigh notes, are stereotypes.

The Last Wave is full of suggestions of impending doom. From the opening scene of a cloudless hailstorm in an outback town to a later scene of torrential black rain in Sydney, the film communicates that something is wrong in nature with water associated with this threat throughout the film (Pike and Cooper

321–22). The central character in the film, White lawyer David Burton (Richard Chamberlain) has visions in his sleep. These visions and his legal work (he is defending a group of urban aborigines against a murder charge) bring him into contact with young aborigine Chris Lee (David Gulpilil) and the older Charlie (Nandjiwarra Amagula). David sees Chris in his dreams. Chris seems to know more about what is pending than he is saying, but it is the elder Charlie who really seems to know what the future holds.

A central issue in the murder trial is whether the accused aborigines are tribal or not. It is a crucial issue because it will determine where and according to what set of laws they are tried. The notion that aborigines living in Sydney are still tribal strikes David's legal colleagues as absurd. However, David senses that these aborigines are and that the murder was tribal justice against one who violated its secrets. As the film proceeds, it is much more these secrets that David is seeking than an acquittal or a change of venue for the men.

Weir introduces viewers to the aboriginal concept of Dreamtime. His presentation of it is, of necessity, a simplification. Mine will be even simpler. Basically, aborigines exist in two times, the present and another that seamlessly merges past, present, and future. In Dreamtime, according to their beliefs, then, aborigines can see the future. In their cave art they often represent the past, present, and future together. Stalking Chris, David discovers that the sewers of Sydney are serving as caves. On one wall, he sees a picture of the great tidal wave that will soon demolish eastern Australia. David's journey out of the sewers takes him into a pipe that leads to one of Sydney's beaches. There, he sees the actual wave.

Weir's film is very much David's story, not that of either Chris or Charlie. They do, however, play major roles. Their roles, however, do not individuate them. The film offers a few details about who they are apart from being visionaries of a sort. These details, however, are distractions in David's and the film's quest for the secret they know. These details, if explored, would tell us such things as where they live, where they work, whom they love, whom they hate—and why; however, we never get an understanding and appreciation of their lives on that mundane a level. Rather, the film's emphasis on their Dreamtime visions results in our knowing them only as two-dimensional figures. They are mystics, and because we do not exist in Dreamtime, we feel estranged from them; we feel that they are "other."

THE CHANT OF JIMMIE BLACKSMITH (FRED SCHEPISI, DIRECTOR, 1978)

Schepisi offers us a much fuller portrait of an aborigine in his adaptation of Thomas Keneally's novel, which, like most of the Australian author's work, is based in fact. We get to know the central character in the novel and film, Jimmie Blacksmith, a half-aborigine who is educated as a Christian and as a non-aboriginal Australian. Because of the education he received, mainly through the Reverend Neville (Jack Thompson) who had adopted the boy, Jimmie (Tommy Lewis) has certain expectations. He believes that, if he works hard and shows due reverence to God, he will be treated decently and will be justly rewarded. The Christian, Australian promise has a great deal of appeal to the boy—more than the aboriginal ways, which the movie shows to have been corrupted through interaction with the colonists. In any event, Jimmie's upbringing has so estranged him from the aboriginal people that living in their manner is simply not an option for the now young man. This estrangement is suggested by Jimmie's inability to thrive in the wild landscape (McFarlane 76–77).

Out in the world, he discovers how false his hopes and expectations were. He works hard and shows due reverence but is nonetheless exploited and abused by the Whites he deals with. They see him as Black, and, no matter what he does, they bring their racism to their dealings with him. As long as he accepts their condescending treatment and remains in his place on the margins of White society, they tolerate him. Jimmie, unfortunately, will not settle for such marginalization.

Two acts threaten the settlers. First, Jimmie marries a somewhat dim-witted White girl named Gilda (Angela Punch). Second, when some of Jimmie's family members come to him for help, he lets them into his house. With the first act, Jimmie seems to have crossed a line. With the second, he poses to them the threat of numbers. They are threatened by Jimmie and his kin, but it would be showing weakness to admit that one is so threatened. So, they claim that Gilda and her child are the ones who are in danger and try to take them away from Jimmie.

Jimmie finally snaps and enacts mindless revenge against the settlers living near him. Schepisi's film shows this violence graphically. Then, Jimmy and his half-brother Mort take off into the countryside. The rest of the film is the story of their pursuit and eventual capture.

What is very much at the forefront of the film is Jimmie's victimization and, then, his revenge, which comes across in the film as justified in theory but not in reality. We feel sorry that Jimmie is pushed to the point at which he becomes violent; however, we cannot excuse the violence per se. The film then offers a true tragedy, not a melodramatic account of racial injustice. That Jimmie might be thought of as a tragic hero deflects just a bit from Jimmie as victim, but it is still the victim's role that he plays. In so playing this role, Jimmie comes closer to being two-dimensional rather than three-dimensional. The film does present Jimmie as an individual; however, the story pulls one's attention away from those details that characterize Jimmie as Jimmie and presents him as an almost stereotypical example of a victim of racial injustice. Schepisi seems to be walking a tightrope here between offering a fully-drawn character and making a strong, generally-applicable political statement and occasionally falling off in the latter direction.

If, for the moment, we can ignore that Jimmie is a victim and that Jimmie is half-Black, we will notice a number of interesting personality traits he has. He loves his freedom and his land. He is competitive, working hard to gain the rewards that hard work leads to. He (and we) feels he is the underdog in this competition, a feeling reinforced every time he is treated poorly, but he fights on nonetheless. Even though he has made some strides into the White world, he is still loyal to family members—his mates, if you will—who need his help. And Jimmie, despite having been taught to be deferential, will defy authority when pushed.

This portrait is very much that of the revised Australian hero sketched in Chapter 3. The excesses of the hero of old are not there, at least until Jimmie commits his crimes; they have been smoothed away at Reverend Neville's insistence. Jimmie is then much like Jim Craig in *The Man from Snowy River* (1982), although one would probably not think to make that comparison. That he is half-Black alters the way we view his story. He is fated to be in a down position; he is fated to be a victim. He is thus somewhat like a few of the female heroes we discussed in Chapter 4. However, Jimmie's story seems more burdened by the expectation that he will be victim than any of their stories.

Portraying Jimmie's victimization is certainly the politically correct thing to do. This portrayal evokes Pauline Kael's glowing review before the term "politically correct" was even in vogue. One would hate to think that White novelists and filmmakers would overlook his and other aborigines' victimization. However, the dominance of that particular "take" on aboriginal life seems to stand in the way of any other characterization. Jimmie Blacksmith has much of the Australian hero in him. However, the understandable insistence on his victimization seems to make it virtually impossible that he will be allowed to play that role. Such heroism may require either the passing of a lengthy period of purged guilt or the filmmaking of an aborigine who could put victimization in a subordinate position in depicting an aboriginal character without being accused of being or feeling insensitive.

Schepisi's film, Kael's review notwithstanding, was not well-received. It was attacked as old-fashioned—another period piece—insofar as it was set in 1901; it was criticized for not being sufficiently commercial insofar as it dealt with a subject that made many Australians uncomfortable and dealt with it in a very "preachy" manner (McFarlane 8; Rattigan 88). The film was also attacked as not being sensitive enough to Jimmie's victimization because it showed his violence—graphically. In fact, the Governor family (Jimmie's adopted family) tried to block the film's screening (O'Regan, *Australian* 59). Schepisi lost a considerable sum of his own money on the film and became embittered toward moviemaking in Australia. The film's lack of success may partially explain why few other films depict an aborigine's story (Stratton, *Avocado* 202). Or, if they do, they avoid Schepisi's "dated" setting, didacticism, and anger-induced violence.

BACKLASH (BILL BENNETT, DIRECTOR, 1986)

Bennett's *Backlash* is contemporary; all of its violence occurs before the film per se begins, and the message is tied primarily to very immediate injustices, not the past, although both the false accusation of murder and a homicide by the police that are the film's concerns are rooted in a legacy of racism. It is not as good a film as *The Chant of Jimmie Blacksmith*; however, it may avoid Schepisi's pitfalls as well as his presentation of aborigines primarily as victims. The primary victim is an aboriginal woman named Kath, whom two police officers are returning to an outback town to stand trial for murder. She is a victim because, as we discover as the film proceeds, she is not guilty. Either she was defending herself against her white employer's sexual attack or she was blamed for what the wife did when she discovered her husband with the aboriginal woman. A secondary victim is a young Black boy who was shot to death, under suspicious circumstances, by a White police officer in Sydney. What ties the two stories—both enacted before the film begins—together is that one of the officers taking Kath back to Quondog, a man named Trevor Darling (David Argue), is the guilty police officer in the Sydney case. In fact, he has been transferred to his current duty shuttling prisoners from state to state by Sydney authorities who want the story of the young boy's shooting to go away.

Trevor's last name is quite ironic because he is far from "darling." As we get to know him on the long drive north, we realize that he is sexist, racist, potentially violent, and drug-using. We feel sorry for police officer Nikki Iceton (Gia Carides) who must make this trip with him and the female prisoner. We are occasionally offered shots of an older aboriginal man who seems to be following the two officers and Kath. In the end he proves to be the father of the boy killed in Sydney. At the film's conclusion, he murders Trevor in accordance with tribal law. Bennett thus resolves the subplot without our really getting to know anything about either the murdered boy or his vengeful father. They are victim and avenger, nothing more.

So our attention needs to focus on Kath. Initially, the drama—largely acted improvisationally—is largely between Trevor and Nikki (Helen Barlow in Murray, *Australian Film* 284; Stratton, *Avocado* 211). However, Kath begins to play a role once the two police officers get lost in the outback after (at Trevor's insistence) taking a supposed shortcut. Kath becomes the resourceful one who gets them out of trouble—finding them, for example, shelter and sustenance. She also exhibits her resourcefulness in other ways. She seduces Trevor and then takes advantage of his postcoital fatigue to escape. She also gains the sympathy of both Trevor and Nikki. One senses they would let her go free if they would not be held accountable for it.

Kath is probably a victim. She is so resourceful that one might doubt the story she tells Trevor and Nikki. However, she wins their sympathy, and that sympathy causes them, in a scene Stratton finds totally unconvincing, to extract a confession from the publican's wife that exonerates Kath (*Avocado* 210). Maybe Kath has shrewdly orchestrated her freedom. If so, then the focus shifts even more from Kath as victim to Kath as person, but that shift already seems to have occurred because so little of the movie deals with the circumstances that led up to her supposed crime.

So, who is Kath as a person? She loves freedom enough to use her body to gain it. She defies the authority the publican thought he had over her body; and she defies the two police officers she is with when circumstances permit her to. If she is lying to them about what actually happened to gain their sympathy, she "plays" them—a shrewd way of defying. She fights, although she is the underdog. During the journey, she seems resigned to her fate, but that resignation does not cause her to give up. And she knows the land so much better than the two citified cops. What ought to be obvious in this portrait is that Kath is very much in the mold of the Australian heroes we have seen in previous chapters. Bennett cannot eliminate from the film our sense of Kath as victim; however, he does manage to focus as much, if not more, on the person she is. What keeps her from being truly heroic is her inability to do much—except for her one ultimately unsuccessful flight toward freedom—insofar as she is physically restrained.

THE FRINGE DWELLERS (BRUCE BERESFORD, DIRECTOR, 1986)

Backlash is not a bad film, but it was clearly beaten in 1986 both in artistry and in presenting aboriginal characters by Bruce Beresford's *The Fringe Dwellers*, a film based on Nene Gare's 1961 novel. Don McAlpine's photography is, as usual, stunning, but, unlike his camera work in Gillian Armstrong's *My Brilliant Career* (1979), which was at times almost impressionistic, his work here is starkly realistic (Stratton, *Avocado* 203). It brings out all of the details, large and small, of aboriginal life in an outback town. Matching McAlpine's emphasis on realism is Beresford's because the director seems intent to present without editorializing in this film. He avoids the temptation to preach—unlike Schepisi in *The Chant of Jimmie Blacksmith*, a characteristic which perhaps weakens that film.

In *The Fringe Dwellers*, we meet an aboriginal family living in a run-down riverside settlement on a town's outskirts. This portrayal of aboriginal small-town life has evoked some controversy, with aboriginal activists claiming it inaccurately shows aborigines from the White man's point of view (Rattigan 135; Stratton, *Avocado* 203). That the settlement as depicted by Beresford seems consonant with documentaries produced at the same time about aboriginal life suggests that the picture may indeed be fairly accurate—although perhaps not what aborigines would choose to have White Australians see. Many who live in the settlement are quite content, but not all. For whatever reasons, the women are less content than the men; the young are less content than the old. Therefore, high-school-age Trilby (Kristina Nehm) is one of the least content. Although the stories of others are told in the film, Trilby's story is the central one in the film.

Urged by Trilby and her mother, the family moves "up" to government-subsidized housing in the town itself. There, they live side by side with

White Australians. They provoke stares from some of their new, non-aboriginal neighbors, but they do not provoke any overt racism. In fact, the woman next door is initially gracious to her new neighbors. The problem is that they cannot fit in amid this new neighborhood: the mother does not understand the culture; Trilby is perhaps too ready to interpret neighborly generosity as charity. Then, the father, never the model of responsibility, gambles away the rent money, and the mother and children are evicted. They move back to the riverside settlement where they came from.

The mother, Mollie, sees herself—and other aborigines—as caught in-between. They have lost their aboriginal language but have not really acquired the language of the "settlers." As a result, for much of their reality, there are no longer words. She seems resigned to this wordlessness and the resulting powerlessness. Trilby, on the other hand, is not resigned to anything. She is proud; she is ambitious. She even thinks that the nursing career her sister Noonah is pursuing represents "settling."

Trilby's rebellious streak, perhaps, leads her into a sexual relationship with horseman Phil. She ends up pregnant. Meanwhile, Phil has taken off, as was his wont. Trilby has the baby, but then drowns the child in a hospital toilet. Perhaps not wanting the scandal, a doctor declares it was an accident. Trilby then finds herself back where she started. The rest of the family seems content in the settlement where they can live comfortably without any White affectations. The father Joe, who left after losing the rent money, returns and resumes an ockerlike life; Trilby's lover Phil returns (Rattigan 135). The family forgives Joe; the family forgives Phil. Trilby, however, leaves home the next morning for Sydney.

Trilby wants to be free. She will defy authority to get what she wants; she will battle, even though she is the underdog, to get what she wants. She is very much the Australian hero insofar as this hero possesses these traits. Her desire for fun also marks her as Australian; however, her desire for material success marks her less as an Australian hero and more a victim of the false Australian dream that affected, for example, Des and Terri Tunkley in *Emoh Ruo* (1985). That she is the hero who has made a wrong turn is also suggested by her fierce individualism. Her attitude toward her sister shows it, as does her absence of mates and her ultimate rejection of Phil. When you combine her materialism and her individualism together, you have at least the potential for a selfishness that goes against the grain of the heroism we have seen throughout most of this book. Selfishness is not, in and of itself, necessarily a bad thing. Sometimes, one must put oneself first, especially if the forces of the world seem to be conspiring to thwart that self. We saw that need, for example, in *My Brilliant Career*. Trilby's selfishness does, however, come across as negative. No matter how much one might admire her spirit, one also must recall the infant she murdered for the sake of herself.

QUIGLEY (A.K.A. QUIGLEY DOWN UNDER) (SIMON WINCER, DIRECTOR, 1991)

Simon Wincer directs entertaining, fast-paced movies. And, with *Quigley*, he gives us a very good one. It is, however, a movie that strikes some as not being especially Australian. The lead actor, Tom Selleck, and the lead actress, Laura San Giacomo, are American; the villain of the piece is played by Alan Rickman, who is British. The situation is also not especially Australian: a hired gun is brought in all the way from the United States to help with a large landowner's particular problem. In addition, lurking not very far in the background are the storylines of Hollywood Westerns, climaxing in the showdown between the good guy (Selleck as Matthew Quigley) and the bad guy—dressed, of course, in black—(Rickman as Elliott Marston). Marston even makes explicit references to these American Westerns. No wonder O'Regan calls *Quigley* a classic example of "Hollywood Down Under" (*Australian* 218).

The film was shot in Australia, largely near Alice Springs. That makes it a bit more Australian, but what really makes it Australian (and, perhaps, not that popular in Australia) is its unblinking presentation of the settlers' treatment of the land's indigenous people. Marston's "particular problem" was the aborigines, and he wanted Quigley to use his skills as a marksman to rid Marston's station (ranch) of these people. Insulted, Quigley turns on Marston. Aided (oddly) by an older aboriginal servant, Marston gains the upper hand. Quigley, and "Crazy Cora," a Texas girl who had befriended Quigley, are then sent out into the desert and dumped, presumably to die.

Quigley will not die. He and Cora will slowly make their way back. At one point, they will be saved from dying by a group of aborigines. At two later points, they will return the favor by defending aborigines who are under attack by Marston's men. One scene in the movie is especially devastating in its effect on viewers. Marston's men are herding the aborigines like sheep or cattle and then driving them over a cliff to their death. We see many die. We also see one young baby survive, and Cora will temporarily adopt this baby as hers. This scene, it is worth noting, is not the scriptwriter John Hill's invention; rather, it is based on fact. Horrific crimes such as what we see in that scene were indeed perpetrated against the indigenous people by settlers, with tacit government approval.

The battle between Quigley and Marston is what the film focuses on; therefore, we see the aborigines more in the background than in the foreground. We see them as saviors: about a third of the way through the film when they save Quigley and Cora and, again, at the end, when hundreds of them suddenly appear and surround the British troops who have surrounded Quigley to arrest him. We see them as victims in the two scenes already mentioned as well as early in the film when we discover that Cora and other white women had been brought out to the station as prostitutes because the men were growing tired of the black women. Although the aborigines are in the background, their story very much informs the film because their story, as saviors and as the saved, has become intertwined with Quigley's.

How then are the aborigines portrayed? They are portrayed primarily as victims. Beneath that compelling portrayal, however, are other elements of note. They are presented as free from many, if not most, of the constraints of "civilization." Their nomadic existence demonstrates this freedom, as does the memorable moment after Quigley guns down Marston when the aborigines on his station all head into the hills to join their people, shedding their constraining "European" clothing as they go. The aborigines are peaceful, but willing to defy supposed authority and stand and fight if need be, even if their "primitive" weapons might make them the underdogs in the battle. We saw that in the scene in which they challenged the British troops who were attempting to arrest Quigley. In that scene, we also see their loyalty to their mate Quigley. As he had come to their aid against the oppressing authority embodied by Marston's men, they were coming to his assistance against the oppressing authority of the British troops, which seem very much composed of men like Marston. The aborigines are also very close to the land. Again, we see that in how they live and also in their ability to draw from the land the sustenance Quigley and Cora need when they are found, almost dead, in the outback.

These characteristics—it almost goes now without saying—are very much the ones admired in the hero figures, both of old and of more recent times. This positive portrayal, however, is very much overwhelmed in the film by the depiction of their victimization. In this case, perhaps more than in the other films examined in this chapter, the aboriginal role as victim is stressed because in this film, unlike in *The Chant of Jimmie Blacksmith* or *Backlash*, we see aborigines as a people and therefore we appreciate the full extent of the victimization. Whereas Schepisi's film tells us Jimmie Blacksmith's individual story and Bennett's film focuses on Kath's, Wincer's *Quigley* depicts genocide.

NIGHT CRIES (TRACY MOFFATT, DIRECTOR, 1989)

By discussing this film, I am departing from the norm of this book. Just as the discussion of *A Town Like Alice* (1981) in Chapter 3 was a departure because it was a television miniseries, not a feature film, this discussion of *Night Cries* is a departure because Moffatt's film is a very important seventeen-minute short, not a feature film. *Night Cries* is important for a number of reasons. It is a well-done film; it is by an aboriginal filmmaker; it serves as a counterpoint to a famous Australian film about aborigines; and it makes a poignant statement about aboriginal life that goes far beyond simply saying that the indigenous people were victims.

Tracey Moffatt is probably Australia's most noteworthy contemporary aboriginal filmmaker. Her output includes documentaries, feature films, and short films. They all look at Black Australian life from the point of view of a person of color; they all are experimental to various degrees; and most provoke controversy, drawing praise and fire from both White and Black commentators. This film is an especially personal one because Moffatt herself was a member of "The Stolen Generation" (O'Regan, *Australian* 328).

As Moffatt explains in an interview with Scott Murray, in the background of *Night Cries* is the story of this "stolen generation." Early in the century, the government decided that the best way to integrate aborigines into mainstream society was to take the Black children away from their tribal parents and give them to White foster parents who would then raise them as if they were a White child. This appalling policy finds its way into the 1955 film *Jedda*, directed by Charles Chauvel. *Jedda* tells the story of a stolen child named Jedda. When she is a teenager, a handsome aborigine named Marbuck arrives at her foster parents' (the McManns') station. Jedda becomes fascinated with him; he with her. So, he seizes her and then takes her, half-willingly but half not, back to his tribal lands. There, he finds rejection—for violating the tribe's marriage customs. He cannot rejoin his people, and, at the same time, an armed group from the McManns' station are pursuing him. With no place to go, he jumps off a cliff with Jedda and they die.

Chauvel's *Jedda* is a tragedy, the lesson of which is, perhaps, Jedda would have been so much better off if she had stayed in the White world that had adopted her. *Night Cries* tests that theory, by giving us Jedda and her very aged foster mother thirty-some years later—on the assumption that Jedda stayed with Mrs. McMann. This, as actress Marcia Langton (who plays Jedda) puts it, is the emotional core of the film. Jedda has mixed memories of her childhood, some positive and some negative, but it seems as if the more recent past has been drudgery that has left Jedda bitter. As she does the laundry, for example, she seems to be taking her anger out on the wash. As she does so, she laughs hysterically. The bitterness has taken her to the brink of hysteria. She stays with her foster mother out of a sense of obligation, but she also feels that her life is passing her by. This feeling is suggested by the image of a speeding train that Jedda wants to send a message by, but the train does not stop.

This brief film contains some puzzling images, but the overall point seems fairly clear: Jedda has been imprisoned by the relationship with her now-needy stepmother. The travel brochure she reads offers her no real escape. The only real escape would be through her stepmother's death, and, so, she waits for that the same way she waits for her stepmother outside the outhouse. Meanwhile, her stepmother becomes increasingly dependent on Jedda, as the old woman's assumption of the fetal position and her crying like a baby signify. This image suggests that there should be a special bond between the two; however, despite some pleasant memories, the overall message of the film is that Jedda is trapped in this relationship with a mother–child who is not hers the same way she is trapped in a culture that is not hers.

This complex, but ultimately bitter, picture is framed by aboriginal gospel singer Jimmy Little singing an upbeat tune called "Royal Telephone." Jimmy is singing the message that the White culture wants the aborigines to believe that God is listening and will address one's needs. Perhaps some aborigines believe this message and take solace in it. The stark contrast between Jimmy Little's singing and the life we watch Jedda living should cause us to conclude that the song's message is false and that those who believe it are deluded and those who sing it have sold out their people (Murray, "Tracy Moffatt"). Who, the film seems to ask, could sing such a song and sing it in such a bouncy way if he or she knew the victimization of Australia's Black people?

In *Night Cries*, we see where victimization ends. We know Jedda stands for a group—for all of the "stolen children" as well as for all aborigines who have been literally or figuratively ripped from their culture; yet, we also know her personal pain as well as her sense of obligation and her few good memories of her childhood (O'Regan, *Australian* 328). Moffatt then manages to depict oppression, but with the fully human dimensions that films such as *The Chant of Jimmie Blacksmith* and *Quigley* cannot communicate because the directors' insistence on making a political statement about oppression obscures them.

As we get to know Jedda, even within the span of just seventeen minutes, we see much that is heroic in the being that she barely manages to suppress: the desire for freedom, the desire to defy the authority that traps her here with her foster mother, the desire to fight against her fate. This being seethes beneath the surface of the film. It is, however, suppressed, and, in the end, we are not sure to what extent she has chosen to suppress it. All we know is that the message she is supposed to hear, straight from her own Jimmy Little, the message that God will address her needs, seems absurd.

RADIANCE (RACHEL PERKINS, DIRECTOR, 1997)

To a large extent, Tracey Moffatt pulled *Night Cries* out of her own pained heart because she had been a foster child to a White mother. Aboriginal director Rachel Perkins, on the other hand, transformed Louis Nowra's stage play into the film *Radiance*. Along the way, Perkins seems to have added a lot of her heart as well as marked feminism because the film blends the personal and the political into a stunning motion picture. Perkins answers Meaghan Morris' complaint in her article in *Communal/Plural* by offering an aboriginal perspective informed by a feminist consciousness.

The film is set in Queensland. The central characters are three sisters: Cressy, Mae, and Nona. What brings them together is the death of their mother. Cressy had gone off "to the city" to become a famous opera singer; Nona had also gone off to the city for wild times and in pursuit of her dreams of singing in a rock band or owning a wig shop. Mae is the one who stayed home and looked after the aging mother. Therefore, from the very beginning, there is tension between Mae and the two sisters who have escaped.

The women seem so very different, but they are similar in many ways. All three want freedom; two fled after it, and the other is bitter that she never had the chance. All three are rebels too. Nona is the obvious rebel—she has lived

Older sister Cressy prepares to escape her Queensland home once more in *Radiance* (1997). Photo courtesy of National Film and Sound Archives. Permission granted by Eclipse Films copyright 1997.

the wild life in the city and has come home pregnant, but is still flirting with every man she sees. Oddly, for being such a rebel, she is the one who wants to follow all the conventions in commemorating the mother's death. Mae rejects those rituals most strongly. Having not rebelled all her life, now she wants to. The most dramatic act of rebellion in the film is one she proposes—burning the mother's house down. The house, you see, did not belong to the mother. It was lent to her by her married lover Harry to keep her quiet. Now, after the mother's death, Harry wants the house back. Cressy's rebellion is the most difficult to see because she keeps so much inside her. Her whole life is a rebellion because she has turned her back on her Black culture, trained her vocal chords until they are rock-hard, and sung in a manner, in a language, and on themes so very far removed from her Queensland upbringing. Cressy was perhaps driven to the point of rejecting her past because she felt her mother never loved her. Her mother, she recalled, had allowed the authorities to take Cressy and Mae away and put them in a convent school. There, Cressy remembers she did laundry on visiting days because her mother never visited them. Cressy's strong sense of what is proper may also be a rebellion against what she saw as her mother's "slutty" behavior. Cressy is, in fact, disturbed to see in Nona some of the same traits, so she slips Nona money—ostensibly for an abortion.

They are all fighters too, although they have fought against the odds in very different arenas. Nona is fighting to stay alive at a time when the cities devour young girls such as her. She is also fighting to achieve her dreams, as silly as they might sound. She is also willing to stick out the pregnancy and fight on as a single mother, even though that life will be so much more difficult than the one she is now living. Mae has been fighting to keep her sanity. Her mother's behavior, as she gradually lost her wits, has almost driven Mae over the edge. Now, she wants to strike out at those who oppressed her mother because, deep down inside, she identifies very strongly with her mother. Thus, she is the one who dresses up in her mother's never used wedding gown. Cressy has fought to the top of the opera world, overcoming (we imagine) a fair amount of prejudice along the way. She has also had to fight out of her mind her nightmare from the past how, at age twelve, she was raped by her mother's boyfriend. She became pregnant, and abortion was not an option then. So, she had the child, and her mother raised that child—Nona—as if she were her own daughter. This secret comes out close to the film's conclusion.

That secret, although certainly the most dramatic, is not the only thing that emerges as the three "sisters" interact. This interaction, with its positive moments and its negative moments, brings the three women closer together. They are brought together by the mother's death, and, by the time the day is over, they can laugh as the mother's ashes spill out of their container all over Cressy and the floor and they have to vacuum "mother" up and then go through the vacuum bag's contents, separating "mom" from "not mom." Also, by that day's end, they are ready, as mates, after a bit of drinking, to burn the house down. They want to commit this final act of defiance and then flee.

The view of the three "sisters" is unmediated through the eyes of White filmmakers. This view is striking in at least two regards. First, they come across as being not "other," but rather Australian. Although the three women have had very different life experiences, they all want freedom, defy authority, and fight against odds. And in the course of the film, they discover their sisterhood, a bond that, like mateship, holds them closely together. The film's closing scene has the three of them driving off together, two of them in disguise, to avoid apprehension by the law. It is almost as if we are back with the Kelly gang or Captain Starlight's men. The happy-go-lucky lawlessness is present, as well as the strong bond among those who have made a stand against "the enemy."

The second striking dimension of Perkin's Black view of these Black women has to do with the identity of "the enemy." Most of the films by White filmmakers have located the enemy within White society. Its violent racism informs *Quigley*; its hypocrisy, *The Chant of Jimmie Blacksmith*; its unequal administration of justice, *Backlash*. In *Radiance*, the enemy is not as easy to pinpoint. Some of that enemy is within the three women in a low self-esteem that prompts self-destructive behavior or in the hatred that helps erect walls of personal isolation. But much of the enemy force seems to be comprised of the men in their lives: the men who have cocreated children and fled, the man who raped Cressy and went unpunished, the man who assuaged his guilty conscience by providing a place for the mother to live. Lurking in the background, however, is the White Australian culture that the Black men are imitating, a culture that calls itself Christian. This culture can ignore its negative side; this culture can pretend that it is good—as long as it can cite Christianity as its basis. As if in response to the veiling role Christianity has played, we see, several times, the picture of Jesus Christ, burning as the house burns. Christianity, then, is presented by the film as part of the enemy too.

After the remains of the mother have been reclaimed from the vacuum bag, Nona places them in a tin can that once contained "Radiance Specialities," a licorice nougat candy. Nona becomes the caretaker of these ashes and eventually sprinkles them on an offshore island she can walk to at low tide. The film, of course, takes its title from this tin of candies. Why? The tin can seems to offer two qualities: oddly, sweetness and light. And the mother, after her death, has brought both of these qualities to the lives of the "sisters." The sweetness is the love for one another they rediscover; the light is the knowledge—the truths—about their lives that they discover. I said "oddly" because this formulation, sweetness and light, takes a student of literature to Jonathan Swift's *Battle of the Books*, in which the eighteenth-century satirist interpolates the fable of the spider and the bee. The bee is said to bring "sweetness and light" through the honey and the candlewax it produces. This sweetness and light is associated with the poetry that has true worth. Perhaps the film's title suggests that *Radiance* is a worthy poem, worthy because it is rooted in the true past of Australia's aboriginal people, not a past oversimplified or romanticized by filmmakers whose people have not lived that past.

Chapter 6
Youth: The Basis for Heroism to Come

Since a primary audience for feature film is young people, one should not be surprised to find that young people are central in many Australian films. Some of these films have their main characters engaging in action we might term heroic, but others offer either coming-of age stories or simply portraits of teenage or young adult life. The question we need to ask of these films, regardless of story line, is—based on the young world they depict—is the culture providing a foundation for a heroism in the years to come that is like that I have sketched in the preceding chapters? If so, does it seem likely that the heroism will exhibit different nuances?

To arrive at an answer to these questions, we need an examination of these films that should consider how the world and authority are depicted in them. If the world and authority are both hostile to youth, then this environment will produce very different heroes than if the world offers many possibilities and authority figures who are friendly. We should also consider whether the young people are inclined to rebel or fight, since both of these activities have characterized the hero but may not be as important in a world that is either totally bleak or totally bountiful. Although too much, perhaps, has been made if it, mateship has been a hallmark of the Australian culture. We need to consider then whether mateship is still evident and, more important, if it is present, how it is different from the mateship of sheepshearers or soldiers. Finally, we need to consider what we might loosely term "lifestyle issues." To what extent do we see behaviors such as alcohol abuse, drug abuse, and sexual promiscuity and to what extent do we see attitudes such as sexism, racism, classism, and anti-intellectualism? These behaviors and attitudes have characterized the heroism we have seen thus far—abrasively so in some films, sanitized to the point where they are barely noticed in others. Whether these behaviors and attitudes are up or down may then determine whether the heroism to come—should there be heroism—has an offensive (like Barry McKenzie) or a brash (like Tony Petersen) or a charmingly politically incorrect (like Crocodile Dundee) tone.

STONE (SANDY HARBUTT, DIRECTOR, 1974)

In Australia, *Stone* has become something of a cult classic. A well-photographed, nicely edited film, done for only $195,000, Harbutt's *Stone* gives us a glimpse of the "biker" culture in Australia during the late 1960s and early 1970s, as, along with undercover cop Stone (Ken Shorter), we join "The Gravediggers" for a while (Pike and Cooper 278).

The film's premise is admittedly weak. Organized criminals (it seems) are targeting politicians for assassination. One of the bikers saw too much. Therefore, the thugs are now knocking off Gravediggers, one by one. It is Stone's job to get to the bottom of these killings by joining the targets for a while. Although this plot is weak, and a tad silly, the portrait of the gang is interesting. It is for that reason one watches *Stone*.

The world the bikers have dropped out of is depicted as dirty, dangerous, and corrupt. The dirty side is seen in the "Extreme Pollution" signs we see; the dangerous side is seen in all the killing that is going on; and the corruption is seen in the vague motives behind the killing. But incipient corruption is seen in how attached to the luxuries of life some members of society seem to be. Stone's girlfriend is a good example: we see her lounging by the pool, annoyed that Stone has to go off on another one of his dangerous missions. The authorities are depicted as either incompetent or unconcerned about people as low on "the food chain" as the bikers. The police, for example, do not even notice that several Gravediggers have been murdered until several hundred bikers from different gangs show up in a display of solidarity at one of the funerals.

The gang's response to this dirty, dangerous, and corrupt world is to drop out—not fight or rebel. They form their own society featuring alcohol, drugs, sex, and Satan. The last, however, does not play much of a role in the film. The other three are, at times, taken to extremes. Nonetheless, there seems to be more nobility among the Gravediggers than in the world they have dropped out of. They are loyal to one another, they live according to the rules they have established, and they refuse to cower in their somewhat safe fortress at South Head and go off to their pub, thereby exposing themselves to danger. They have even, at one nightclub, played the role of "good guys" by driving off the protection racketeers who were harassing the owner.

The sexism that characterizes the gang is a disturbing note. Only males can vote, and the females who travel with the gang are clearly sex objects and possessions. On the positive side, gang rules insist on fidelity in its male–female relationships. Furthermore, gang rules permit females to end a relationship, so the women do have some rights. There is also, we note, one aboriginal in the gang, and he is in a relationship with a White woman. So, the film makes at least a nodding gesture against racism.

The gang members then are not unlike male heroes we have seen in countless films. The mild sexism, the substance abuse, the camaraderie, and the refusal to back off are typical. So is the competitiveness they exhibit with regard to bike riding, making Stone prove his worth on a bike before he can join the gang. What distinguishes these proto-heroes from what we have seen before is the extent to which they have dropped out of a society they dislike and fashioned their own. As Stone notes at the film's end, there is a lot of good to be found in their counterculture society. There are also two tendencies, either of which would give the "hero to come" a different slant: their tendency toward disengagement and their tendency toward violent assault. Both of these tendencies are present in heroes we have seen before but perhaps not to the extremes we see in *Stone*.

PICNIC AT HANGING ROCK (PETER WEIR, DIRECTOR, 1975)

The film that put Australia back on the moviemaking map—Weir's *Picnic at Hanging Rock*—is two motion pictures intertwined. Based on Joan Lindsay's novel (termed "banal" by McFarlane), it tells the story of growing up, complete with all the emotional turmoil (72). It also depicts how the mysterious forces of nature will inevitably resist repression.

Beautifully filmed by Russell Boyd, *Picnic* tells a semi-true story of a mysterious event that occurred on St. Valentine's Day in 1900 at a girls' boarding school. The air is already tense with sublimated erotic tension before the girls go off on an excursion to Hanging Rock, a somewhat phallic rock that surged upward from the plain thousands of years earlier. The heat of the day is such that most of the girls and the others who have journeyed to the rock just lie there languidly. A few girls, and one teacher, are drawn to the rock. As they climb, it seems as if they fall into a trance. They take off their shoes and stockings—scandalous by 1900 standards—and climb higher. One girl, the least attractive one, panics and stays behind in a crying fit. The three girls remaining then vanish, as does a teacher who was doing her own exploring.

There are many suggestions of lesbian love, most with an innocent tone. So, one might read the phallic rock's captivation of the girls and the woman as the reassertion of heterosexuality, the natural passion that the girls-only atmosphere of the school denied. However, a teenage boy, who becomes drawn to the girls' beauty, is also battered by the rock when he goes up it alone in search of the girls, especially the angelic-looking Miranda. So the force that the rock represents seems less heterosexual than just sexual. This reading of the rock is perhaps confirmed when one of the girls, Irma, is found and the foremost question on people's minds seems to be if she is still "intact." Weir denies that there is a sexual dimension to the film, but most have found that denial ingenuous (McFarlane 73).

The mystery is never solved. But the events of that February 14th have a devastating effect on the school. Already teetering on the brink of financial insolvency, the school—another monolithic intrusion onto the landscape—collapses as parents begin withdrawing their daughters out of fear that there is some menacing force nearby (McFarlane 72). One young girl, Sara (Margaret Nelson) who had been especially enamored of Miranda, kills herself (or is murdered) when she is told she must leave the school because her tuition is considerably overdue. We move from her battered body to news that the school's headmistress, left largely alone at the school, has gone to Hanging Rock and become lost there as well. The events on the 14th seem to have started a process of collapse, and, in the end, the posh girls' school is no more.

The world of this film is a repressed place. Its surfaces are prim and proper, but beneath the surfaces, tensions—erotic and otherwise—exist. The denial of these tensions causes the place to be a hypocritical one. The film suggests that such hypocrisy cannot endure. It will destroy one who is too caught up in it as it brings down the facades that it had previously erected. This repressed place will prove so destructive because that which is repressed will, much like the rock, erupt. That the film is set at the turn of the century is perhaps relevant here, the suggestion being that repression has characterized an epoch and the mysterious events signal the beginning of something new. One feels as if transported to the end of Yeats' "The Second Coming," facing the new but not knowing precisely what it is. And I suspect that Weir did not want the film to have an answer.

Some characters in the film cannot face what has been repressed. Others are, however, lured into it. In giving way to it, they rebel against the rules and the standards of their time. The girls lured up the rock were not supposed to climb it; they certainly were not supposed to remove their stockings. And the teacher who ventures onto the rock was found, in a confused state, even more undressed. In this film, seduction and rebellion go hand in hand. One is drawn to the repressed; one rebels against the societal chains; one is further drawn; one further rebels.

The rebelling, at least as it occurs on the rock, is done in a group. Erotic tension has already rippled the surface of any mateship that might exist among the girls. There is also tension between those who are beautiful and those who are not—seen when the heavy girl, Edith, is treated with scorn when she retreats from a higher climb—and tension between those devoted to Miranda and Irma, who, upon her "intact" return, cannot remember anything that will help return the beloved Miranda to them.

There is also tension between the two teenage boys who admire the ascending girls from a distance. They are separated by social class, but, in the heart of the February afternoon, that does not seem to matter as they share an intoxicating drink. But drinking together, a ritualistic first step to mateship, does not lead to an enduring relationship. What splits them apart is the way one is pulled to find out what happened to the girls on the rock and the other is not. Class seems to play a role in this split because concern about the girls' fate seems to be beneath the more English-acting boy.

With Weir's *Picnic*, we are dealing with the year 1900. Thus alcohol, drugs, and sex—let alone rock 'n' roll—are not issues. Alcohol appears tastefully, and we have moody panpipes, not electric guitars. Sexism seems to affect the boys no more than normal for 1900, and everyone's concern for the girls' virginity also seems appropriate for the date. What does surface in a nefarious manner is classism. Implicit in it is the belief that some are more worthy than others—based on birth and wealth. Classism separates the two would-be male mates, it is partially behind the ill treatment of Sara, and it seems to haunt the personnel at Appleyard College who seem to believe that they are in some way inferior and, thus, doomed to defer to those who are better and play the acceptable subordinate role as educators.

"Heroism" is probably not the word that springs to one's lips when thinking about *Picnic at Hanging Rock*. Nonetheless, there is something heroic about those who defy authority and yield to the sensual power of nature. They are rebels, although at times they seem more entranced than iconoclastic. The pettiness and the unnaturalness of the girls' school environment and the power of social class in turn-of-the-century Australia inhibit mateship. If the rock symbolizes nature—defined in the broadest way so as to include sexuality—then Appleyard College, the building itself, symbolizes those hierarchical structures humans have superimposed on it—class being one of them. Then, the collapse of the college suggests that the power of class, as well as other barriers dividing humans, is diminishing as we move into Australia's initial century on her own. Weir's film was clearly intended more to suggest than to state; nonetheless, it may be stating that the new Australian nation, confederated in 1901, will be premised much more on nature and egalitarianism than the unnatural and class-conscious environment that defines Appleyard.

THE DEVIL'S PLAYGROUND (FRED SCHEPISI, DIRECTOR, 1976)

The male counterpart to *Picnic at Hanging Rock* may well be Fred Schepisi's *The Devil's Playground*, a depiction of repression at a boys' seminary in the early 1950s. It does not feature stunning photography, it is not at all poetic; instead, it is a rather bleak (and rather quiet) look at growing up male in an environment that denies the natural just as much as the Victorian environment in *Picnic* does. The denial in Weir's film takes the form of romanticizing the natural, so that what is natural comes across as pretty. The denial in Schepisi's film, on the other hand, takes the form of condemning the natural, declaring it to be ugly. Given this difference, it is appropriate that the surface of *Picnic* be strikingly pretty and the surface of *The Devil's Playground* plain.

One of the first scenes in *The Devil's Playground* has one of the brothers scolding a young boy named Tom Allen for daring to shower in the nude. This scene, in many ways, sets the tone: anything concerning the body is to be considered sinful and shunned. The atmosphere that this extreme repression creates is not a positive one. Several of the brothers at the school are very aware of how negative the atmosphere is. At a game of pool, one remarks that such an atmosphere is the breeding ground for poofters. As it turns out, he is correct because there has developed among the older boys an elite "bodily purification" society that practices sadism, masochism, and homosexuality.

When the secret society is discovered, some of the brothers point to it as an example of what the school's rules and atmosphere can result in. Others say that the society was just the idea of a few bad apples. One brother, Brother Francine (Arthur Dignam), strongly denounces the others for not seeing the evil in the school's ways. He says if the body is denied, then the mind will sin, the sin will be worse, and it will haunt one, making life hateful. This brother knows what he is talking about because, when he and some other members of the order go into town, he goes off to the civic pool to leer at the women and girls in their bathing suits. Later, he suffers erotic nightmares.

The world of the film is then a repressive one, and the authority figures in it either know that there's a problem and ignore it or are so oblivious to human nature that it is almost comical. For example, one visiting brother (played by author Thomas Keneally) gives Tom, who is having a problem with what the brothers insist on calling "bed wetting," water from the shrine at Lourdes to help with the problem. Some live their own lives in near-hypocrisy, tempting themselves with the forbidden but staying just on the "right" side of sinning. I mentioned Brother Francine earlier. Two other brothers go into a pub, "pick up" women, but then flee before the flirtation leads to anything physical.

Tom rebels against this repression by an innocent flirtation with a young girl, Miss Cochran. They exchange letters, the contents of which are quite innocent. The brothers reprimand him severely and tell him he must cease the correspondence immediately. This event and others such as Tom's discovery of the older boys' secret society and the expulsion from the seminary of Tom's friend Fitz finally cause Tom to try to escape. He prays to God for help and begins hitchhiking away from the school. Unfortunately, he gets picked up by two brothers on their way into town to watch a footy (Australian rules football) match. They take him along to the game and—as I read the film—then back to the seminary (see McFarlane for a more liberating reading [141]). This turn of events suggests that, rebel as he might be, Tom is trapped. Just as freedom for the brothers is a short time away from the place, so will it be for Tom.

There would seem, on the surface, to be mateship in the seminary society. I would suggest that what we see either runs shallow or runs askew. The brothers play billiards together; they go off into town together. Their behavior in the latter case reveals that they are not really mates. As soon as they reach town, one goes off on his own. The other two go to the football match and cheer together like mates, but, in the pub afterward, they quickly split ranks when faced with the very aggressive women they have met. One flees, leaving the other to wheedle his way out of the situation on his own. The brothers then, I would argue, display the illusion of mateship. A similar illusion is perhaps present if we look at the camaraderie among the school boys. But, due to the seminary's repressive atmosphere, this camaraderie seems too often become perverted as in the case of the older boys' secret society.

Alcohol and drugs do not play a role in the seminary society the film depicts. Neither does sex per se. However, homosexuality and masturbation—what society would deem perversions of sex—do. The youth who emerge from this school atmosphere, then, are not likely to have a predatory sexist attitude like that of the stereotypical ocker. However, they are likely to have an unhealthy attitude toward sexuality.

The hero who might emerge from this environment would be a rebel. This rebel would justifiably believe that the condition of the world and the behavior of authority figures in that world justify battling against them. However, this hero might also feel that the fight is futile. Tom does, after all, end the film as he begins. And although sex, drugs, and/or alcohol will not probably play a defining role in Tom's heroic persona, an unhealthy attitude toward sex, the body, and even women may.

THE GETTING OF WISDOM (BRUCE BERESFORD, DIRECTOR, 1977)

The girls' boarding school to which Laura Tweedle Rambotham is sent in Bruce Beresford's adaptation of the Henry Handel Richardson "classic" nineteenth-century novel is not as sexually repressive a place as either that in *Picnic at Hanging Rock* or that in *The Devil's Playground*. There are hints of lesbian liaisons in Beresford's film, but they do not play a major role in the evolution of Laura's character. Social class plays a much larger role.

Laura comes from an outback town, from a family very different from most of the families who have sent their daughters to the exclusive school. Most of the other girls recognize that Laura's background is different. As a result, she is teased and, sometimes, excluded. Her response to the girls' behavior toward her is to try desperately to fit in. She even invents a romantic intrigue with the school's young chaplain to gain a kind of status with these girls who constantly remind her that, in the social order, they have status and she does not. Against the authority figures who try to enforce the elite class' standards of behavior on her, she often rebels. To the extent that some of these standards enforce a patriarchal society's view of what is proper and possible for a young woman, her rebellion is directed at sexism as well as classism. However, as both McFarlane (170) and Rattigan (140–41) note, *The Getting of Wisdom* is a far less feminist work than *My Brilliant Career* (1979), although both are scripted by Eleanor Whitcombe.

One needs to keep in mind, however, that Laura is a young girl. Thus, at the same time she rebels, she also conforms and even sometimes finds herself quite intrigued by the "finer" ways and "finer" things. In mixing these responses, novelist Richardson, screenwriter Whitcombe, director Beresford, and young actress Susannah Fowle, all offer us an authentic portrait. As the story unfolds, the rebellious side of Laura becomes more dominant. Her academic work at the school proves to be excellent. Perhaps that success, as well as maturation, gives her self-confidence she lacked when she arrived at the school. With this self-confidence, she no longer needs to worry about pleasing others so much and can be herself. And being herself means rejecting some of the notions being forced on her by "polite" society.

In the end, she wins both literary and music prizes. As part of the celebration of the latter, she performs. She chooses, however, not to perform one of the sedate pieces deemed suitable for a young female pianist; rather, she plays a difficult, passionate piece. Her defiance shocks, but her performance earns applause. Then, she leaves the school. She runs across a park near the school, flinging her hat and her gloves away. Her act may not seem especially rebellious, but, in the context of the film, it is, for she has been taught by the polite society that young women do not run and that one's hat and one's gloves are emblematic of decorum and modesty. Her run through the park, then, represents her rejection of these "rules" in favor of a freer life.

The Getting of Wisdom is a more optimistic movie than either *Picnic at Hanging Rock* or *The Devil's Playground*. In the former, we see a collapse, which to some extent is that of a British-based class system superimposed on the more egalitarian Australia; in the latter, we see an older order—this time that of the Roman Catholic Church—continue on, despite its repressions, hypocrisies, and perversions. In the former, we have two missing girls who may have found a mystical "something," but not much else that is even vaguely uplifting; in the latter, we have Tom, still a prisoner in the seminary. In *The Getting of Wisdom*, we see the older, class-based ways get pushed aside, and we see Laura joyously move onward, a process that parallels that of the Australian nation, suggesting that the story may be vaguely allegorical (Rattigan 139).

Laura's move is hers alone. There is, however, a touch of mateship in her life at the school. It is there in her very close relationship with Evelyn, an older girl Laura much admires. It is also there in her befriending of Sarah, another "country" girl who comes to the school. In these relationships, there is only a touch of mateship. The relationship with Evelyn is not an equal one because Evelyn is older and more sophisticated and therefore venerated by Laura. The relationship with Sarah is also not equal because Laura has acquired a degree of acceptance with the elite. In addition, the relationship is not sustained: Laura's loyalty to Sarah runs hot and cold. So, to a large extent, *The Getting of Wisdom* depicts a more individualistic triumph than a collective one.

The excesses of life are not at all in the film's foreground. Even though we are at a school, the intellectual side of life is not prominent. The arts are, and, in this arena, the film embraces both the elite and the somewhat less so. Laura, we imagine, will do her own thing in writing and in music, even if doing so means defying sexist norms. Laura will probably not discard the writing and the music favored by the elite class she rejects. She will not reject what the establishment presents as "the best" or "the appropriate"; rather, she will combine these "finer" things with the passionate or even the popular frowned on by the social class that dominates the school and, it would seem, Melbourne society at that time.

THE F. J. HOLDEN (MICHAEL THORNHILL, DIRECTOR, 1977)

Beresford's *The Getting of Wisdom* is a period piece. Don McAlpine's "soft" photography helps create the mood of a "classic" and, in many ways, that is what the film was—the film version of a classic—because Henry Handel (really Ethel) Richardson's novel was standard high school reading fare in Australian

Mates Kevin and Bob sharing many late night beers in *The F. J. Holden* (1977). Photo courtesy of National Film and Sound Archives. Permission: Michael Thornhill.

schools and, to some extent, *the* classic nineteenth-century novel that students read and used as the basis of their sense of what a novel was. The mood of Michael Thornhill's *The F. J. Holden* is quite different. We are in the mid-1970s in what McFarlane calls "the desolate western suburbs" of Sydney, in Bankstown to be specific (98). The film softens or romanticizes very little. It is realistic—"grim" and "austere," according to Pike and Cooper—in its depiction of youth culture—so realistic that the film, rather than suggesting where heroism might emerge from, suggests that heroism might no longer be possible.

The adults depicted in the film seem inept. Parents stand to the side, prim and proper, while teens drink themselves into oblivion at parties in these parents' home. One father takes his son to a club, where father–son male bonding occurs in the context of overeating and casino gambling. No female role models seem to exist for the girls (McFarlane 150). The police seem especially condescending and insulting toward the young people in the film, whether the young people are guilty of any wrongdoing or not. If these are the adults who are supposed to be leading the youth by example or by advice, we can understand why the youth exhibit the behavior and attitudes they do.

One perhaps should not make too much of this representation of the adult world because, to some extent, such a representation is almost conventional in "teen" films. Since young people would be the primary audience and since young people, being rebellious and irreverent, enjoy seeing the parents and other authority figures depicted negatively, filmmakers, wanting to turn a profit, load teen films down with such depictions. That having been said, I also should add that Thornhill, although he willingly works in B movie genres, is not the typical "B movie" director who puts together a film mindlessly, and, as a consequence, *The F. J. Holden* is a well-done motion picture. Therefore, I think we have to assume that the negative portrayal of the adult world is not just pandering on the director's part but, rather, his statement that, if youth are troubled, then some of the blame belongs with those who should have been molding the young people, not standing off to the side.

The trouble we see in *The F. J. Holden* also suggests little pandering on Thornhill's part—no orgies; no rampant drug abuse; no despairing suicides—rather, we see girls and boys who seem lost. Let us consider the boys first, because, in the film's world, the boys' behavior has negative effects on the girls.

The two central male characters are Kevin (Paul Couzens) and Bob (Carl Stever). They fancy themselves mates. Being mates means, primarily, that they drink to excess together. It also means they share Anne (Eva Dickinson), at least initially. Perhaps because she finds sex slightly more enjoyable with Kevin than with Bob, she chooses to have an exclusive relationship with him. However, as Kevin's mate, Bob is always around, even to the point of being in her parents' living room watching as Kevin and Anne make love a few yards away in her bedroom. Not surprisingly, Anne is upset because Bob is always present.

She, perhaps, wants privacy; but more important, she wants time alone with Kevin to develop a relationship with him that goes beyond sex.

Her being upset leads to a confrontation at a party at a friend's house. Kevin arrives at the party already drunk, and his foul language and obnoxious ocker behavior cause the hostess' father to demand that Kevin leave and, when he will not, to call the police. Kevin and Bob evade the police, only to be arrested later, at home. Meanwhile, the two mates end up drinking some more. Their discussion about women as they drink is revealing. Bob, who seems to be less attractive to the girls, says he will not waste his "grog money" on women. He consoles Kevin, who has now lost Anne, by saying that they are "still mates" and noting that "you may have lost a bitch, but . . ." (he does not finish the sentence). The scene is interesting insofar as it shows how mateship, even if not comparable to what, for example, Archie Hamilton and Frank Dunne exhibit in *Gallipoli*, is still important in the male culture Kevin and Bob inhabit. The scene is also important insofar as it suggests that mateship is a weakening institution. Bob, the one who cannot get a woman and the one who ends up watching, does the talking about mateship, not Kevin, who has lost Anne. Furthermore, Bob cannot voice what it is that Kevin has gained to compensate for the loss of "the bitch." Implicit in the scene is that Kevin may not entirely share Bob's assessment of how mateship provides more than the relationship that may have been possible with Anne.

The girls in the film seem to define themselves primarily in terms of the boys they are with or might be with. They do not have meaningful jobs. So, partly to please the boys and partly to escape the boredom of the suburban community, they join in rebellious activities. The alcohol, the drugs, and the sex in the film all seem to be ways of "acting out," but it is not always clear what either the boys or the girls are acting out against. The rebellion seems mindless. It also does not seem to get anybody anywhere. The young people seem trapped in the rebellious world they have chosen. Despite how important the car is to the culture they are in, they seem rather immobile.

In *The F. J. Holden*, rebellion seems empty just as mateship seems somewhat empty. The adult world offers little; the youth world offers alcohol, pot, and sex, but not much in the way of fulfilled lives or meaningful relationships. Thornhill's film has a quick pace. One might even say it has energy. This energy is in stark contrast to the malaise that seems to have settled on the suburbs. Dinner conversations lacking real communications; school and jobs lacks interest; sex is mechanical and lacks pleasure. The world of *The F. J. Holden* is not one from which much in the way of heroism can be expected to grow. The film moves quickly, just as, at times, the cars move quickly. But, for all the movement, the film depicts characters who are standing still.

MOUTH TO MOUTH (JOHN DUIGAN, DIRECTOR, 1978)

Equally bleak is John Duigan's *Mouth to Mouth*. It is the story of two teenage girls—Carrie (Kim Krejus) and Jeanie (Sonia Peat)—who escape from a reform school for girls and live on their own in a blighted section of Melbourne. Not too long into the movie, they pair up with two unemployed boys—Tom and Sergio—and, from that point on, the film is more about a quartet than a duo.

The film has a gritty quality. Tom Cowan's photography is a tad grainy; the dialogue is so heavy with slang and an urban Australian accent that a dubbed version of the film was needed for widespread distribution. Duigan, whose style can be sentimental or melodramatic, seems intent here on stamping this film with the word "reality." The film's low budget of $129,000 may explain some of this feel, but not entirely: Duigan seems intent on challenging the nostalgic, romantic view of the nation with contemporary documentary realism (O'Regan, Rattigan 216; *Australian* 242).

The film focuses on the quartet, but especially on the girls. We see the world they inhabit as a cheap one that countenances prostitution, massage parlors, and urban violence. We do not however, see many authority figures. Their absence is striking. We are not shown cruel reform school matrons or brutal police or inept parents. There is an emptiness in the film; the inclusion of these almost stock characters of the teen film genre would have filled the void. Implicit is Duigan's choice to do something much closer to a documentary than to a motion picture of that genre. He wants us to see the world of these youth as they experience it—mixing in some good with the bad. That experience just simply does not include many members of the older generation except for a down-and-out old man who lives near the quartet and befriends them. He helps bring Carrie home one night when she gets drunk and ends up lying sick in a rail yard. But he is not the missing older-generation helper because he needs their help as much as they need his, especially when Carrie's old boyfriend reappears and beats the old man to death because he is a supposed derelict.

With the older generation almost completely absent, the youths' actions become not so much indicators of their rebellion as mechanisms for survival. We never find out much about what the boys do; in fact, it almost seems as if these two mates are living off unemployment compensation and/or off Carrie and Jeanie. We do find out what the girls do: they try shoplifting; they try door-to-door sales; and then they try prostitution. Jeanie cannot handle it; Carrie says she can. But Carrie ends up drunk and sick in the rail yard when what she is doing finally hits her. Although not rebellious, the girls are fighters. The odds seem very much against them, especially since in the background lurk bad economic times in general, but the film ends with the two still out there fighting, maybe even acquiring some steely determination at the old man's funeral.

The boys' mateship we can only guess at, because, although they are on the screen a great deal, their stories are not really told. They seem in the film more to react to Carrie and Jeanie than anything else. The boys do claim mateship. The two girls, on the other hand, demonstrate repeatedly that they are mates.

They care for each other; they cover for each other. Perhaps the scene that shows them as mates more than any other is their initial try at prostitution. When they arrive at the hotel where they have their "dates," Jeanie decides she cannot go through with things. Carrie, however, can and does. Rather than having her mate go it alone, Jeanie joins her. Throughout the scene that follows, it is very clear that Jeanie does not want to be there and does not want to be doing what she is doing. Nonetheless, she is there with her mate.

Sex, of course, plays a role in the quartet's life. The sex, however, seems to be meaningful as the relationships between the girls and the boys develop (Rattigan 216–17). Despite the film's grittiness, the sex does not come across negatively. Alcohol and maybe drugs are present, but they are not defining characteristics of the youth culture the way they were in *The F. J. Holden*. In fact, to the extent the quartet can be independent of the larger world, their lives seem oddly wholesome, despite the depressing environment they live in. There also seems to be a fair measure of wholesome equality among the four.

This odd wholesomeness gives us hope, as does the mateship we see between the girls. The fact that the girls are also battlers gives us hope. They may have the makings of heroes. Two elements of the movie, however, qualify this hope. The first is that the girls seem to have a lot more going for them than the boys. We will, in fact, in these youth movies as a whole see a gender difference, with the girls showing initiative and a fighting spirit and the boys showing much less. The second is that the world the girls (and boys) are battling in seems to have entrapped them: outside, there seem fewer and fewer opportunities to "score"; so, soon, they will have to face the bleakness of their situation.

PUBERTY BLUES (BRUCE BERESFORD, DIRECTOR, 1981)

Puberty Blues is also primarily the story of two teenage girls; however, it has a very different feel to it. Beresford's direction is lively; Don McAlpine's photography sharply depicts suburban Sydney, especially the beachfront of Cronulla. Despite this very different feel, the film delivers somewhat the same message as *Mouth to Mouth*, but with a much more upbeat ending.

Whereas Duigan's film purported to tell real stories, *Puberty Blues* does. Two young Sydney girls—Kathy Lette and Gabrielle Carey, encouraged by coproducer Margaret Kelly, who was their creative writing teacher—wrote a scandalous series of sketches about what life was really like for young teen girls caught up in the surfing culture of Sydney's beaches. The sketches were based on the realities they knew. Margaret Kelly worked them into a fuller, more coherent story. Kelly and the other producer Joan Long talked Bruce Beresford (fresh from his phenomenal success in *Breaker Morant* [1980]) into directing. They all thought that both teens and adults ought to consider seriously the picture that Lette and Carey had presented. They also knew that to get people

Mates Debbie and Sue getting dressed for a night of Crunulla "excitement" in *Puberty Blues* (1981). Photo courtesy of ScreenSound Australia. Permission granted by Limelight Productions.

to the theater they would have to mix the light with the dark and thereby offer an entertaining film that delivers an important message nonetheless. They also knew that dealing with the sex in the girls' book was going to be a problem. They wanted to shock audiences with the prevalence and the emptiness of teenage sex, and, to do that, they had to make it clear what was happening. However, they did not want to be overly explicit because, given the film's theme, exploitation of the young actresses was offensively contradictory. Furthermore, explicitness would result in a rating that would prevent young teens from seeing the film (Brown 435). Beresford worked closely with the Australian film censors as he directed the film. The team also increased the girls' ages from fourteen in the book to seventeen or so in the movie, diminishing the shock somewhat but making the film less objectionable to the censors.

These tensions are worth considering because, with them in mind, one can discern how the film walks a tightrope rather successfully. Some of the ways Beresford handled this tightrope walking have not pleased some people. For example, some think the ending has a "fake" feel; some think the bikinis worn by the girls are far too abbreviated. These criticisms are muted considerably if one keeps in mind that the filmmakers were trying to be entertaining while making a social statement and were trying to shock while not being exploitative.

In line with the teen film genre, *Puberty Blues* depicts "authorities," such as school officials and parents, as somewhat oblivious to what is going on in teens' lives and largely unable to do much about even what they do know about. The parents of Debbie (Nell Schofield), the central character, see her going out with a boorish young man whose woody (wood panelled station wagon popular with surfers) is decorated with *Playboy* centerfolds and stickers proclaiming his dislike of virgins. They act as if nothing is even slightly wrong and wish the boy and her a good time. The film is undoubtedly making the point that authorities do not know the extent to which alcohol, drugs, and sex are playing roles in teenagers' lives. However, the film makes these authorities come across in a comic way in line with the conventions of teen films.

Some might say that the situation I just described is nothing new. Teens have always done more than teachers and parents realize. And there certainly is some truth to this observation. However, the world that Debbie and her friend Sue (Jad Capelja) inhabit goes beyond occasional beer parties, a toke or two of pot, and once or twice going "all the way." Parties are frequent—in homes and at the beach—and beer and liquor are plentiful. Pot is plentiful too, but so are harder drugs: one of Debbie's boyfriends dies of a heroin overdose. And sex is routine: sex between girlfriends and boyfriends as well as gang sex with less attractive girls who can be convinced or almost forced into trading their bodies for a few minutes of popularity. In assessing this world, do keep in mind that the characters in the book were fourteen, not seventeen or therabouts as depicted in the movie. If this thought seems to take one beyond the movie per se, remember that the Australian audience for the film would have, for the most part, been aware of this fact.

A world dominated by alcohol, sex, and drugs is the background to the film's story. What is more central is the surfing culture. This culture was, at the time the film was set, male-defined. Only males surfed; the role of females was to sit on the beach, tanning, while ooh-ing and ahh-ing at the moves the males were making on their boards. In this culture, the females who were "in" were the surfie chicks. To be among them, you had to behave as they did. And you had to have a surfer boyfriend, with whom sex was expected, if not required. You had to be subservient to the males, waiting on their needs; you also had to scorn all those who were not part of this "in" group. We, of course, see this culture as very oppressive of women. However, Debbie and Sue, at age seventeen, see this culture as *the* one to be part of. The story is much more Debbie's than Sue's, so we watch her make her way into the culture from the outside, doing all that is necessary to be accepted as a surfie chick.

From very early in the film, we can see that Debbie is not happy with her situation. She does not watch the males surfing as she should, although she lies about seeing them and then dutifully trots off to get the males their food. Beresford occasionally has Debbie narrate events, but the narrative voice is from years later. So, in this particular beach scene, we get the narrator Debbie commenting negatively on how the girls had to conform to certain behavioral norms, while the character Debbie comments on how "great" a time she is having. Despite her then-and-there positive comments, however, we see in her actions a degree of rebellion against those norms.

Three events seem to make Debbie more the rebel. She witnesses how an unattractive girl named Frieda is dumped on the sidewalk by a bunch of guys after they essentially gang-rape her. Debbie is told to stay out of it by her boyfriend, and she does. But one can tell from the expression on Debbie's face that the incident has had an impact. The second is when her boyfriend is rushed away in an ambulance. He is dying from a drug overdose. The third is when she thinks she is pregnant and, finally, discovers that she is not. All three events suggest where the culture might lead.

These are all dramatic events. Less dramatic is a rainy-day scene. There is no surfing, so the surfers sit around playing cards. The girls' role is to watch—or, maybe, bake a cake the surfers will devour. Debbie finds this sitting around rather mindless. She wants to do something and says so. Both surfers and surfie chicks scorn her for daring to express her discontent.

She is rebellious enough to speak her mind in that scene. A bit later, after the pregnancy scare is over and after her dead boyfriend's surfboard is ritualistically sent to sea, Debbie and Sue buy a surfboard—Debbie determined, Sue a bit unsure. When they take it to the beach and announce their plan to surf, both surfers and surfie chicks scorn them. They are told "girls don't surf"; they are told they are "bent," suggesting psychological and gender role confusion on their parts. Interestingly, as they walk to the surfing area of Cronulla, Debbie says hello to Frieda, the girl who was gang-raped. A surfie chick would not even talk to someone like Freida, but Debbie rebels against the "rules." She signals that this day will not be usual.

She and Sue do surf. Sue does fairly well, Debbie quite well. Some of the boys who initially scorned them start offering them advice. Boys and surfie chicks on the shore take note of their moves. The scene is set up so that we almost think Debbie and Sue have effected a revolutionary change in the culture; however, this is not the result. The culture does not change that easily, and, in any event, as Anna Gul noted, the step is a small one (in Murray, *Australian Film* 81). They nonetheless proved that women can do exactly what men can do—in the surf and, by extension, elsewhere. If the surfing culture sees their performance as just a blip without consequence beyond those few hours, the motion picture audience, years later, grasps the message in their surfing.

Another important message is presented in *Puberty Blues'* last scene. Debbie and Sue, triumphant, are walking back along the beach from surfing, alone. The one says to the other, "Guess we're dropped," indicating their awareness that their act has severed them from the surfing culture, not transformed it. The other says, in response, "Who cares." With that remark, we are a long way from the Debbie and Sue at the film's beginning who wanted nothing more in the world than to be surfie chicks.

Debbie is clearly the more prominent character in the film. She is more naïve in the beginning; she is more rebellious throughout and at the end. She experiences more shocks than Sue. That is one reason why she is more iconoclastic. The early high school scenes make something else very clear: she is one of the brightest students in the class. As an aspiring member of the surfing culture, she hides her academic credentials a bit, especially since she does far better than her boyfriends. We, however, remember her intelligence and attribute some of her decision to resist the culture to the fact that she is too bright to tolerate its mindlessness and the demeaning messages it sends to and about women.

Although the film does focus on Debbie and makes the rebellious decisions seem as if they are hers, we should note that Sue is there with her all along. Sue is at her side when they are both trying to get in the "in" group. Sue is there getting drunk with Debbie; Sue is there helping Debbie handle all of the issues, like sex, that come with having surfer boyfriends; Sue is there to console Debbie at trying times such as when she thought she was pregnant; and Sue is there buying the board they will share and taking her turn on it. Debbie and Sue are very much mates. All of the elements of the usual-male relationship are present right down to the liquor and the sharing of sexual exploits. One gets the impression that many of the rebellious decisions were primarily Debbie's. By going along with Debbie, even though she is perhaps a good bit less gung ho, Sue is risking being tossed out by the school's most prestigious clique. No matter—loyalty to her mate takes precedence over her desire to belong.

Debbie, then, is very much in the mold of the Australian heroes sketched earlier in this book. She has the potential to play that role in stories to come. The lifestyle of the youth culture she has aspired to could drag her down, but she seems to have learned about that lifestyle's traps through Freida's gang rape, her boyfriend's death, and her own near-pregnancy. So, the only barrier is the sexism that she can dent but not destroy. In facing sexism, however, she is much like many of the female heroes discussed in Chapter 4. One feels, given Debbie's strength in the concluding surfing scenes, that she will be one of the women who is not thwarted by the sexism she inevitably will have to overcome repeatedly.

STARSTRUCK (GILLIAN ARMSTRONG, DIRECTOR, 1982)

There were rumors that Gillian Armstrong wanted to follow-up *My Brilliant Career* with *Puberty Blues*. An interview with the women behind the latter film suggests, however, that this was just a rumor. One can understand, however, how the rumor might get started because in many ways Debbie is like

Sybylla Melvyn. Rumor had it that Armstrong's commitment to another project, *Starstruck*, was the reason why Beresford, not she, directed *Puberty Blues*.

Starstruck allowed Armstrong to direct unknown Jo Kennedy playing Jackie, another very strong female character. But *Starstruck* is a very different kind of film from either *My Brilliant Career* or *Puberty Blues*. Whereas the former was a period piece and the latter a bit of social reality lightened a bit by some humor, *Starstruck* is a rock musical that asks questions that anyone familiar with Hollywood will find quite familiar: Will Jackie become a star? Will someone be able to save the Harbour View Hotel (pub) from financial ruin (Rattigan 282)?

The setting of *Starstruck* is as urban as that of *Mouth to Mouth*. The one is Sydney; the other Melbourne, but that is not the crucial difference. The difference is what the camera allows us to see and the mood that is thereby created. Whereas we see rundown sections of Melbourne in photography that stresses the gritty tones, we see The Rocks, the business district, and the Opera House in Sydney in shots (by Russell Boyd) that are vibrant with color. At times, the setting seems overdesigned by the same artist who did Jim Sharman's *The Rocky Horror Picture Show* (1975) (Stratton, *Avocado* 114). In such an exciting Sydney world, the natural impulse is to try to get ahead. There is, in the financial problems of the pub, evidence that not all is as bright as the scene, but our attention is focused on the dynamic Jackie, who is trying to work her way to the top of the rock music world in a buoyant environment that causes us to think her dream plausible. Furthermore, she might even save the pub at the same time. In this case, the film's musical comedy genre sets up the expectation as much as the generally positive setting.

When we see Jackie perform, we become convinced that she exudes energy on stage and may even have some genuine musical talent. However, she is young (eighteen) and an unknown. Her fourteen-year-old cousin Angus (Ross O'Donovan, another unknown) becomes her promoter/manager. He has her do nude (supposedly) tightrope walking at Circular Quay to gain the attention of television rock music personality Terry Lambert. The stunt works, but, when she goes on Lambert's show she flops because she allowed Lambert's people to "package" her, choosing her music and her "look." One of Jackie's own songs is "I Don't Know My Name." There is a sense after flopping on Lambert's show that she has lost both her direction and her identity. Angus helps her recover both and manages to sneak her onto a televised New Year's Eve show at the Sydney Opera House. There, she and her band, "The Wombats," present the "real" Jackie, not the packaged one viewers saw on Lambert's rock music program.

Those responsible for the Opera House show, however, pull the plug on Jackie—literally. She had, after all, stolen the climactic spot on the show from "The Mainliners." The "authorities" wanted Jackie off and the popular "Mainliners" on. That group's name is perhaps doubly significant. It suggests that the band is following the well-trodden path; it also suggests that the band's performance either is drugged or acts as a drug. Jackie's music is set against theirs because hers is outside the "established" norms and is full of natural energy, not druglike highs and lows. Angus finds a way to re-empower Jackie. The authorities, responding to the crowd, let her show go on. We presume that the musical future is now quite bright for Jackie. She has also won $25,000 in the New Year's Eve battle of the bands, money that does indeed save the Harbour View Hotel from ruin. She succeeds; the pub succeeds. The odd person out is Angus, who, at fourteen, is too young to accompany Jackie onward and upward. Originally, the script was a love story between Jackie and Angus. As the project developed, it became much more Jackie's story, leaving Angus marginalized throughout, not just at the very end (Murray, "*Starstruck*" 115). Relatively late in the film's production, Armstrong added scenes to the ending showing Angus' romantic meeting with "the roller-skating girl" outside the Sydney Opera House. Armstrong wanted Angus to have a happy ending too.

Jackie is clearly a battler. Even though she makes mistakes, she fights on. Initially, her fight seems to be against the odds. As the film progresses, the fight is much more against the authorities. They try to regulate her performance on "The Terry Lambert Show"; they try to stop her from singing at the Opera House contest. She is very much the underdog in this battle. However, as is not the case for many Australian heroes, there is no cloud of inevitable failure hanging over her head. Largely because of the expectations set up by the film's genre, there is an aura of eventual success there instead. If, then, Jackie is a bit atypical of the Australian hero because of this optimistic aura, she is very typical insofar as she needs the help of her loyal mates to succeed. Her band members, the entrepreneurial Lambert, and especially cousin Angus push her on. She does, however, seem a bit less loyal to them than they are to her. She does not protest much at all when "The Terry Lambert Show" insists she perform with the house band instead of her "Wombats," perhaps because, at that point, she has a crush on him. Then, she seems to distance herself from both Lambert, once he proves to be gay, and the too-young Angus. She thus seems more of an individualist and an opportunist than the Australian norm.

She fights her fight in a context happily devoid of urban problems or cultural problems that are evident in other films. Neither drug use nor sexual excesses are issues in the film, and alcohol consumption, at least in the context of the Harbour View Hotel, comes across positively. Beer and camaraderie and Australia join in a usually celebratory mood in the pub. Racism and classism are not striking; neither is sexism. Jackie's barrier is that she is unknown, not that she's female. Like Debbie in Beresford's *Puberty Blues*, Jackie's potential to be a hero seems high—maybe even boundless.

BMX BANDITS (BRIAN TRENCHARD-SMITH, DIRECTOR, 1983)

Starstruck is a rather light, very high-energy, and very optimistic film, so is Trenchard-Smith's *BMX Bandits*. Its central characters are more Angus' age than Jackie's; thus, the film has a more innocent feel to it. Male–female relationships in *Starstruck*, for example, can be serious, but not so in *BMX Bandits*. There, the young teens toy with boyfriend–girlfriend scenarios but, in reality, they are all just young mates, regardless of gender.

We have already seen the horse-loving culture evident in films such as *The Man from Snowy River* (1982) and *Phar Lap* (1983) become the car-loving culture in *The F. J. Holden* or the motorcycle-loving culture of *Stone*. Yet another transformation is into the fast bicycle-loving one in *BMX Bandits*. The young teens are never very far from their bikes. Their speed and versatility combine with the kids' very good knowledge of the suburbs north of Sydney to allow them to get in and out of trouble with facility.

The kids, led by Judy (played by a young Nicole Kidman), get into trouble with villainous characters who seem to have stepped right out of British television. They are, of course, a potential danger to the young teens; however, the villains are scripted and acted in such a way that they seem comically inept, not genuinely threatening. The good side of the adult population, parents and police, to the extent they are even present, are similarly comic and inept (Rattigan 63). That both the forces of bad and the forces of good are largely incompetent opens up the space in which the Bandits operate, overcoming the inept "baddies" in the aid of the inept "goodies." The "Bandits," it should be noted, work very well together as a team. They are also fiercely loyal to each other, exhibiting the positive aspects of mateship. The mateship crosses gender lines and is nothing at all like the drunken mateship we saw in *The F. J. Holden*.

The kids are less rebellious rather than just free. What strikes one is not that they break rules or thumb noses at" authority" figures but that they move freely through the cityscape with speed and smarts. They—young larrikins—seem to very much enjoy this freedom (Rattigan 63). That it is overdone is a reflection of the motion picture's being a "teen film," which can overemphasize the desired level of freedom for the viewers' vicarious enjoyment. The inept portraits of the adults, which puts the kids on a higher level of competence, are also a reflection of the film's genre. One should, therefore, not make too much out of either the kids' freedom or the adults' incompetence. Nonetheless, probably because of the film's highly kinetic quality communicated through well-photographed chase scenes, the freedom is striking (Stratton, *Avocado* 341).

This freedom becomes channeled in the film into the task of defeating the bad guys. Should the freedom continue to be part of the kids' make-up as they mature and should that more mature free spirit be channeled into less comic heroic tasks, they have much potential. Since the film is targeted at a young teen audience, neither alcohol, drugs, and sex nor racism, classism, and sexism play a role. The film is innocent of abuses and negative "ism'" s—healthfully so. The absence may, however, be a reflection of more than just an attempt to avoid unpleasant subjects. Sexism, even in males this young, could have surfaced and been directed at Judy who very much plays the leader's role among the Bandits. Trenchard-Smith and writers Patrick Edgeworth (script) and Russell Hagg (original screenplay) seem to choose to omit this complication. As a result, the film sends a very positive message about male–female relations to the young people who view the film.

MOVING OUT (MICHAEL PATTINSON, DIRECTOR, 1983)

Pattinson's film depicts a group of somewhat older teens. The portrait offered of this group is interesting, as are the two other "plots" of *Moving Out:* the central character's (Gino) coming to terms with his Italian ethnic heritage within an Australian context and his finding himself as an artist. The film's major flaw is that these three plots are not as well-integrated as they should be.

The group Gino hangs out with mixes genders and ethnic backgrounds. The members hang out in the abandoned cars in their Fitzroy (close-in section of Melbourne) neighborhood. There, they smoke, drink, and talk about sex. Their interaction is not, therefore, as innocent as that among the kids in *BMX Bandits*; however, it is not at all what we will see soon in a film such as *Dogs in Space* (1987). The group steals automobile insignias off cars for kicks. The group mocks sex as they tumble about at the bottom of a playground sliding board. Then, they go further: breaking into a house so that one couple, Gino and the very un-Italian Sandy, can get beyond mock-sex in one of the big house's bedrooms. There, the police catch them. So, the group does get into trouble. However, we scarcely feel we are dealing with future felons when watching Gino, Sandy, Renato, and Helen.

Most "authorities" in *Moving Out* are treated neutrally. Both school officials and police officials seem competent and fair, not inept and/or abusive. But these are not the relevant authority figures in Gino's story and, to a varying extent, those of the other group members. The relevant authority figures are the ones who try to force a strong ethnic identity on these young Australians. Gino, for example, is urged to speak Italian, which he denounces as a "wog" language. He's compelled to attend an Italian party for immigrants of all ages rather than Helen's beer and rock-'n'-roll gathering. These authority figures who urge Italian words and gatherings on him are depicted in neither a positive nor a negative light. They are human, dealing with the tension between their homeland and their adopted "Oz" as best they can.

Gino's rebellion against these authority figures comes to a head when his parents plan to move from Fitzroy to an outer suburb, Doncaster. Gino wants to stay because Fitzroy is where his group is. However, the move would be a move up and away from the more ethnic close-in neighborhoods. So, in rejecting the move, he is rejecting integration into the broader Australian society. Paradoxically, that integration is precisely what he wants, but his group is familiar to him and the outer suburb is not. Further complicating the decision is the growing attraction between Gino and an Italian girl,

Maria, who has just arrived in Melbourne. She gives him yet another reason to want to stay in Fitzroy.

Another kind of rebellion is brewing within Gino. In high school, he is not doing well in his English class, despite considerable ability. He is not doing well because he is not committed. What seems to be at the root of his problem is his inability to connect with the Australian literature he is being "forced" to learn. This inability to connect is a hint that he is less Australian than he claims to be (Rattigan 219). He is then, perhaps accurately described as being in between—rebelling against the ethnic as he is still drawn to it; paradoxically rebelling against a move that would take him further away from the ethnic because he feels safe where he is; paradoxically rebelling against Dorothea McCullough's "A Sunburned Country" and similar Australian literary classics, not realizing what this rebellion might suggest.

Gino seems to find a way to cope with the tensions within him through art. He is good at sculpture. He is also serious, so much so that his sympathetic art teacher gives him keys to the school's art room. His first finished piece of work is a fist, which he paints red. The fist would seem to suggest Gino's determination to fight; the red, either the passion he will bring to the fight or the blood he anticipates the fight will spill. Once he takes this fist home, he guards it carefully. Rather than prompting more defiance of the pending move, the fist seems to push him away from defiance and toward compliance. The fist, which he cradles in his lap as the truck he is seated in pulls away carrying the family's possessions, may then symbolize the inner battle he will fight to reconcile all of the pulls in different directions he feels.

The film ends with Laura Brannigan's rock hit "Gloria." Sometimes rock music is used in teen films such as *Moving Out* just to create atmosphere. Not so here. The song in this case represents the reconciliation Gino is striving for. It is not the lyrics that matter, but other things. First, the song is a piece of Australian-produced popular music; second, the song is sung in Italian, not English; and third, "Gloria" is the name Gino's Fitzroy group gave the wrecked Plymouth Valiant where they hung out. The Australian Gino wants to be part of the Italian ethnic heritage he halfheartedly wants to reject, and the safe camaraderie of the Fitzroy gang and by extension that entire neighborhood all merge in the rendition of "Gloria" at the film's end. And the song is by its very title a song of praise and joy.

Gino's fight is a complex one. Nothing is simple in the film: there are pulls in different directions, and, although the directions are clearly opposed, they do not seem simply good on the one hand and bad on the other. Authority is not a one-dimensional oppressive force, and mateship, although valuable, is also a route to trouble, as Renato's drift into more serious trouble than breaking and entering suggests. There is also alcohol, drugs, and sex in Gino's world to deal with—not as much as in a film such as *Dogs in Space* or *Mouth to Mouth*, but certainly more than in *Starstruck* or *BMX Bandits*. Gino's fist may allow him to be ultimately heroic, but he has tensions to deal with in his life before a "Gloria" seems totally appropriate for him.

GOING DOWN (HAYDN KEENAN, DIRECTOR, 1983)

The overall message in Haydn Keenan's *Going Down* is summed up nicely in the film when a character observes that it is a dog-eat-dog world but that there is not enough dog to go around. At the lower end of the economic continuum, Keenan's characters, who are in their late-teens or twenties, have to make do somehow. We see various choices, including theft and prostitution. We also see the drug- and alcohol-induced oblivion the characters stumble into once the sun sets. As if to underscore how low the characters have reached, the screenplay features much vomiting. The movie also depicts one deep kiss that immediately follows vomiting, offering viewers a notably disgusting moment. And the movie depicts two of the girls, working as prostitutes, urinating on their wealthy client at his request, offering viewers another notably disgusting moment.

The world depicted in *Going Down* does not seem to offer the characters much at all. The male characters seem no longer able to function. They seem to be playing stereotypes such as nerd or ocker without the role-playing having much connection to their day-to-day lives. It is as if the day is a subway train on one track and their role-playing a train on another, with the two heading in opposite directions. The best that can be said for the male characters is that they are "there"; the worst is that they are drug dealers and drug addicts who will steal from both charities and their female friends. The female characters are depicted somewhat more positively. In fact, four girls—Karli, Ellen, Jackie, and Jane—are the movie's central characters. As we swirl through the Sydney night, thanks to camera work by Malcolm Richards that at times seems to punch us about, we follow their stories as best as we can (McFarlane 102). Alcohol and drugs and sex do play roles in their nighttime leisure and, in Jackie and Jane's case, employment. However, they are not as disconnected from reality as the males are. Jane tries to dissuade Jackie from prostitution; the three (exhibiting mateship) follow Ellen when she, drunk, leaves a club with a group of men who, the girls fear, might rape her. Of the four, Karli (Tracey Mann) seems the most connected to reality. That is why she is planning to leave Sydney.

"Authorities" do not play a major role in *Going Down*. Police do make an appearance, and their behavior seems unnecessarily harassing. But, for the most part, the young characters drift through the Sydney night without much interference. Parents seem almost entirely out of the picture, with the exception of Karli's father. He, perhaps recognizing what the prospects in Sydney are, gives his daughter $3,000 at the beginning of the movie so she can go to New York City. By helping her leave, he is playing a positive role. However, he seems very much on the margins of her life, and his help will create further distance—literal distance—between the two of them.

There is not much hope in *Going Down:* the world depicted is bleak; the characters' lifestyles are debilitating. Therefore, the upbeat music and cinematography as dawn comes to Sydney are difficult to decipher. We think initially that the mere fact that they have survived another night may be the cause of the sudden optimistic turn the film takes. More likely, the optimism is tied to Karli's story. She manages to retrieve the $3,000 a male friend has stolen from her. Then, she steals the car of a just-married couple and speeds her way to the airport. The "Just Married" sign perhaps connotes how she is embarking on a new life herself. Once she arrives at the airport, she abandons the stolen car and quickly makes her way through customs. We feel good for her that she has escaped; however, we feel badly because Ellen, Jackie, and Jane were her mates and she is leaving them without even a farewell. Karli, however, gives us a more optimistic ending by coming back through the customs checkpoint to meet the three mates who have rushed to the airport to bid her good-bye. They give her gifts, including a little money to help her along in New York. They reach the communal conclusion that at least "one of us has got her act together."

The optimism at the film's end is, however, deceptive. Yes, Karli has realized that she is getting caught up in a scary world in Sydney, and, yes, she has rebelled against this world. However, her rebellion removes her from that world: from the father who tried to help her and from her mates. There seems to be no way to rebel against the bleakness of urban Australian life and thereby reform it. It is either stay in and go down or get out. Karli gets out, but the others we meet in the film are still there in Sydney going down.

SLATE, WYN, & ME (DON McLENNAN, DIECTOR, 1987)

With McLennan's film, we are no longer in Melbourne or Sydney; rather, we are in a small outback town. The place is not as big as the town depicted in *Shame* (1988), nor as small as the town depicted in *Razorback* (1984), but it has some of the qualities of both. The men all seem ockers, and none of them seems to be going anywhere. The place also seems oppressively boring. Most of the men and the women in the town do not seem to notice the oppressiveness. Two brothers, Slate and Wyn Jackson do, however. Their way of dealing with the oppressiveness is to get the money necessary to get out of town by robbing the bank. They do, but things go wrong. Wyn ends up shooting a police officer, and the two boys end up kidnapping a girl named Blanche who witnessed the killing.

Off the trio goes on the road, destination not entirely known. They act as if they are heading to the border. In the United States, this might make sense: north to Canada or south to Mexico. But their flight to remote Queensland only makes sense if you buy the stereotype of Queensland as backward and assume that, therefore, they will be safer there than in the more southern states.

They are not too long on the road when Blanche (Sigrid Thornton) begins acting more like a mate than a hostage. Her character is the most difficult of the three to figure out, perhaps because some of her ideas and feelings were lost when the story was transformed from a novel by Georgia Savage. The film, with Blanche less in the foreground than in the novel, tries to divide its attention equally among all three characters. As a result, we do not know whether Blanche less is as desirous of escape from the town as the boys, whether she alternately loves the one and then the other, or whether she is playing games with them, all in an attempt to gain her freedom. We do not know whether she is fed up, fickle, or manipulative.

Why the Jackson brothers wanted to escape is fairly clear (although the demons in Slate's head from his service in Vietnam destabilize and thereby complicate his character). What is also initially fairly clear is that they see themselves as mates: no matter what turn the flight from the law takes, they are in it together. Strongly suggestive of the bond is Slate's willingness to share with Wyn the responsibility for killing the police officer even though Slate was not at all at fault.

What these mates do not, however, anticipate is the effect Blanche will have on their bond. First, she becomes both of their mates. Then, she becomes close to Wyn; then, lover to Slate. As she shifts from man to man, the tension between the two mates increases, and mateship vanishes. When she gets her chance, she turns on both. The ensuing police raid kills Slate. Wyn, on his own, is committed to avenging his brother–mate's death by killing Blanche. When he finally finds her, she, in the eighteenth-century manner, "pleads her belly," saying she's carrying Slate's baby. Whether true or shrewd, the tale saves her.

Slate and Wyn never should have ended up as they did. They wanted out, which is understandable given how oppressively boring their town seemed to be. So, they decided to leave. After that, they seem less decisive agents and more just acted-upon malcontent boys. We are supposed to understand that the gun that killed the lawman somehow just fired. Then, we see them drift down the highways, heading generally north while the radio plays Chuck Berry's "No Particular Place to Go." Then, we see Blanche, perhaps, "play them" this way and that, crushing their mateship (Joanna Murray-Smith in Murray, *Australian Film* 229). They do keep on going: there is enough of the fighter in both of them to keep them ahead of the law as best they can. However, we do not detect much in the two boys that would prompt decisive action in a crisis should such action be necessary. They are, in other words, without much heroic potential beyond their discontent, their desire to survive, and their too easily undermined mateship. If anyone has potential, it might be Blanche, but we do not have enough insight into her in the film to make a good assessment.

THE YEAR MY VOICE BROKE (JOHN DUIGAN, DIRECTOR, 1987)

Duigan's film is set in a small town not unlike that in *Slate, Wyn, & Me*. It breeds its share of ocker types as well as the women who fawn all over them.

The teenage girl in the movie—Freya (Loene Carmen)—is a more intelligent, more sensitive version of these women. Yes, she has her macho boyfriend in Trevor, but she also has a soul mate with whom she can share ideas and feelings in the slightly younger Danny (Noah Taylor). The town also has a secret much as the small town in *Shame* does. The secret is the story of Sarah Amery, who committed suicide at age seventeen. Sarah's reputation with the kids is that of a witch; her now-abandoned house is thought to be haunted. The reality is that Sarah was "the town slut," and her house functioned pretty much as a brothel, one that most of the men in town visited at one point or another.

Danny is also more intelligent and more sensitive than most of the young boys in the town. Being such and being smaller in size, he gets bullied a great deal by the macho males. He very much wants to escape the town, but sees no immediate way to do so. Once upon a time, he escaped by going to places away from the town per se with his friend Freya. Danny tries very much to keep that shared retreating alive, but Freya has begun to move on—out of young adolescence. Danny lingers behind. He is obsessed with Freya—sexually so—but he is not as mature as she is and is, therefore, not thought of by her in romantic or sexual terms. She arranges dates for Danny with her younger stepsister. Freya seems to be trying to keep the mateship of Danny and herself going in a more mature double-dating context. But the new context is fraught with tension that only Danny really understands, since the source of the tension is his love of Freya.

Freya is trying her best to fit into the community and its norms. She seems genuinely fond of and attracted to Trevor, despite his wreckless behavior and jovial stupidity. It is not altogether clear whether the relationship has a future because Freya's sexual license causes her reputation to suffer to the point that she no longer feels welcome or happy there. What Freya does not understand is why her reputation sinks so very rapidly. Danny discovers the explanation and shares it with her: she was Sarah Amery's illegitimate daughter, and the townspeople—guilty about how they had treated her mother—see in Freya's recent behavior proof that she is just like her mother. Rather than confront their guilt, they displace it on her, making her the new town slut, rather than just a passionate young girl. Even the Olson family, who had adopted her, now view her as a moral reprobate and want her gone before she has a negative effect on their younger daughter.

Perhaps Freya's intelligence and sensitivity would have driven her out of the town eventually. But now, she is driven out because she knows the truth about the town based on how it treated her mother and how it treated her. As she boards the train to leave for the city, she and Danny talk. She finally realizes his love for her, but she cannot stay and he cannot go. So, the realization is for naught.

There is certainly much in the outback town to reject. Danny's rebellion is thwarted; Freya's is forced. Neither character defies the ways of the town: Danny sidesteps; Freya lets the town determine what she must do and then she does it. Furthermore, their mateship does not give either of them enough support to do anything else: Freya is no longer always there for Danny; Danny cannot yet reconcile sex and friendship as he wrestles to redefine their relationship. The mateship gets hung up as if on a rock at the point in time when Freya discovers her sexuality, while, maturely a bit behind her, Danny's voice breaks.

As Duigan's film ends, we do not feel fully depressed. Freya is leaving to a place where she can start anew without people knowing she is Sarah Amery's daughter and expecting her to act accordingly. Danny has matured a great deal, and we have hopes for him. He may soon escape. But what is depressing is that they have lost each other and, with that, all the potential their relationship had. Under different circumstances, that potential could have sent them forward, fighting and winning, but the circumstances were not right this particular year.

DOGS IN SPACE (RICHARD LOWENSTEIN, DIRECTOR, 1987)

Lowenstein's film takes us far, far away from the rural setting of both *Slate, Wyn & Me* and *The Year My Voice Broke*. We are taken to a seedy counterculture section of Melbourne, specifically to a single house in which a variety of youth characters live and an even greater variety hangout and party. The film immerses us in the house, taking us through three weeks in its life. We do not have much in the way of plot, but several stories do emerge. We have, for example, Luchio, who is trying to study for his engineering exams at the University of Melbourne, only to be visited by his very pregnant girlfriend from back home. We have a young runaway, who drifts into the house and almost becomes trapped in its environment of alcohol, drugs, and sex. And we have Anna (Saskia Post), suburban girl in love with a junkie. She dies of a tragic heroin overdose at the film's end.

Luchio's story, and a few others, serve as a somewhat comical counterpoint to an otherwise dreary succession of people trapped by what the house, as a symbol of the counterculture, offers. If there is an oppressive force in the film, it is this culture. It is not authority. However, "authority" does not come across in the motion picture as offering any useful direction to the youths who are trapped. Parents, when they appear, are ineffectual or worse. A glance at Anna's parents suggests that they are too preoccupied to figure out why their girl has gone away. A longer scene involving drug addict Sam's mother has her delivering food and drink to her son at the house only to be treated like a servant and then verbally abused. She seems to be acting as if being obsequious and begging Sam (rocker Michael Hutchence) will get him off whatever he is on and back home. Police are curiously depicted in the film. There are many films in which the police are rude, if not worse, to characters such as the ones who live in this house. The police in *Dogs*, however, are extremely polite and, as a result, extremely ineffectual at dealing with problems they ought to be dealing with such as rampant drug abuse, offensive loudness, and flamboyant violence.

Since authority is so weak, it is difficult to talk about challenging it. The characters in the house, however, certainly do not look as if they could challenge much. They are simply too far gone: lost in a haze of alcohol, drugs, and sex. Only Luchio, by studying, seems up to a challenge.

To emphasize the characters' lack of fighting spirit, Lowenstein introduces political threads into the film. When the band "Dogs in Space" (that some of the house's residents are a part of) is asked to perform at a concert being staged to benefit a number of political causes the band members ought to be interested in, they ask how much money they will make. When an activist visits the house and shares her feminist, pro-aboriginal, pro-environmental ideas, her words are largely lost in noise. Those who can hear are too far gone on drugs and alcohol to care. The subtlest political touch is the "East Timor" sign on the house's kitchen wall. When we initially see it, we can read its political message, calling for support of dissident elements there. Later, it is largely covered over with notes and other debris. Still later, it is more covered and half falling down. The sign's fate suggests how such causes fare with this group. The members ought to be willing and able to fight for these various left-wing causes, but they are quite clearly not.

Similarly, they are too far gone to be much of mates to each other. All we see are vestiges of mateship. We see a group go off on a road trip to Ballarat. They "capture" a lamb and bring it back to Luchio. We see Anna offering cautionary advice on sex to the young runaway. We do not see much more than these few moments of camaraderie or care.

Throughout the film, we hear about how pieces of debris are falling from space. This falling space junk helps give the film an apocalyptic feel (Raffael Caputo in Murray, *Australian Film* 214). The sky is literally falling, and the residents of the house mirror this oblivion by having fallen into their own alcohol- and drug-induced oblivion. Out of this oblivion, there is little chance that anything even vaguely heroic might emerge.

MULL (DON McLENNAN, DIRECTOR, 1989)

McLennan's film, based on Bron Nicholls' novel *Mullaway*, is much more hopeful than *Dogs in Space*. Nonetheless, McLennan's film shows us all of the problems a young person must face when growing up.

The young person in *Mull* is teenage Phoebe Mullens (Nadine Garner). She has to quit high school and play a major role in caring for her family because her mother is quite ill (dying, in fact) and her father has developed a religious obsession that preoccupies him. McLennan does a good job capturing—through rare voiceovers and Phoebe's words and facial expressions—the essence of her first-person narration (Stratton, *Avocado* 363). We thus see and hear her work through various problems—her own and the family's—relatively well, despite the fact that the supposed "authority" figures are incapable, for one reason or another, of offering her much in the way of guidance. Her father offers nothing; her mother offers advice about birth control so that Phoebe does not become pregnant and have to marry as the mother did. Only a former teacher, who urges "Mull" to return to school and do something creative with her life, offers her any words that are at all upbeat.

Mull fights her way through much—big and small. She must deal with not being asked to be a bridesmaid by her close friend Helen because, Mull thinks, she is not pretty enough. She must deal with being rejected by Guido, who, it turns out, is her older brother's gay lover. She must deal with her younger brother's developing obsession with religious purity, which comes to a climax when he has a "wet dream" and believes it is a punishment from God; she must deal with—reject on her behalf and that of her younger siblings—the religious fanaticism that has taken over her father's life. And she must deal with the fact that her mother is dying of cancer.

Mull manages to deal with it all. There are times when she becomes angry or depressed or drunk, but she gets by. After her mother's death, she comes the closest to giving up. She has a long talk with her father. She tells him she quits, and goes off, for a short period, to stay with a deaf boy she has developed a loving relationship with. But Mull returns and commits herself to doing what has to be done for the family—on the condition that the father changes his ways and does his share. She decides to return to school too, determined to do something with her life. "I Can See Clearly Now," sung by Marcia Howard, concludes the film at this point. The song suggests that Mull has won her battle.

Mull, it should be noted, fights pretty much on her own. Her older brother Steve is little help: one suspects that he is busy struggling with his homosexual orientation in a macho Australian culture that will undoubtedly give him grief. Her friend Helen proves to be very much a fair-weather one. Toward the film's end, her deaf boyfriend George does provide needed emotional support. However, the energy and determination Mull needs pretty much must be mustered from within, not derived from supportive mates.

Mull exhibits, then, heroism as she helps her family survive. Her determination to do something with her life suggests that she has the potential for heroism in years to come. But she will, it seems, have to be heroic without much support from either those older and wiser or any mates. She will have to go it alone, much as she did during the year *Mull* chronicles.

ROMPER STOMPER (GEOFFREY WRIGHT, DIRECTOR, 1992)

Mull was set in St. Kilda, a beach suburb of Melbourne. To some extent, the setting lightens the environment somewhat, preventing the problems that face Phoebe Mullens from coming across to viewers at least as overwhelming.

Romper Stomper, on the other hand, takes us into the heart of Melbourne. Its prevailing grayness causes the picture of youth culture in Wright's film to come across as foreboding.

Romper Stomper focuses on a neo-Nazi youth gang. In the early scenes, we see the neo-Nazi skinheads attacking Vietnamese who are "taking over" businesses in the neighborhood. Then, we see the Vietnamese counterattack the skinheads. During all of this violence, the police are absent. War among ethnic groups seems to have settled on urban Melbourne. And it is not just white supremacists versus encroaching Asians because the Vietnamese are fiercely anti-Greek in a city that has the second largest Greek population in the world. In addition, the neo-Nazis are opposed to what they term "hippie degenerates." We have, in O'Regan's terms, "dystopian multiculturalism," a general atmosphere of ethnic hatred in which neo-Nazism and anti-Asian sentiment are not developed ideologies because they function as "us vs. all others" banners, not as thought-through political positions (*Australian* 152).

The leader of the neo-Nazi gang is Hando (Russell Crowe). He takes in—and takes to bed—a young epileptic girl named Gabe (Jacqueline McKenzie). Her life has been scarred by a rich father who has sexually abused her. Most of the girls in the gang are passive; not so Gabe. She leads the gang in a revenge attack on her father and his posh house. The attack, however, becomes mindlessly and sadistically prolonged, giving the father a chance to free himself and call the police. When the police arrive, they are brutal toward the skinheads.

"Authority" does not come across positively in *Romper Stomper*. When Asians and skinheads are brawling, police authority is absent; when it comes to Gabe's father's rescue, it is unnecessarily brutal. Parental authority is depicted, in the one case where we see it, as horribly abusive. The rebellion against this authority does not, however, come across positively either. And the rest of the gang's violence is not rebellion but rather hatred, unless one wants to see their racist assaults as representing defiance against the government's immigration policies. And it might be, in a perverse way, because Hando compares the skinheads' endangered status to that of the aborigines run over by the early settlers.

Mateship also seems present only on the surface. The gang members seem loyal to one another, but there are tensions apparent. All of the brawling among themselves is not just for fun. In addition, one has a difficult time imagining that the girls are completely content being put in a subordinate position and being "used," often brutally, for sex. Gabe manages to bring some of these tensions to the surface because she is not a passive follower of Hando's regime. When they clash, she reveals how shallow her commitment to the gang was by seducing Hando's chief ally Davey (Daniel Pollock) away from the group and then turning the gang in to the police.

In perhaps the film's only positive moment, Gabe joins Davey in the little cottage he lives in next door to his grandmother's house. They make love. As O'Regan notes, when they have sex, she is on top and she climaxes, as opposed to when she and Hando had sex with her pushed face-first against a wall with Hando hammering her from behind (*Australian* 151). The differences in these sex scenes speak volumes about Hando's all-encompassing hatred and Davey's contrasting openness to something more loving as well as the two males' very different attitude toward women. But the positive interlude does not last. Next thing we know, we are on the road with Hando, Davey, and Gabe and, then, on the beach. The scene is in many ways incongruous. In a culture dominated by the beach and the sunbathers and surfers who hang out there, one has certain expectations for beach scenes. This one defies them because we have two leather-clad skinheads along with punk-looking Gabe. The incongruity is a bit humorous, but the scene is not. Hando appeals explicitly to mateship in trying to get Davey to rejoin the gang and join him in killing and then disposing of Gabe, who was a snitch and now knows enough to get the two mates jailed. Davey responds to this appeal by killing Hando.

The film's concluding scene is violent, just as the bulk of the preceding scenes. There is no sense of romance at all as Davey chooses Gabe and potential love over Hando and mateship. Rather, there is a bleakness, added to by the bleak gray day—and hopeful desperation. Adding a bizarre note is the group of Japanese tourists who arrive at a nearby scenic overlook. They excitedly watch and film the confrontation on the beach below—almost as if it were being staged as a tourist attraction. The effect of their presence is to suck any meaning there might have been out of either Davey's choice or Hando's death. We are left with meaninglessness.

Romper Stomper then offers little hope for heroism emerging from the youth culture it depicts. What further emphasizes this hopelessness is the alcohol abuse and the sexual abuse among the neo-Nazi gang members. Their culture, even at its "matiest" moment, is ugly. Senseless violence seems its almost natural consequence, not any kind of heroism. Serge Grunberg notes Wright's "hatred of [an] Australian ideology" with its "suffocating . . . well-meaningness" (31). Wright manages in *Romper Stomper* to undermine this idealism quite effectively.

Chapter 7

Playing with the Concept

Some who study what is popularly called science fiction are fond of the alternative generic name "speculative fiction." The alternative name gets at what the works of fiction or film are trying to do, which is not to tell stories about where science may take us but, rather, to ask the question what if: What if aliens attacked? What if the aliens are already among us? What if a totalitarian government took over? What if there were nuclear war and only a handful of people—of course, in Australia—survived? These questions are posed because the writers of such works want to know, not the details of the threatening event, but, rather, the effect the event would have on everything else. They want to speculate about that effect.

One such effect of such surprising or catastrophic events would be on heroism. Would it still be possible? Would its essence change? In this chapter, we will examine several films that ask "what if." We will consider what the event—be it contact with aliens, a nuclear war, a right-wing plot, or total commercialization—does to heroism.

SHIRLEY THOMPSON VERSUS THE ALIENS (JIM SHARMAN, DIRECTOR, 1972)

Sharman's directorial career has taken him from the cult classic *The Rocky Horror Picture Show* (1975) to an adaptation of Nobel laureate Patrick White's "The Night of the Stranger." Somewhat closer to the former in style is the *Shirley Thompson versus the Aliens*, a film that predates *Rocky Horror* by four years. The film will, at first sight, strike viewers as strange. It does not proceed in chronological order; it jumps back and forth from black and white to color; and, through visual and audio special effects, tries to create the illusion of seeing events through the eyes of someone on the brink of insanity. From the swirling film, one can extract its basic premise and story.

When Shirley (Jane Harders) is sixteen years old or so, she and a group of friends go to Luna Park, an amusement park (now closed) tucked under the north approach to the Sydney Harbour Bridge. The park was closed, but they sneak in. There, in the "River Cave" ride, aliens appear to them. All but Shirley flee. She is zapped by the spaceship and given a special power and a special mission. The latter is to help the aliens warn the world of its imminent destruction. However, the world, the message goes on to say, can still save itself.

The rest of the film shows attempts to communicate this important message to the public, the public's inability to grasp the message, and Shirley's eventual insanity when she realizes that she cannot fulfill her heroic mission and help the aliens warn humankind. The aliens try to warn people using a radio message. Few hear it; some, for example Shirley's fiancé Harold, dismiss it as a Fascist ploy. Then, the aliens try to call a meeting at Luna Park, but no one comes. So, Shirley and her friends decide to have one of the statues of someone famous and well-respected at the wax museum come to life (in a sense) and deliver the warning. Since Prince Philip is visiting Australia to open the 1956 Melbourne Olympiad, they choose his statue. Looking just like the Prince himself, the statue speaks, but no one seems to be paying any attention to his specific words. They cheer on, oblivious to what he said. Their placid oblivion may be, as Pike and Cooper suggest, a satire on the sullen complacency of the Menzies era in Australia (263–64).

Shirley's fight to get people to pay heed to the aliens' message is parallel to her fight to escape marriage to Harold, the man her parents picked for her. She seems a bit more successful in avoiding Harold than in communicating the aliens' message, but, in the end, she loses the marital battle as well. The film then flashes us forward to 1960, showing us Shirley unhappy; to 1964, showing us Shirley mourning her mother's death; to 1968, showing us Shirley distressed that her little sister has become a go-go dancer; and to 1972, showing us Shirley in a psychiatric ward. When we are with Shirley in the ward, we tend to see the world from her point of view. Thus, it is at this point that we have to work our way through some of the most bizarre footage in the film. It seems as if Shirley is raped by a bandage-wrapped man while in the ward. Whether a nightmare or a reality, the scene suggests her total disempowerment. In fact, he says to her that when he pulls his penis out of her, all the power will flow out. This remark returns us to what the aliens said to Shirley. She was just an ordinary Australian teenage girl. When they chose her to help deliver their mission, they said that they were putting within her—making her almost pregnant with—the power to do the job. The rape, then, takes this power (that had made her gifted) away from her.

THE CARS THAT ATE PARIS (PETER WEIR, DIRECTOR, 1974)

Sharman's film is difficult to figure out because of the way it is filmed. Weir's *The Cars That Ate Paris* is filmed very straightforwardly; instead, it is the plot that makes the film difficult to figure out. Gradually, if one closely follows the plot, a conspiracy is revealed. The number of road accidents near the town of Paris has increased dramatically. Several drivers report blinding flashes of light before they crash. The crash victims who survive often find themselves in the town's expanding hospital, expanding because it has become a center for medical and psychiatric research. The surviving crash victims are the subjects. They populate the hospital—which is described as consisting of "veggies," "half-veggies," and "quarter-veggies." It seems as if nobody who drops in to the hospital via a road accident ever leaves Paris.

One would think that some evil physician was behind the conspiracy. As the movie continues, we discover that it is not a physician but, rather, a gang of bizarrely decorated cars that are in control. Their "game," perhaps, is to transform all humans into "veggies" of one degree or another. These cars have the people of Paris cowed, and the cars make sure that anyone who comes to Paris either conforms or is eliminated. Both Pike and Cooper (277–78) and Rattigan (78–79) pin the blame on the delinquent drivers, leading the latter to complain about two not very well integrated plots of medical experimentation and youthful rebellion. I think they fail to see the truly bizarre satire of Australia's car culture and the send-up of horror movies implicit in having the cars be the enemy.

Into Paris comes our hero with the unheroic name of Arthur Waldo (Terry Camilleri). He survives a wreck and the hospital. When he tries to leave Paris, two older cars scare him back into the town. He later witnesses a gang of cars playing out in the open while the people of the town are in church, but Arthur does not realize completely what he has seen. He later goes for a walk into the countryside. A sinister-looking car, "driven" by the mayor, follows, keeping tabs on Arthur. The mayor seems quite fond of Arthur; so he arranges for Arthur to assume the job of superintendent of parking. For reasons not entirely clear, the cars dislike this arrangement and attack the mayor's house.

Emboldened, Arthur, like a hero in an American western, challenges the cars. Of course, he thinks he is challenging their youthful "drivers." The mayor, with a soothing gesture toward one of the cars, causes them to back down. But they do not stay pacified for long. They appear finally in their bizarre glory and surround the town of Paris, making wild animal noises. The cars then attack, and the townspeople fight back. Arthur, in the midst of the battle, flees. The music at least suggests that Arthur will make it back to "civilization," but the mayor's distraught look suggests that the townspeople are about to be devoured by the monstrous cars.

Arthur Waldo's heroism, then, is very limited in its effect. He can save himself from the marauding cars, but he cannot save Paris. This failure could be read within the conventions of the horror film genre in which it is not unusual for the forces of evil to triumph over all except the fortunate few who escape. Most, however, think Weir is doing more in this film than writing and directing a horror film. Insofar as it is cars that are the attacking force, Weir may well be suggesting how the car culture has taken over Australia, turning the people into zombies of a sort because, as they tool along in their little metallic conveyances, they rarely interact as they did once upon a time.

As noted earlier, not all who view the movie see the cars as being, at crucial moments, unmanned. These viewers put angry young people always at the wheel, even though at times our view of them is obscured. If this viewing is correct, then Weir may well be suggesting how the youth culture has taken over Australia, turning adults into figures of impotence. In conjunction with this interpretation, it may be relevant that the Australian economy was suffering at the time the film was made. In the film, both the prime minister and the mayor talk lamely about how there is "a light at the end of the tunnel." Perhaps this empty rhetoric is Weir's way of showing how impotent the adult generations have become in an arena—economics—more serious than the absurd battle fought against young people and their bizarre automobiles depicted in *The Cars That Ate Paris.*

MAD MAX (DR. GEORGE MILLER, DIRECTOR, 1979)

Mad Max was an incredibly low-budget film. It attracted a fair amount of attention in Australia, but not much outside the country. *Mad Max II* (1981), with a somewhat higher budget, quickly attracted international attention, especially attention in the United States, where it was released as *The Road Warrior.* That attention led to the re-release of *Mad Max* abroad and inspired *Mad Max beyond Thunderdome* (1985). The three films are, therefore, linked by their production history as well as by the presence of Mel Gibson in the lead role. However, as the discussion in this chapter should suggest, the films are strikingly different. Max as hero comes across very differently: in *Mad Max*, he is an avenger; in *Mad Max II*, a hero for hire; and in *Mad Max beyond Thunderdome*, a reluctant hero. These differences are, to some extent, because the situations in the three films are not the same.

Each film takes us further into the future. We discover in *Mad Max II* that nuclear war has driven the world into anarchy, but that premise is absent from *Mad Max.* In the initial film, anarchy has settled on Australia; however, we are not entirely sure why. We just know that we are somewhat in the future—although not too far—and anarchy reigns on the highways. Two groups are competing for control of the roads: an evil-looking gang and a uniformed force. Appearances suggest that the former represents lawlessness, the latter law. However, the situation is not that simple because, in the anarchic world, the law oftentimes behaves just like the lawless. In fact, revenge seems to be the primary motivating force behind the actions of both groups.

Max Rockatansy (Mel Gibson) patrolling the anarchic highways in *Mad Max* (1979). Photo courtesy of National Film and Sound Archives. Permission granted by Kennedy Miller Productions.

If the gang kills a member of Max's "highway patrol," Max gets even. If a member of Max's group kills a member of the gang, the gang gets even. What tilts the audience more in favor of Max's side than the other—than it already is, based on their appearances—is that the gang goes after Max's young wife and child. The gang's brutal murder of them makes it easy for the audience to collude with Max and overlook the violent revenge Max then enacts. We might think that in a world where innocents are murdered, we need avengers such as Max, a world fit for the likes of Clint Eastwood's character Harry Callahan (McFarlane 48–49; Rattigan 191). If we so think, then we probably find the highway patrol chief's speech to Max about the world needing heroes rousing. However, we should note that no sooner does Fifi, the chief, deliver the speech than he himself makes fun of it. The world we have entered in *Mad Max* is not one characterized by easily identified "good guys" versus easily identified "bad guys." Heroism is, therefore, no longer a matter of wearing the right colored hat.

The world is characterized by fast-moving cars and fast-moving motorcycles. Weir, in *The Cars That Ate Paris*, and Miller, in this film, suggest how attuned to fast cars the Australian culture is. But whereas in Weir's satire the cars have succeeded in blotting out much in the way of human feelings as one by one people become transformed into zombies either through being the victims of medical experimentation or by serving as the emotionally numb experimenters, in Miller's *Mad Max* human feelings are still alive. We see them in the anger Max feels when those he loves are killed; we see them in the loving scenes shared by Max, his wife, and his son. But racing vehicles are on the screen far more than these emotional moments, suggesting along what lines this future world is developing. If heroes are laughable now, what will they be down the road when anarchy and violence become not just common, but normal?

MAD MAX II (A.K.A. *THE ROAD WARRIOR*) (DR. GEORGE MILLER, DIRECTOR, 1981)

Miller's film takes us several years further into the future. We are told at the film's beginning how the world became the place it is. We are also told that Max, because of the emotional impact of the murder of his wife and son, is now emotionally dead, drifting from place to place in his modified (to increase its speed) automobile. He has become a scavenger, living off of what he finds as he drifts. An especially valuable commodity is fuel. He needs it for his car, but whole societies seem to need it to rebuild life after the nuclear catastrophe that a war over oil seems to have set in motion.

Max (Mel Gibson) defends himself against the gyropilot (Bruce Spence) in *Mad Max II* (1981). Photo courtesy of National Film and Sound Archives. Permission granted by Kennedy Miller Productions.

While scavenging, Max stumbles upon a community that has a large supply of oil because it has mining and refining capacity. The people in this community dress fairly normally. They have marriages and families; they believe in law and democracy. In other words, they strike Max (and us) as embodying the values of "the time before." These people are under attack by a marauding gang that appears very different, with spiked hair, lots of leather, lots of chains, and lots of bare skin. The gang is violent, and that violence (a murder and a rape) confirms us in our judgment that the gang is the "evil" side in the battle. However, the gang clearly features close human relationships (even if homoerotic) among members and closely observed laws. The audience easily chooses sides; however, on closer analysis, the two sides are less "good" and "evil" and more two different ways of regulating living: one familiar; the other "other."

The audience chooses sides before Max does. Max simply wants fuel for his car. He does the bidding of the familiar or good side not because he believes in their society or in their right to the oil but because they are willing to pay him. When he finishes the job, he expects to be paid and allowed to leave. Although some in the society want to compel this "hero" to stay, the leader keeps his word, pays Max, and prepares to send him back to the outback desert. Unfortunately, the marauding gang's presence outside the community's gates makes it all but impossible for Max to leave safely. Meanwhile, the community is planning to leave en masse for a safer location on Australia's north shore. The community wishes to take the stockpiled oil with them because it will be necessary to the economy in their new location. If Max stays behind when they all flee, his chances of survival are minimal. So, he chooses to drive the oil carrier for them. Max, it should be noted, is choosing his best chance at surviving, not heroism.

The concluding twenty minutes of *Mad Max II* is the exciting chase through the desert, as the marauding gang tries to stop Max's truck and he, and accompanying members of the community, try to get the oil through. Max fails and succeeds in his mission. He does not get the oil through, mainly because his truck was filled with sand, not oil. It was a diversion, and, as such, it worked because going another way, most of the community and the oil make it to the north shore. Max himself simply vanishes into the desert. As the voice of the community's future leader tells us, he was never seen again—at least by that community. The voice, however, makes it clear that Max is chronicled by his people as one of its heroes.

Max's success in *Mad Max II* exceeds his success in *Mad Max*. In the original film, he successfully gains revenge against those who murdered his wife and child; in *Mad Max II*, he helped an entire people survive and thrive. His success far exceeds that of Shirley Thompson, who cannot get the people to listen to the aliens' message, and Arthur Waldo, who gets himself out of Paris but no others. In general then, these films that ask what if, end by showing very limited space for heroism in the scenarios they create. And, as in *Mad Max II*, when there seems to be space, the hero does not want it, and the people are not entirely honest about the task he is to take on.

Mad Max II may not be "one of the finest films ever made in Australia" (Adrian Martin in Murray, *Australian Film* 78); however, it is not worthy of the condemnation of Phillip Adams' review in *The Bulletin*, the French banning of the film, or the "R" rating based on its overall tone (qtd. in Stratton, *Avocado* 82–83). It has tinges of the traditional American western mixed with elements of Kurosawa's Japanese warrior films (Rattigan 197; Stratton, *Avocado* 83). And it is no more distressingly violent than either. In addition, it is masterfully filmed by Dean Semmler. The negative responses it received in some quarters may simply be because it was not another beautiful period piece.

GOODBYE PARADISE (CARL SCHULTZ, DIRECTOR, 1983)

Schultz' film is a campy cross between Bogart and speculation. The film takes us to Surfer's Paradise on Queensland's Gold Coast. There, amid the glitter and the seediness of a resort not unlike Raymond Chandler's Los Angeles, we follow a former deputy police commissioner named Michael Stacey (Rattigan 144–45). He is writing a book, purported to be something of an exposé, which is attracting the unwanted attention of those who fear what he might say. He is also working for an ambitious senator, whose daughter has become "lost" in the Gold Coast's seediness. Senator McCredie wants Stacey to find Kathy before she causes a scandal that undermines his ambitions.

Stacey is not successful in finding her. Instead he finds a look-alike who has become a prostitute and tries to help her deal with the alcohol- and drug-induced state she is in; however, she dies under mysterious circumstances during the night in a hotel room Stacey had rented. On his way home, Stacey is badly beaten by thugs. Once he gets home, he discovers that his apartment has been vandalized. Then, McCredie tells him that his services as detective are no longer needed. But Stacey does not give up. Perhaps because he is not about to let others think he can be intimidated, he continues his search for the girl and finds her in "New Eden," a commune built in the Queensland mountains by former Senator Todd. He convinces Kathy to leave the commune for a few days and go see her distraught parents. When Stacey and Kathy arrive at her parents' house, they find that McCredie has died under mysterious circumstances.

Ray Barrett plays the lead role in a manner that consciously evokes Humphrey Bogart. The use of Stacey's voice as occasional narrator is also reminiscent of Bogart's film noir ventures. Instead of Casablanca, however, we get the Gold Coast, but its seediness and its danger seem exaggerated. Instead of a posh resort strip, we get decadence. The decadence lures some, such as Stacey, into alcoholism and many younger others into a world of drug addiction and prostitution. Schultz, of course, played off of elements that can be found along the Gold Coast; however, he deliberately exaggerated them, speculating about how things would be should the decadent touches become the prevailing color.

Speculating about increased decadence is not the only speculating scriptwriters Denny Lawrence and Bob Ellis and director Schultz do. They also speculate along political lines. Queensland, as Australians would know, has been fertile ground for right-wing politics down through the years. In fact, right now, the reactionary "One Nation" Party finds most of its strength in this northeastern state; then, it was the similar Bjelke-Petersen National Party government (Stratton, *Avocado* 235). So, in keeping with this political image, the filmmakers posit, first, political activism for a Gold Coast free state—free of Queensland and maybe even free of Australia—and, then, right-wing military activity that will make this free state a reality. The new state's economic boon will be offshore drilling for oil, something that Australia as a whole seems opposed to for environmental reasons. Keep in mind that the shore under discussion here is just south of the Great Barrier Reef, the fragile ecosystem that is one of Australia's treasures. That the new state will have significant oil has, evidently, prompted some American involvement on the side of those who are planning to launch a coup and proclaim Gold Coast independence.

McCredie has been involved in this right-wing political activity, but has evidently tried to withdraw when the plans turned violent. Thus, he was assassinated. "New Eden" is but a cover for the base that is training those who will stage the coup, although many of the commune's residents are totally unaware that their paradise has this sinister side. Stacey stumbles into these political goings-on while he is searching for Kathy. He is enough of a cop still to sense what he has inadvertently discovered.

Can he do anything, however? The answer is not much. He saves his own life—barely—but he cannot save some of the people he loves the most. And his assistance in stopping the coup seems unnecessary. In an over-the-top ending that screenwriter Ellis hated but director Schultz loved, the Australian forces already know and are readying a preemptive strike—to the tune of the "1812 Overture," used at the time of the filming in Australian army recruiting advertisements—against the rebels (Stratton, Rattigan 146; *Avocado* 235–36). Rather than being a hero, Stacey is reduced to being a surviving spectator.

Stacey's relative impotence in the situation he stumbles into is perhaps signaled in the film in two ways. First, he is not at all making progress writing his book; in fact, his missing of deadlines set by the publisher has put the entire project in doubt. Second, his excessive consumption of alcohol has caused the blood flow to his brain to slow, causing him to suffer occasional blackouts. Thus, for physical reasons as well as, perhaps, psychological and emotional reasons, Stacey just does not have the "stuff" to be a hero.

There are two ways, then, to read the answer the film offers to the question of the possibility of heroism in the future world it projects. The first would treat Stacey as an isolated case and draw no conclusions about heroism, in general, from his failure. The second would treat Stacey as a product of this future environment and draw a general conclusion from his failure. I would suggest that the latter reading seems truer to the film, which creates in its depiction of Surfer's Paradise an atmosphere of fatigue, ennui, and seediness that fits Stacey quite well. As a reflection of what the place, accurately read as more than just a corner of Queensland, has become, Michael Stacey suggests that the heroic spirit is no more. We do not have room in this film's what-if future for the Australian hero we have seen in many motion pictures. We only have comically overblown rebels and patriots who absurdly battle while audience members think of "Quaker Puffed Oats," long advertised with the overture as its theme music. If only the political speculation was entirely absurd, then the film would be entirely campy. As it is, *Goodbye Paradise*, is campy with a scary twist.

THE RETURN OF CAPTAIN INVINCIBLE (PHILIPPE MORA, DIRECTOR, 1983)

Mora's film may have been pitched primarily at an American audience (an orientation made even more pronounced when producer Andrew Gaty re-edited the film to make the U.S. version even more American in content) (Stratton, *Avocado* 79). Thus, its campy hero, Captain Invincible (Alan Arkin) is an American superhero, and the evil that he will eventually encounter is presented as taking place in the New York metropolitan area. Australia, however, lurks in the motion picture's background. Not only is it the setting for much of the film, but it seems to be very much what Mora has in mind when offering the United States. The United States then becomes Australia in disguise. Perhaps the disguise was indeed an attempt to attract American viewers, but it may also have been a way of veiling Australia's problem from Australia—just long enough to get the film's Australian audience over a knee-jerk reaction against the film's political message.

When we first meet Captain Invincible, he is drunk, lying near the Harbour Bridge in Sydney. What has driven this hero to drink and to Australia? Flashbacks, creatively using newsreel footage, show us how Invincible, a hero in the American World War II effort, was victimized in the 1950s by U.S. Senator Joseph McCarthy's investigations into supposed Communist activities. Being labeled a Communist, Invincible left the United States. He thinks that, since then, the United States has changed for the worse. Rampant greed has taken over, replacing the patriotic spirit best represented by Kate Smith's "God Bless America." So, he came to Australia, stayed, and, falling prey to alcohol, became a drunk.

The film then takes us into the future. The evil villain Mr. Midnight (Christopher Lee) has used the giggle gun to capture the hypno-gun. With this weapon, Midnight is convincing people from various "other" cultures to buy land and a home in a new waterfront development in the New York City area. Once Midnight has them all gathered there, his plan is to commit genocide, thereby ridding the United States of these unwanted "others." As one of the film's many mediocre songs (most written by the same duo that scored Jim Sharman's *The Rocky Horror Picture Show*) tells us, "What the world needs right now is a hero." Therefore, Invincible is recruited and reeducated in heroism.

His reeducation is not easy. He has lost almost all of his superhuman powers, and he is so depressed by what he sees in the world that he is not extremely well motivated to do the work necessary to regain them. In addition, alcohol has gotten its clutches into Invincible. Kate Smith's singing "God Bless America" over the "American Eagle Network," broadcasting one last time, rouses Invincible, and he saves the day, defeating Mr. Midnight's genocidal plan.

So, the hero triumphs in this what-if scenario. However, a number of elements prevent one from taking Captain Invincible's heroism seriously. The general campiness of the film, seen especially in its costuming and its musical numbers, deflates the heroism. So do Invincible's periodic very politically incorrect sexist remarks and the fact that he is barely able to rise to his former greatness—ironically, only rising because of a woman's inspiring voice—and defeat evil. However, if we cannot take the heroism seriously, we can take the evil seriously. Although Mr. Midnight's plot is presented somewhat comically, it is clearly premised on a racism and a xenophobia that are so extreme that they lead to potential mass murder.

The United States is not without its racism and xenophobia. However, given Australia's "White Australia" policy and the resentment of many when the policy was changed, the evil depicted in the film seems to be more Australian than American. Therefore, since the film also shows the heroism necessary to overcome the evil in almost parodic terms, the film seems to be suggesting that there is an ugly problem in Australia that cannot be easily overcome by summoning a superhero. There is no Mr. Midnight planning something Hitleresque. However, Australians watching the film should not forget that their ancestors were responsible for attempts to exterminate aborigines back in the nineteenth century, and their elders were behind the "White Australia" policy that ruled supreme early in the twentieth.

Peter Carey's fiction has proven popular, in and out of Australia. Its bizarre humor and its far-fetched scenarios are probably two of the reasons for its popularity. Both of these defining characteristics makes it difficult to translate his work from print to film. In the next chapter, we will consider how Gillian Armstrong attempts to do so in *Oscar and Lucinda* (1997) by making the film much more of a pure period piece than the novel. In this chapter, we will consider two other directors' attempts to effect the transformation: Ray Lawrence's in *Bliss* and Brian Trenchard-Smith's in *Dead-End Drive-In* (1986).

BLISS (RAY LAWRENCE, DIRECTOR, 1985)

Like many postmodern writers, Carey gives us a time that is not past, present, or future and a place that is not Australia or America or any other place in particular. The film *Bliss*, because it must render time and place in more definitive visual terms, rejects this postmodern vagueness for a time slightly in the future and a place that is clearly Australia, although Carey and his advertising agency mate Lawrence, who collaborated on the screenplay, do not stress the place that much so that the film's satire might have a broader reach. The future scenario the film offers features greed, derived largely from America, as having pushed decency aside. Most of the characters are caught up in this greed, some in bizarre ways. Bettina Joy (Lynette Curran) wants all that money can buy, as does Bettina's husband's American business partner. The two of them celebrate their mutual devotion to money by carrying on an affair behind husband Harry Joy's (Barry Otto) back. Harry and Bettina's children are also affected. Son David (Miles Buchanan) is heavily into drugs—not using them but selling them to his peers. He even sells them to his little sister Lucy (Gia Carides) in exchange for fellatio. Somehow in this future world, money, sex, and drugs become merged in an evil that seems contagious. Even Harry Joy has become caught up in the evil until the day he has a near-death experience. That experience causes Harry to become a changed man.

Harry Joy rejects the materialism that he sees all around him. That rejection, as well as some of Harry's admittedly bizarre behavior, results in his wife's institutionalizing him in a mental asylum. She acts against Harry to save the advertising agency. Such acting, however, also makes it easier for her to carry on her affair with partner Joel (Jeff Truman).

Along the way, Harry meets Honey Barbara (Helen Jones), a free-spirited hippie from a lush valley amid mountains. Unfortunately, financial problems in that valley have forced Honey to the city, where she is selling her body to make money to send back home. Honey does not allow her spirit to be sullied by what she is doing, however. And that spirit inspires Harry to break totally free from the urban environment that has become infected with materialism.

Unfortunately, to break free, he must first get out of the mental asylum. The only way out is a corrupt business deal with Bettina, a deal that represents a betrayal of Honey Barbara. The deal done, Honey flees for the mountains. Harry flees after her, intent on earning her trust and love again. He spends eight years, living near her and growing trees. When the trees are mature enough to flower and feed her bees, she tastes in the resulting honey his repentance and re-embraces him. They live a long life together in that edenic mountain valley until Harry dies, ironically killed by one of the trees that he had planted. His soul this time rises from his body, not to return into it as had happend before.

Harry is an unlikely hero. When we first meet him, we would undoubtedly say he does not look the part. His behavior is so wishy-washy that we would also conclude he does not and could not act the part. Experiencing near death, seeing the corrupt world for what it is, and meeting Honey Barbara change Harry. He becomes heroic. His heroism, however, is largely that of renunciation. It does take courage to renounce the only world he has ever known. I do not want to slight the act. However, such renouncing has little effect on anybody else. The world goes on, perhaps on a self-destructive course (as proves to be the case with Bettina), but Harry's action does not push the world one way or another. So, his heroism, if measured in worldly impact, seems minimal.

Measuring in terms of worldly impact, however, is precisely what the film wants us not to do. And the film (and book) offers other terms: for example, the years of tending young trees that Harry Joy spends to win back the love of Honey Barbara. He fights no battles. The typical ways of talking about heroic fights—the arduousness and the odds against him, for example—do not quite fit. He does work hard, but what he demonstrates as hero is not labor as much as love. In embracing love as he does without any guarantee at all of receiving anything in return, Harry totally rejects the evil that had surrounded him in his earlier city life. The quiet embracing of this love makes him heroic, but in terms that are different from those we have seen elsewhere in Australian film. This is not to say that love has been absent from the picture, but that love in films such as *The Man from Snowy River* (1982), *Cool Change* (1986), *Crocodile Dundee* (1986), and *The Lighthorsemen* has been accompanied by action, not ever-patiently waiting.

MAD MAX BEYOND THUNDERDOME (DR. GEORGE MILLER AND GEORGE OGILVIE, DIRECTORS, 1985)

The transition from *Bliss* to the third film dealing with "Mad Max" would seem to be one from ever-patiently waiting back to action. However, *Mad Max beyond Thunderdome* is less of an action film than its two predecessors. In *Mad Max*, Max chose to enact revenge; in *Mad Max II*, Max is hired to do the bidding of a society he stumbles upon and then "chooses" to do the further bidding of because the alternative is probably death. The degree of choosing is, I would suggest, diminishing. It further diminishes in *Mad Max beyond Thunderdome*, in which Max tries to choose not to act. Max acts—and the film features action—only because he is virtually compelled to.

Mad Max beyond Thunderdome has a tripartite structure. In the first part, we are in Bartertown (filmed near Sydney), a place whose politics are difficult to figure out. Max wanders in. He is "recruited" by Aunty Entity (played by rock diva Tina Turner) to fight Blaster in Thunderdome. At stake seems to be control of Bartertown, the political contest being between Aunty Entity and a dwarf named Master who usually sits atop Blaster's shoulders. Aunty Entity, as she talks with Max, makes it seem as if Master is the evil force, she the beneficent. So, when Max is forced to fight for Aunty Entity, we are not unduly upset. The coercion may disturb us, but at least he is on the "right" side.

As the battle game in Thunderdome progresses to its end, we see Aunty and Master–Blaster differently. Blaster is but a feebleminded child. Max, therefore, in violation of the rules, will not kill him. One of Aunty Entity's followers does, however, leaving Master with his beloved Blaster's body to cry over. Aunty then declares that, since Max violated the rules, he must "face the wheel" that will select his punishment. As we read the choices, we realize that most entail Max's death. At this point, we begin to see Aunty as the "evil" one and the grieving Master as the "good one." However, we also begin to feel that the future world we have entered in this film is not as simple as "evil" versus "good."

In the second part of the film, Max is rescued from imminent death by a group of teenagers and children who are living together in an oasis of sorts in the desert (filmed in the Blue Mountains). Max had been sent out into that desert by Aunty, bound and blinded by a clown's head stuck on his. The teenagers and children—"The Waiting Ones"—believe Max to be their long-anticipated savior Captain Walker. They have preserved orally the story of what had happened to the world of skyscrapers and how they all escaped from that world to the place they now live. They have drawn pictures on the walls of caves; they even have a viewmaster and a few slides of the time before. The Waiting Ones now expect Max, as Captain Walker, to fly them back to the city. They even have the aircraft waiting for the return trip.

Max has to disappoint The Waiting Ones: he has to tell them both that he is not Captain Walker and that the world they wish to return to is gone. They do not want to believe the disappointing news they are hearing. At this point, a disgruntled group of Waiting Ones takes off for Bartertown. Knowing that they will not survive there and owing his life to them, Max chooses to lead a rescue mission.

The third part is the rescue mission (filmed primarily near Coober Pedy in southern Australia). The rescue becomes entangled with helping those who are trying to rebel against Aunty Entity. Thus, Max becomes a hero not just to The Waiting Ones he is saving but to those who have been oppressed under Aunty Entity's rule. As in *Mad Max II*, the last twenty minutes or so is very kinetic. Basically, two groups are trying to flee. The oppressed of Bartertown, including Master, have joined forces with The Waiting Ones. First by rail and then by Jedediah's airplane (not Captain Walker's 707), they try to escape. Max is fending off the onslaught of Aunty Entity's forces that are intent on stopping the flight. Max succeeds in fighting off the pursuers, allowing the joined forces to go off and found a new society. Max will be remembered in its legends as a hero. However, at the end of the film, Max is left behind, standing with Aunty Entity. Rather than kill him, she and her forces just leave him there alone. We imagine he might die or he might wander into another settlement, such as Bartertown, out there in the wasteland. Before leaving Max, Aunty says, "Ain't we a pair." She seems to be recognizing that they are both without commitments, doing whatever is necessary to survive.

More often than not, the music over a film's closing credits is not an important part of a film. In this case, the music may sound an important final note. Tina Turner sings "We Don't Need Another Hero." In her role as Aunty Entity, the title line suggests that, in the grim circumstances of the post-nuclear-war world, heroism is a silly idea. The world is populated by those who survive and those who do not. She and Max are of the former sort, but not heroes. But later in the song, The Waiting Ones sing the same line. Their message seems different. They do not need another hero because they have two: Captain Walker, who led them out of the dying city of Sydney, and Max, who helped them return. The film, however, makes it clear that neither Captain Walker nor Max are what The Waiting Ones' legends make them out to be. They are heroes in those legends; in reality, they are something different. This discrepancy calls into question the whole notion of heroism, just as Aunty Entity's "take" on the common bond between herself and Max does.

DEAD-END DRIVE-IN (BRIAN TRECHARD-SMITH, DIRECTOR, 1986)

Much more heroic is the story of Crabs in *Dead-End Drive-In*, a film adapted from Peter Carey's short story "Crabs." The film takes us several years into the future. Something has clearly gone wrong, but as in *Mad Max*, it is not entirely clear why Sydney or Australia has descended into borderline anarchy. All we know is that automobile crashes seem to have increased in this "car culture" and that, whenever there is a wreck, a gang of Karboys battle a group of tow-truck operators for "the remains." As in the first two "Mad Max" movies, we tend to side with the tow-truck operators because they look less bizarre and act more normal than the crazed Karboys. However, viewed objectively, there is not the stark difference that there initially seems to be between the two groups.

The government must think that there is a threat from youth in general because when would-be tow-truck driver named Crabs (Ned Manning) goes to the drive-in theater with his girlfriend Carmen, he falls into a trap that the government has set. The drive-in, you see, is not really a drive-in but a prison of sorts. The young people who go in cannot leave and must therefore form some sort of society in the drive-in, living in their cars and eating their meals at the drive-in's snack bar. The society they form is a parody of Australian society at large. The film targets the competitiveness and superficiality and the sexism of much Australian society, as well as the readiness of members of the society to conform to whatever the latest norm is. Thus, most of the male residents become concerned with who is in charge when, really, none of them are in charge, while most of the female residents are concerned with their hair and their makeup. The one event that brings male and female together is their outrage and opposition when the government carts in wrecked automobiles and then Asians to live in them. The residents' reaction and the meetings they hold are the film's satirical glance at the "White Australia" movement and how that movement's sentiments are still alive today, even among the nation's young.

The film, and the Carey story it was based on, is satirical. In that satire, the futuristic, speculative dimension of the motion picture sometimes gets lost. The film is clearly making a statement about Australian society in 1986, but it is also asking what if: What if society loses its glue, gangs roam the streets making them unsafe, and the government must crack down, rather indiscriminately, to maintain a semblance of order? The answer the film seems to provide is that most will simply surrender to whatever the "new reality" is. Some may even squabble over social or political position in it, even if it is a rendition of the "old" but with many of the freedoms of the "old" lacking.

The exception in the film is Crabs. He refuses to conform. He confronts the theater's manager, trying to find a way out and, then, berating him for keeping the drive-in's inmates docile by dispensing drugs. He confronts his girlfriend about how willingly she is conforming. Initially, Crabs wants to get out because he has his brother's car and is afraid of what his brother will say and do when he discovers it is gone, especially if it does not come back intact. So, Crabs initially prowls the grounds looking for Chevy wheels to replace the ones that have been pulled off the vehicle to immobilize it. Gradually, Crabs' focus seems to shift from getting wheels for the sake of getting wheels to getting wheels because they are necessary to escape to freedom. Then, the desire for freedom takes over. The Chevy, now without a motor, is irrelevant; gaining freedom becomes his chief desire. What others who have settled into the drive-in environment think does not matter; what Carmen thinks does not matter. The Asians, for example, are not the enemy to Crabs but fellow prisoners (Philippa Hawler in Murray, *Australian Film* 189). He will escape; he will gain the freedom that "the authorities" have taken away from him.

The last twenty minutes of *Dead-End Drive-In* are as kinetic as the endings of *Mad Max II* and *Mad Max beyond Thunderdome*. Crabs steals a police tow truck and the chase is on, around and around the drive-in grounds, with crashes causing fires, which quickly spread. Panic seizes the residents. As they watch Crabs' escape attempt, it is not at all clear whether they are cheering him on or jeering his destruction of their happy surrogate homes.

Finally, Crabs finds a way to leap—a record leap for a stunt car driver—the electrified fence that keeps those in the drive-in from escaping on foot (Stratton, *Avocado* 287). There is a gleam in his eyes as the truck lands beyond the fence and he finds himself on the road back to Sydney proper. The film then ends on what seems to be a positive note.

As I suggested in a 1999 article in *Antipodes*, those who have read Carey's story might read the ending differently. In the story, when Crabs makes his leap he finds himself, somehow, back inside the fence. He wanders for a bit in the truck, but, when he finds his way to a drive-in gate, he strangely finds that he is still on its inside. Carey is, of course, playing with reality a bit, suggesting, in a "Twilight Zone" twist, that one can never escape the drive-in. There are, however, few if any hints of this ending in the film. There are, nonetheless, a few notes that should, on reflection, cause one to be a little less happy at Crabs' escape. As already noted, through his escape he has probably destroyed the drive-in society, a comfortable if oppressive home to hundreds. His escape to freedom has had a price that others will have to pay. Furthermore, he has escaped into a society that is so anarchic that the government felt imprisonment of youth to be necessary. It was Karboys versus tow-truck drivers before.

Crabs, harassed by the former, was judged too "small" to be among the latter. That situation has not changed during the days he has been "at the movies"; in fact, it may have worsened. There may be a pitched battle being fought in the streets, and Crabs is vulnerable, not being a member of either side. At the drive-in, Crabs was safe; out in the streets of Sydney, he may become a victim—either an innocent one or one targeted by the Karboys because they know Crabs is tow-truck driver Frank's little brother.

Dead-End Drive-In is scripted and filmed so as to suggest a flight, literally, to freedom. Just as Carey's story very clearly takes away the illusion of freedom it gives to make the point that freedom is no longer possible, Trenchard-Smith's film may plant disturbing notions in viewers' minds so that, after the exhilaration of the ending fades, they begin to think about what Crabs' escape has cost others and what Crabs' escape has gained Crabs. To the extent these notions bother viewers, then Crabs' heroic fight for freedom becomes less something to celebrate and more something to regret. In other words, Trenchard-Smith may be counting on viewers to get themselves to the point that Carey's story very clearly leads readers to: the point of rejecting the heroism on display as Pyrrhic and empty.

DALLAS DOLL (ANN TURNER, DIRECTOR, 1993)

In Ann Turner's film, American comedienne Sandra Bernhard plays a foreigner (an American) who has come to Australia, ostensibly as a motivational speaker who helps people deal with postmodernity by conducting soul-baring group sessions. This visitor, named Dallas Doll, is preceded by her reputation as a champion golfer, and, during an early "therapy" session, she reveals the sad story of her life. As it turns out, neither the golfing legend nor the sad tale proves true, leaving both the people she is visiting and the audience wondering about her true past. As the film progresses, talk about aliens increases. And, at the film's end, an alien spaceship lands. Although the film never commits itself one way or the other, the implication is that Dallas Doll is not the American she claims to be, but an alien invader.

If she is an alien invader, what is the nature of her invasion? She initially seems to have a liberating power, causing the family she stays with to lose its inhibitions. She seduces both the father and the son. Then, after a game of indoor strip golf, she seduces the mother. Only the daughters in the family—both young—do not succumb to Dallas' spell. The daughters, in fact, resist Dallas' influence as if they, in some way, intuit that she represents something otherworldly.

Sexuality is not the only area in which Dallas loosens things up. The mother, who is rather wealthy, is seduced into shoplifting just for the thrill of it. The son is taught, by Dallas' example, how to lie and manipulate his way to the top of the business world.

What Dallas seems to be able to do is not lead people against their wills but, rather, cajole them into taking courses they deep inside want to take but do not. She, in other words, removes inhibitions. As a result, people become their core selves, as opposed to presenting various facades to the world. Thus, what Dallas reveals is that the adult family members are sexually repressed: the mother wants a few thrills in her otherwise safe, predictable life, and the son is really very deviously power-hungry and greedy.

The game of strip indoor golf, although silly, is perhaps emblematic of what goes on in general in the film. Because of Dallas' influence, characters strip off facades and stand in their "nakedness" before themselves and before others. But what, you may ask, does this process have to do with Australia? The family Dallas visits, I would suggest, represents upper-class Australia. For this class, the facades are many. What the film reveals, then, is the repression, dullness, hunger for power, and greed that may characterize this class. *Dallas Doll* is very much in the tradition of satire. Thus, one should not conclude that Turner's point is that all Australians who have made it to the socioeconomic top are truly repressed and so forth. Instead, what Turner is suggesting is that many are.

Dallas' influence, it might be noted, is not restricted to the family she stays with. She also has an influence on the town. Perhaps that influence shows less in her convincing them to convert fields to golf courses and more in her convincing them to move the war memorial, found at the center of town, to the shore. They move it to the shore so that it can defend Australian shores against the onslaught of Asians. In so convincing the townspeople to move the statue, Dallas has stripped away their surface political correctness and revealed the lurking racism and xenophobia they still very much possess. Again, as satirist, Turner is not suggesting that all Australians are fiercely anti-Asian but that this prejudice is there in the hearts and minds of many.

As the film draws near its conclusion, people become progressively less and less comfortable with Dallas' presence. The son, Charlie, becomes so power-hungry that, seeing Dallas now as a rival, he decides he must find a way to discredit her. The mother, on the other hand, gradually begins to see that Dallas' influence is not altogether positive. In the end, she drives Dallas off with a shotgun. After Dallas' death, at the "hands" of either alien invaders and/or stampeding cattle led by the dog Dallas earlier shot, the mother is still hostile. She refuses to sell her family land for the golf course complex Dallas had inspired the town to plan. Although O'Regan suggests she finds herself through the liberating lesbian relationship with Dallas, I would suggest she reclaims her much earlier farm-girl self after she sees that Dallas' influence, although eye-opening, is ultimately reductive to the worst motives of human kind (*Australian* 299). She then finds herself in reaction against Dallas, not in her liberating embrace.

The mother's role in the film is the only positively heroic one. Most of the characters fall under Dallas' spell and stay captivated or, as in Charlie's case, become so influenced that there is no longer room for the both of them. The world that Dallas reveals when she strips away the polite facades is so "seedy" that it cannot produce heroism of any sort. The mother manages to escape this moral mire and drive both Dallas and her ideas off.

Chapter 8

Eccentrics

Others who have written on Australian film, most notably Susan Dermody and Elizabeth Jacka, have used the term "eccentrics" to refer to directors who followed a path other than certain well-trodden ones such as filming period or social realism films (*The Screening*). For example, Paul Cox, who typically does quiet, very European pieces about relationships, or Philippe Mora, who does more experimental films than the Australian norm, would be considered eccentrics.

I want to use the term somewhat differently. I want to focus not on the films' directors but on the films' central characters, the ones who are structurally, at least, heroic. Some of these characters are eccentric in the very literal sense of falling outside the circle this study has thus far inscribed to contain the variety of characters one might consider heroic That circle is big enough to include characters as varied as Tony Petersen, Archie Hamilton, Jim Craig, Mick Dundee, Darryl Kerrigan, Sybylla Melvyn, Kate Dean, Jeannie Gunn, Dotty Stubbs, and Asta Cadell as well as embrace younger characters such as Laura Rambotham, Debbie Vickers, Jo Kennedy, and Phoebe Mullins, almost embrace Black characters such as Trilby Comeaway and the three "sisters" in *Radiance* (1997), and theoretically embrace "future" heroes such as Max Rockatanksy and Harry Joy. Despite how big this circle is, it defines a type: a freedom-loving, iconoclastic, battling-against-the-odds lover of the land, horses or cars, drink and sex, and one's mates. It defines a type that is prone to embrace sexism and reject intellectualism, a type that is given to excesses, a type that will probably eventually lose whatever fight he or she is in.

Not all characters central in Australian film are of this type. Those who fall outside the circle are there either because they embody some characteristic of the Australian hero to an extreme or because they embody some quality that Australia does not seem to value. Either way, these characters and the screenwriters who create them offer a satirical look at the Australian culture. If the central character is one who takes a characteristic to an extreme and thereby falls outside the circle, then the satire is directed against that characteristic. Someone who, for example, is anti-intellectual to the point of extreme boorishness might well be a satirical glance at the anti-intellectualism of the Australian culture. If the central character, on the other hand, is one who represents some quality that the Australian culture ignores, then the satire is directed against the culture for ignoring it. Someone who, for example, values the beauty of art might well be a satirical reminder of how little a role aesthetic awareness seems to play in the Australian hero's life.

STORK (TIM BURSTALL, DIRECTOR, 1971)

Stork is one of the most striking characters in Australian film because of his height. At 6'7", Stork (Bruce Spence) towers over the other characters in this low-budget film, especially his eventual romantic interest Anna (played by petite Jacki Weaver). His size in a way suggests how he functions in both the film and the David Williamson play the film was based on. Stork is an exaggeration of the Australian hero's character: he is an extreme example of ockerism, and he is an extreme example of naïveté.

The ockerism is perhaps most evident in his rendition of the smoked-oyster-up-the-nose routine at an avant-garde art show and in his "chunderscapes" made from his beer-induced vomit. The naïvete reveals itself in his relationships with women: Anna, whose promiscuity baffles Stork, and Elaina, whose feminism scares Stork. And both ockerism and naïveté combine when he fails to grasp what is and what is not appropriate at a job interview and ends up confessing that he could not manage his bowels until he was five and therefore would not be especially good in a management position.

Both the ockerism and the naïveté are, of course, satirized. The naïveté, however, softens the ockerism somewhat, allowing Stork to function, somewhat like Voltaire's Candide, as a vehicle through which many aspects of the Australian world are mocked. He mocks academic life by (rightfully) accusing a psychology professor of "perving on the moll" (sexually harassing a coed). He unknowingly mocks pretentious art connoisseurs not only through his chunderscapes but through the serious examples of art that inspire his bizarre art form. Burstall mocks feminism through the character of Elaina, who spouts feminist ideas but, in the throes of sexual arousal, throws those ideas all away in favor of being viewed and ravaged as a sex object. And Stork and Burstall mock the institution of marriage by staging Anna's. She is pregnant, but she does not know which of the four boys she lives with is the father. She picks one and another serves as best man, while Stork first denounces the hypocrisy of this marriage and then the oppressiveness of all marriages. Through Stork's radical words and other glances at university demonstrations, Burstall sends up the radicalism of the late 1960s and early 1970s.

Stork is a rather episodic film. It lacks focus as it moves from scene to scene. It also lacks focus in what it satirizes. It almost seems as if in Williamson's and Burstall's minds, anything was fair game. In general, though, the film seems directed at those who pretend to be a noble thing but are really something less: the professor who is really a lecher, the artists who are really junk welders, the feminist who is really a wanna-be sex object, the bride who is really four boys' occasional lover, and the radicals who are really slogan-chanting, sign-wielding slugs. The point of the film, as far as the Australian culture is concerned, is that a good dose of this hypocrisy seems to characterize it.

PATRICK (RICHARD FRANKLIN, DIRECTOR, 1978)

Patrick is a horror film directed by Richard Franklin, a former University of Southern California film student and a former intern with Alfred Hitchcock (O'Regan, *Australian* 191). And a horror film may really be all it is. Good performances by Kathy Jacquard as Susan and Robert Thompson as Patrick, an effective score by Brian May and effective photography by Don McAlpine have caused commentators to take the film more seriously than perhaps they should. The film may be nothing more than entertainment, not, as McFarlane puts it "one of the liveliest films of the Australian revival" (in Murray, *Australian Film* 22). Finding an even semi-serious point in the film may be a futile task.

The central character is eccentric because he has virtually given up living. He has been comatose for years. The only demonstration that there is life in him is his periodic spitting. Dismissed by his doctor as nothing more than a muscle spasm, the spitting strikes us and several characters as having a deeper meaning. Patrick seems to be communicating his disgust for the world by spitting at its representatives.

Then, Patrick begins communicating by using psychokinetic power to operate a typewriter in his hospital room. He is inspired to communicate because he finds a soul mate in his latest nurse Susan Penhaligon. The question then is what links Patrick and Susan together. The answer might be that they have both been rejected. Patrick, like many male characters in horror films, was very attached to his mother. When he caught her with her lover, he, feeling rejected, murdered them both. Kathy is just out of a somewhat abusive relationship and on her own. Patrick may sense in Kathy a fellow victim or a fellow believer that love should be something pure and noble. Thus, he opens up to her.

No matter how much a believer in love Kathy might be, the world is still an unloving place: one of lust and betrayal. Therefore, Patrick, once roused, turns dangerous. In addition, Kathy has begun another relationship, making her just as much a traitor to him as his mother was. She is now in danger just as others are. Fortunately, those who are trying to stop Patrick do so before he succeeds in harming Kathy. The horror film, then, has its happy ending: the character we most care about survives. The film also has its kicker because there are hints that Patrick has only been temporarily stopped. Franklin certainly knows the horror genre's conventions quite well.

If *Patrick* has a message to deliver (if it is not just a horror film), then the message concerns the world Patrick escaped into a coma from which, the world that is causing Kathy problems as well. The depiction of this world as unloving may well be a comment on Australia at large. On the assumption that nothing is incidental in a film, a viewer might note that the radio broadcasts we overhear in the background talk about police corruption. These broadcasts may be another indication that things are not right with the world Kathy inhabits and Patrick has virtually withdrawn from, only to occasionally spit at it.

TIM (MICHAEL PATE, DIRECTOR, 1979)

Most people who watch *Tim* these days watch it to see Mel Gibson's pre-*Mad Max* (1979) performance in an adaptation of a Colleen McCullough novel. In the film, Gibson plays a mentally handicapped young man who gradually finds himself in a loving relationship with an older woman, the American Mary Horton (Piper Laurie). This situation could have had an "odd" feeling because of the difference in mental capacity and age. However, in general, Gibson and Laurie enact the two roles in such a way that we do not feel she is in any way "perverted" when she takes Tim as her lover and husband. The film's music by Eric Jupp is rather overdone, making the melodramatic even more. But the melodramatic touches in the film are probably what prevent the relationship from seeming perverse; the music directs us to see genuine affection, not perverseness.

The plot of the film largely centers on Tim. His family—mother, father, sister—are very close and have always been rather protective of Tim. Thus, when Tim begins spending more and more time with Mary Horton, at least the sister suspects Mary's motives. Their angry confrontation is a melodramatic moment. More so are his sister Dawnie's wedding and his mother's death. Tim is so simpleminded that both of these events have to be explained to him as if to a very small child. Then, when Tim sees Mary hugging his father (Mr. Melville) out of sympathy, Tim becomes jealous and runs off—another melodramatic moment. Mary becomes close to both father and son: in different ways, they become emotionally dependent on her. Then, after seeking a counselor's help, Mary proposes marriage to Tim—yet another melodramatic moment. Then, the marriage; then, the wedding night; then, Mr. Melville dies; then Tim tries in the spirit of love to reconcile his sister Dawnie to Mary and his marriage.

This plot summary does point to one interesting dynamic in the film as it progresses: Tim changes from being acted upon to acting. The plot less frequently swirls around Tim and more frequently finds Tim playing crucial roles. The suggestion of the film is that love has wrought this particular transformation. In fact the film is largely about the power of love.

Tim initially is left out of activities by supposed mates. We see fellow day laborers leave him behind as they go off for an after-work beer or two. He is embraced by his family, especially by Dawnie, but the embrace is an overprotective one. The family members seem happy to allow Tim to do various tasks to keep himself occupied, tending to treat these tasks much as one would treat a child's chosen games. Seeing Tim as child and treating him as such, they do not allow him to grow and experience the emotions, including love, of a man.

The film implies that the way the family treats him is very much the way society treats him, that is, not as an adult. He is often treated kindly, but implicit in that kind treatment is the assumption that he is, and will forever be, childlike. Mary Horton is not of this society. By age and by national origin, she is separate. Even though she has been living in Australia for many years, she still seems remote from it. Not, then, a fully integrated member of the society, she can depart from its assumption about Tim and embrace him in a different way. She can treat him more like an adult and thereby let him, for the first time, experience a range of adult emotions. The film hinges on her decision to treat him in this manner. With that decision, it becomes a romance with a happy ending (as in McCullough's novel) rather than an exploration of societal attitudes toward the mentally challenged (Peter Lawrance in Murray, *Australian Film* 49).

Tim grows into the adult emotions Mary evokes. At the film's conclusion, he is a much more mature and a much stronger character than in the beginning. These positive changes occur, in a sense, outside his society. The implication is that neither the trust nor the love that changes Tim really existed in the world he was living in, that he needed to find them in another world, that which gentle Mary created. This observation is certainly not a strong satirical indictment of Australian society—far from it. Nonetheless, it does cast that society in a shadow because Tim needed the sunshine of the outsider Mary to thrive.

WINTER OF OUR DREAMS (JOHN DUIGAN, DIRECTOR, 1981)

The eccentrics in Duigan's film are arguably more "normal": they are not outrageous or comatose or mentally handicapped; rather, they are thirty-year-olds who have made swerves in their lives that have taken them outside the circle. Lou's swerve was into the King's Cross district of Sydney, where she is a prostitute: Rob's was into a safe life as the proprietor of a bookshop and the denizen of a trendy Balmain neighborhood. These swerves, as different as they were, took these two outside of lives that mattered and into lives that simply drifted along.

What causes them to realize that they have drifted and what brings them together in the film is the death of thirty-year-old Liza. Her body was found dead in Sydney Harbour. Both are connected to her, but in different ways. Lou (Judy Davis) is living in Liza's former apartment and is the inadvertent custodian of some of Liza's things, including her diary from her university years. Rob (Bryan Brown) went to school with Liza in the country and on with her to the University of Sydney. There, Rob became Liza's first lover.

Liza takes Rob back to days when causes mattered more. As a result, he feels increasingly that his life almost ten years later is empty. He adheres to the liberalism of old by selling "alternative" books and magazines and by maintaining an "open" marriage with his wife Gretel. He begins to realize, however, that these are just the superficial trappings of the engaged politics that once informed his being. Because Lou links him back to Liza, Rob becomes increasingly interested in her. Initially, his interest seems to be more in Lou as a cause—a drug addict whom he can help straighten out. Later, his interest turns sexual.

Lou sees in Rob a way out of the drug addiction she suffers from and the prostitution she has turned to to feed the drug habit. She genuinely seems to want "out." But, when she goes to Rob and Gretel's home for help, she becomes distracted by their material wealth and ends up stealing money for drugs, not getting the assistance she needs. During her second time there, she goes through the nightmare of withdrawal and leaves a changed person.

Rob has lost his engagement in things that matter: Lou has lost her engagement in life. Their relationship has the potential to revivify both of them. Her way of reaching Rob is first through sex. When that does not seem to be enough to really get him into her life, she starts to play the role of Liza, almost restaging moments in Rob's relationship with the girl that Lou knows of from reading Liza's diary. This tactic seems to scare away Rob. When she invites him to lunch at her (and Liza's) flat, he declines at the last minute because earlier he had made a commitment to play in a sports match. So she ends up sitting alone in the apartment that she and Liza share. Then, she walks down to Circular Quay where an antinuclear demonstration is being held. These are the kinds of events, she knows, that engaged Rob and Liza, but her face suggests that she is disengaged still. A relationship with Rob offered her not only a way out but a way into something meaningful. She is left at the film's somewhat open conclusion temporarily out but still without meaning.

Rob chose the sports match over the lunch with Lou when he could have just as easily chosen the other way. As it turns out, he does not even play in the match. He sits in the locker room, staring. He knows he has been a coward, that he has turned his back on a relationship that might take him back, at least in spirit, to where he was ten years earlier as a university student. But rather than taking the risk, he has chosen the safe, disengaged course.

If they could become engaged in life again, Lou and Rob could be heroes. They could even be heroes as they fought their way toward engagement. Lou tries to fight, but she chooses to do so not as herself but as the deceased Liza. Her quest almost seems doomed from the start by her not yet being comfortable enough with herself to pursue life as her own person. Rob, at a crucial moment, chooses safety over the risks inherent in being engaged in life once more. The two of them are, at best, would-be heroes.

What goes wrong? They have departed from the circle in two very different directions, both typical of many Australians. Lou has chosen the decadent route, losing herself in all the King's Cross neighborhood has come to stand for: alcohol, drugs, sex. Rob has chosen the materialistic route. He has kept alive the facade of his former self in the nature of his business and the openness of his marriage; however, his focus seems to have been very much for the past decade on the accumulation of wealth and things. These are two eccentric routes, and, in the sadness of the film's ending, we can see that these two routes are being held up by Duigan as dead ends.

LONELY HEARTS (PAUL COX, DIRECTOR, 1982)

Paul Cox's film, like Duigan's *Winter of Our Dreams*, features a couple of eccentrics. In Cox's film, the "he" is middle-aged Peter (Norman Kaye); the "she" is thirtiesh Patricia (Wendy Hughes).

Peter's eccentric swerve is due, probably in equal proportions, to his advancing years (evident in the balding head he covers with a toupee), to his never quite fitting into the macho male culture of Australia, and to his being dominated too long in life by his mother. He is a quiet man who has lived with his mother until her recent death. His great passion in life is the theater, but one finds it difficult to imagine that he has or feels free to express great passion.

Patricia's case is somewhat similar. Her eccentric swerve (that is, her not fitting the Australian hero stereotype) is because of her somewhat shy personality, her inhibited attitude toward sexuality, and her being dominated too long in life by her father. She has, in fact, just moved out of the family home, but mother and especially father seem reluctant to give her independence at long last. They call; they visit; they worry.

Peter, now fifty, meets Patricia through a dating service. Although it scarcely seems as if anything is developing between the two, something is. Either that or they are both so desperate for the companionship of the opposite sex that they pretend something is developing. The courtship is slow: in fact, the pace of the film is very slow—a characteristic of Cox's films that makes them less-than-box-office phenomena. However, the courtship does seem to offer them both a way to connect to a life that they have largely let slip by. Perhaps the event that kicks the relationship from low gear into high is Peter's getting Patricia involved in a community theater production of Strindberg. Having their daughter do theater really panics Patricia's parents. They say it is the "theater people" they are worried about; but, instead it seems that what they are most worried, even frightened, about is the self-assuredness their daughter has acquired by stepping on the stage. Before they have an opportunity to undermine the show and Peter and Patrica's relationship, sex does the undermining for them.

Patricia proves inhibited and awkward as a lover. Rather than understand her feelings, Peter becomes upset—probably because he feels just as awkward at his age and finds it easier to blame her than to confront his own discomfort. The two split: she quits the show and he turns to liquor, prostitutes, and shoplifting. This descent on his part is handled somewhat comically by Cox: thus, we never find ourselves disgusted at Peter's behavior, just saddened. Aided by the Strindberg play's flamboyant amateur director, the two reconcile. Symbolically, Patricia makes it clear to her father that she is her own person now; and Peter decides to sell his mother's old house and get a place of his own.

So, the two embrace life and end up as heroes battling for freedom against "authority"—living and dead—and grabbing hold of fading youth and all its pleasures. As O'Regan notes, their ending up together is atypical of Australian films in which couples are more often doomed to eventual failure *(Australian* 199). What makes *Lonely Hearts* even more compelling is how far "gone" Patricia and Peter were before they began reengaging. Their story is interesting because they were pushed outside the circle by forces of authority that we have seen depicted again and again as "the enemy." Thus, in baffling lingering parental control, they do what many heroes have done—just rather late in their lives. But they were also pushed outside by the Australian culture itself that values youth, activity, vigor, and verve. Growing older, neither Peter nor Patricia exemplified activity, vigor, and verve. Doubly eccentric, they nonetheless prove triumphant.

MAN OF FLOWERS (PAUL COX, DIRECTOR, 1983)

There is definitely a directorial signature evident in *Lonely Hearts* and *Man of Flowers*, as well as in the 1984 *My First Wife*. Some have termed the style "European," meaning that plot per se is less important than the development and interaction of characters and that the film lacks the bright lighting and expansive feeling characteristic of many Australian films—the softer lighting and the more enclosed space being thought more appropriate for personal and interpersonal explorations (O'Regan, *Australian* 62–63, Rattigan 209).

The character doing the exploring in *Man of Flowers* is a middle-aged man named Charles (Norman Kaye, who played Peter in *Lonely Hearts*). As the film progresses, we discover more and more about Charles' upbringing. As a youth, he was told he was retarded. That was certainly a blow to his ego. Then he had a number of erotic experiences, all tied to his mother, whom he loved very much. She was, of course, forbidden to him. Furthermore, he received the message that women's bodies were, in general, forbidden to him. So, now on his own after his mother's death, Charles finds himself still intensely attracted to women's bodies but only as a voyeur: he looks but does not touch. When we first meet Charles, he is directing model Lisa as she strips naked before him. He watches, increasingly diverting his eyes. As the encounter (for which she is paid handsomely) ends, he runs off to the church across the road. There, in one of the film's heavy-handed moments, he plays the organ and (we imagine) reaches sexual climax. More usually, he climaxes before the girls he hires are completely nude.

Charles' problem is one that should be treated; and it has been: he has been institutionalized. But now that he has considerable money because of his mother's death, he has been able to buy his way out of the institution by overpaying his psychiatrist to say that Charles is sane. We are, however, not unduly concerned by his freedom since he seems a menace to neither others nor himself. The only problem, in fact, that we foresee is others' taking advantage of his naïveté and his obsession.

Charles' sexual problem merges with his much more positive love of beauty. He particularly sees beauty in flowers; and he sees women as beautiful flowers. After his mother died, he spent money on flowers—beautiful women conceived of as flowers as well as literal flowers and artistic renderings of flowers. He is, in fact, taking art classes himself so that he can draw and paint things, such as flowers, that are beautiful. It is through the art class that he meets model Lisa.

Charles' sexual problem certainly makes him eccentric in the sense of "odd." His love of beauty, however, seems to make him eccentric in the sense of not fitting the Australian norm. The culture, although certainly appreciative of the arts, is not an arts-oriented one. Sports stadiums and pubs are the focal points, not galleries or museums. The film further suggests that the art world that does exist has embraced the bizarre and replaced genuine creativity with a desire for money. Lisa's artist boyfriend David epitomizes this perversion of the arts. The more we get to know David, the less we like him. He is jealous, he is unfaithful; and he is opportunistic. Lisa also seems to like David less and less as the film progresses.

Lisa, however, also has an opportunistic streak. And it is David's and Lisa's opportunism that lead to the film's double climax. Lisa thinks that if she can get $100 for just stripping, she can perhaps get $2,000 if she and lesbian lover Jane spend a weekend with Charles and "perform" as he watches. He reluctantly agrees, his reluctance signaling that it is beauty he finds arousing, not sex acts. While they are with him, he asks them to kiss and touch. He is trying to find a beauty in these acts of love that he denies himself, but he cannot seem to make the leap from seeing Lisa's static body as beautiful to seeing her lovemaking body as beautiful. He has, unfortunately, been too often pushed away from an active eroticism.

David thinks that any man who will pay $100 to just watch Lisa undress would also be a good customer for his large bizarre paintings. He tries to sell some to Charles. When Charles resists, since the paintings are clearly not what Charles likes, David tries to blackmail Charles into buying. Charles, however, is not to be blackmailed. The only art he will buy is pictures of flowers. David then makes his artistic stand: he does not paint anything as realistic or "pretty" as flowers. However, not very long afterward, David forgets this artistic stand and shows up at Charles' house with a huge painting of flowers.

Both Lisa and David go against Charles' eccentric notion of beauty. Lisa corrupts it by misunderstanding it to be more purely sexual than it is. David corrupts it by producing a grotesquely large painting of flowers—the larger the painting, the more money. These violations of Charles' aesthetic sense end up costing Lisa and David. Lisa, after the weekend she and Jane spent with Charles, is told by Charles that he now wants their relationship to be nothing more than just a friendship. She is no longer the beautiful flower in his eyes. She weeps at his request, not because she has lost her $100 per strip or because she has fallen in love with him but because she now is beginning to understand his sense of beauty and is finding it more compelling than any of the notions circulating in her artistic circles. Unfortunately, she lost her chance to be a part of that beautiful world. David's fate is worse: the giant painting he has done falls on him and kills him. He is, in a sense, killed by the flowers (the beauty) he has rejected through his bizarre art, through his poor treatment of the beautiful Lisa, and his crassly commercial appropriation and distortion of the flowers in the painting that kills him. Beauty is avenged. To make the revenge complete, Charles has David physically transformed into a bronze sculpture, which he gives to the city. David becomes, eternally, the beauty he never understood or embraced.

Lisa and David then, much like the culture they are to different degrees a part of, are criticized in the film for their corruption of beauty. The eccentric Charles embraces beauty, despite his sexual deviance. Lisa and David are too much of their larger culture and of the world to fully (in Lisa's case) or even partially (in David's) to do so. So, Lisa ends up in tears, and David ends up dead. Charles, on the other hand, dissolves at the film's end into a Renoir-like painting. He then becomes art, becomes beauty.

MALCOLM (NADIA TASS, DIRECTOR, 1986)

Tass' debut movie charmed Australian audiences. It also suggested, through the eccentric character Malcolm (Colin Friels), some qualities that the Australian culture (and its hero) had lost.

Malcolm, like Tim in the Michael Pate movie of the same name, is, for lack of a clinical diagnosis, simpleminded His mental capacity reveals itself in a very different manner, however. Whereas Tim seemed slow across the board, Malcolm is "slow" when it comes to matters of the world but a genius when it comes to anything mechanical: he is an inventor of amazing devices, such as a car that, on necessity, splits in half along its front-back axis.

One of the reasons Malcolm is naïve when it comes to matters of the world is that he has led a very sheltered life with his mother. As in both Paul Cox films just discussed, his mother has recently died. This death has left him alone without a great deal of money. Those close to Malcolm decide that the solution to the problem is for Malcolm to take in a boarder. The person he takes in is Frank (John Hargreaves); and shortly thereafter comes Frank's girlfriend Judith (Lindy Davies).

Both Frank and Judith have experienced much of what the world offers and are somewhat jaded as a result. Frank is a typical heavy-drinking, brawling ocker, whose rough edges and criminal inclinations are perhaps somewhat explained by an upbringing spotted by his mother's death and his father's murder by an inmate at a lunatic asylum. Judith is the more open of the two. She befriends Malcolm and encourages Frank to treat Malcolm as his mate. They end up becoming a family of sorts.

They are linked together not only by proximity and some measure of affection, but also by their unemployment. It seems as if Frank prefers consorting with criminal elements rather than holding a steady job. Judith and Malcolm, on the other hand, would like jobs. Malcolm had a job he loved—conductor aboard a Melbourne tram—but was fired because he embarrassed the company by building and then taking for a spin his own mini-tram. Judith also had a job and also was fired because Frank came to the restaurant where she was working and started a fight with men who were flirting with her. Unemployment leads the trio to plan and execute a rather comic bank robbery. What makes the robbery comic is the extent to which it relies on mechanical devices Malcolm has engineered for the very purpose.

The film is a lighthearted comedy. So, not only do we see Frank and Judith become less jaded as they interact more and more with Malcolm, but we see the trio succeed in their robbery, ending up together with the money in Portugal.

Malcolm's spirit, then, is contagious. It is also very non-Australian and, as such, provides a useful corrective to things that have gone awry in the nation's culture. Malcolm uses his mind, not his brawn. Malcolm drinks when he is thirsty, not just because he's at a pub. Malcolm shares his fantasies about trains and trams with girlfriend Jenny rather than rushing her into bed. Malcolm's differences, although presented in a lighthearted way, do offer a satirical glance at Australian society and its heroes. Malcolm is very different from, for example, Foley in *Sunday Too Far Away* (1975) or Handcock in *Breaker Morant* (1980). Not a man's man, with all that that term implies, Malcolm causes one to question, although not reject, a heroism that seems to have such macho roots.

TRAVELLING NORTH (CARL SCHULTZ, DIRECTOR, 1987)

Carl Schultz' adaptation of David Williamson's play focuses on a civil engineer named Frank. He has been a cantankerous man his entire life. Now, at retirement age, he is even more so. In both his pre-retirement life and his life now that he is leaving Melbourne and heading north to the warmth of Queensland, Frank has embodied many of the qualities of the Australian hero. He has, however, exaggerated many of them.

He loves his freedom. That love has probably prevented his sustaining the important relationships in his life—with his first wife, his son, and his daughter. That love of freedom reveals itself in his politics—for a long time he was a Communist, even though this affiliation cost him the chance to get elected to public office and cost him lucrative engineering contracts. Going north to Queensland is probably a reflection of this love of freedom because he will not be dependent on his daughter and he can live as he wants to: listening to the music he loves and fishing on the lake his cottage borders.

Being a Communist was a good "fit" for Frank, because Communism, at least in the beginning, had a strongly iconoclastic bent. One of Frank's favorite pastimes, it seems, is attacking icons. After he arrives in Queensland with his somewhat younger lady friend Frances, he attacks her rather traditional ideas about God and Heaven. There, they have a rather too friendly neighbor named Freddie. Freddie had served in the military, and it does not take long for Frank to attack patriotism and some of the ventures, such as the war in Vietnam, that patriotism and an ill-advised foreign policy got Australia involved in. Communism, as we know, also acquired a pronounced dictatorial quality. Throughout his life Frank has had such a quality himself: he drove his wife and son away by barking commands at them. His daughter is able to tease him about his authoritarian manner most of the time, but, in a poignant scene fairly late in the film, she confronts him with the damage his authoritarianism has done to others and his relationships with them.

His gruff dictatorial ways exhibit themselves in Queensland as well: he angrily confronts Saul, the town's only physician, demanding more information about the doctor's diagnosis and prescribed drug regimen. Frank has developed a weak heart, but he will not accept the doctor's judgment. Instead, he has to read up on heart disease and pharmaceuticals himself. Frank also will not accept all of Saul's advice about moderating his diet and, especially, his behavior. He drives, although the doctor tells him he should not; he travels south to Melbourne so Frances can visit her family, although the doctor advises him to stay in Queensland: late in his life, he travels to Sydney to marry Frances and have a lively honeymoon with her, although the doctor advises him to stay put. Frank's defiance of the doctor highlights several aspects of the man's personality: anger, intelligence, stubbornness—not entirely a negative portrait. Frank's gruff dictatorial behavior toward Frances, however, does not have any redeeming qualities. He attacks her family; he mocks her love for her children; and he orders her about the cottage.

Frank is unlike the stereotypical Australian in that he is attuned to the arts and is able to carry on a very intelligent conversation about the matters of the world. But, like other male Australians, he enjoys his drink, and he enjoys his sex. Sex is an important part of the relationship between Frank and Frances. Although the very idea shocks Frances' daughter, the couple is sexually active from their second date onward. Frank's heart ailment, however, brings their sex life to a screeching halt. The drugs cause depression, and the depression causes a degree of impotence. But, as the doctor tells Frank, the impotence is probably a blessing in disguise because sexual activity (vigorous, since Frank would hear of no other) would probably kill him. When Frank tells Saul that he and Frances made love in Sydney during their honeymoon, Saul is genuinely surprised that the intimacy did not bring Frank's life to a crashing halt.

Frank, because of his behavior, has placed himself outside the circles of life: he stood outside his family; he stood outside the Australian political world; he stood outside Frances' family. And, by traveling north to a remote town, Port Douglas, in tropical Queensland, he stands on the edges of Australia. He is eccentric because he has taken certain characteristics of the Australian hero to the extreme where they do damage—to himself and to others. Frank, then, serves as a warning to other would-be Australian heroes. When we look around the world that the film depicts, it is obvious that Australia needs such a warning. We do not see or hear of a good marriage. Although the women in these marriages are not always passive victims, they are always victims of men who belittle, berate, and betray them. These men all seem to have their own measure of what Frank has in extreme.

The film ends with Frank's death. Oddly, this is a positive note. Freddy has convinced Frank to apologize to Frances, who has left Frank and returned to Melbourne. Somewhat surprisingly, she chooses to return to Frank. They marry. They have a wonderful honeymoon, crashing a private art exhibition, dancing at a disco, and making love. They have a pleasant last month or so together, for Frank's heart is weakening and he and she know he will not live long. In Frank's typical dictatorial manner, he leaves, in several numbered envelopes, precise instructions to be followed after his death. He wants no priest and no piety; he wants Frances to go home to Melbourne and not entangle herself with any other old men (such as Freddie and Saul) who may just be waiting to snare her up in Queensland. He also wants those he has left behind in Queensland to drink a magnum of champagne each in his memory. When Frances and Freddie do, it is actually an uplifting moment.

This moment, however, does not negate the critique the film offers. Frank is a fully drawn character. Therefore, it is reductive to say that he is a type of anything. Nonetheless, he does represent many of the qualities of the Australian hero and the Australian culture carried to an offensive extreme. Frank allows us to see this extreme and see all the damage such a character does—to himself and to others. Thus, the film is a cautionary tale. Frances is a good woman. She made some mistakes earlier in her life that have caused strains to still exist in her family. Despite these mistakes, she is a very good woman. And the love of her redeems Frank—somewhat. That this redemption is possible is the film's important footnote to the cautionary tale.

RIKKY & PETE (NADIA TASS, DIRECTOR, 1988)

Tass followed up her success in *Malcolm* with this film. There is a touch of the character Malcolm in the character Pete: both do not quite fit in; both are mechanical whizzes. However, the eccentricity of Pete is more complex, and, in the film, it is paired with Rikky's very different type of eccentricity.

Pete and Rikky (portrayed by two virtual unknowns: Nina Landis and Stephen Kearney) are brother and sister raised in a wealthy Melbourne family. To different degrees (Pete more so), they reject this upbringing. They also, to different degrees (Rikky more so), reject the neat pigeonholes that Australian society has arrayed before them.

Pete fancies himself as "Evil Donald," a prankster. He chains police cars together, gaining revenge against a police officer who accidentally hit his mother and put her in a wheelchair. He invents a device for a posh art exhibit that tosses eggs at patrons. These patrons certainly are not pleased, and neither are the police. These pranks, however, do not reveal a criminal mind, just irreverence. Pete's irreverence seems rooted in his upbringing. He does not have a clear sense of what is right and what is wrong because the amoral world of wealthy Melbourne seems to have blurred the two together.

Rikky's story is different She is a walking contradiction: a very feminine woman who has opted for a stereotypically male career as a geologist. She is a scientist but pursues singing and painting as avocations. She is an urban dweller where rock music is preferred, but she is into country and western. There are so many facets to Rikky that she is difficult to define. Perhaps symptomatic of this difficulty is her performing under different names: in an outback town as Eartha Kitt with the backup band "Dumbdog": in Galena (supposedly near Mt. Isa but actually the much photographed Broken Hill) at the Eureka Hotel as Rikky Mendoza.

Finding Melbourne not to their liking (and with the police in pursuit of Evil Donald), the two hit the road into the outback. There is a sense of their starting over out there in a place with stronger values than the city. Although the values in Galena might be more honest than those in Melbourne (as Rikky tells her parents), the outback is not without its problems: drunkenness, violence, greed, general weirdness, and rampant sexism. The last is illustrated by Rikky and Pete's job-hunting misfortunes. Rikky applies for a job as a geologist. According to the sexist boss, she must start at the bottom, labeling bottles for samples. Her immediate supervisor is a woman, and Rikky catches this woman performing fellatio on the boss to maintain her position at the mine. Pete, on the other hand, without any qualifications whatsoever, gets a job he cannot really do. A miner working with Pete notes this inability and tries to blackmail Rikky into bed by threatening to expose her brother as a fraud. When she rejects his "offer," he then seeks her help in stealing minerals from the mine

Having left Melbourne partially because of its corruption, Rikky and Pete are now faced with something comparable in Galena. In the meantime, Pete has found Flossie, a Fillipino woman. So, the three of them conspire to outwit the Galena crooks. They purchase a piece of land, quickly mine it out to the tune of $1,650 (using a super, new mining machine designed by Pete), let word get out about how rich the plot is, and then auction it off to the highest bidder. Their plan works, but Pete, meanwhile, has found his way to jail (apprehended by pursuing Melbourne police). Rikky and friends have to break him out or pay his way out because he did quite a bit of damage before finally being incarcerated. The plot then turns slapstick and quickly dissolves into silliness and a confrontation between the siblings and their stern, but dishonest parents.

In any event, finding neither Melbourne nor Galena places of true worth, Rikky and Pete head home. Pete has Flossie. They motorcycle south. Once there, now more content because he has love, Pete designs a fleet of automatic newspaper delivery trucks, and he and Flossie live off the proceeds. Rikky seems determined to make her life work in the city, now that she knows that the outback offers no more noble a world. She chooses the more conventional route back—an automobile—and, once there, she gets a job as a geologist, working not on mines or quarries but on the foundations of a new city building.

So, the ending of *Rikky & Pete* is upbeat. Their eccentricity was a vehicle that allowed the director to reveal some of the ways the world, be it urban or rural, disappoints an idealist who thinks that goodness and justice and love ought to simply *be*. The film, however, does not beat one over the head with the world's limitations. They are there; we should know they are there. But, like Rikky and Pete, who initially try to stand apart from this world, we can find ways to make life work.

SWEETIE (JANE CAMPION, DIRECTOR, 1989)

Campion's debut feature film offers us eccentrics of rather opposite sorts. Sister Kay (Karen Colston) is thin and introverted. She has largely disengaged from life because life seems to terrify her. Her intense fear of trees is symbolic of this larger fear because trees seem to symbolize life to her. She wants things to be very predictable. Trees, because they root every which way, are terrifying, then, because they suggest that life is just not that predictable. Sister Dawn, nicknamed "Sweetie," is fat and extroverted. She has thrown herself into life so much that she is beyond control. That lack of control wrecks the order of her parents' marriage, causing the mother to leave the father and the father then to move in with Kay, and wrecks the order of Kay's life when Sweetie (Genevieve Lemon) moves in with her.

The cultural norms of Australia seem to lie somewhere in the midst of all of this. For a moment, assume that trees represent not just life but those norms. The link is in the fact that the norms are very social and very alive: good-natured competition, camaraderie, boozing, always doing. And just as trees send out roots that knit themselves into the land, the cultural norms also hold things together. If trees so symbolize life and culture, then we can see Kay and Dawn pursuing two very different paths with regard to the Australian society they live in. Kay is afraid of it, hiding from it because the culture is too social and too unpredictably kinetic for comfort. Dawn, on the other hand, is excessively caught up in it and is therefore on the brink of leaving the norms behind and swerving into chaos, taking others along with her.

Near the end of the film, Sweetie reaches chaos. We find her up a tree, naked, painted black, and barking like a dog. No one knows how to respond. Then, she falls out of the tree, killing herself. Note how the tree is still symbolically functioning as life and culture. Sweetie goes so far to the extremes of the culture that she finally falls out of it. As she does so, she not only leaves the culture's liveliness but also life.

Sweetie's death seems to push Kay closer to the center of things. It is almost as if Sweetie represents a side of her. Once it has been exorcised, she no longer feels pulled by it and therefore no longer needs to push herself in the opposite direction. She can find the center. This reading of the film makes it sound very Aristotelian, with Kay and Sweetie as the extremes and where Kay rests at the film's end as at least the beginnings of a cultural "golden mean." Read in this manner, the eccentricities are the problem. Either disengagement or over-engagement are behaviors to be avoided.

One must ask, however, what in life and culture causes these behaviors to be triggered? We are compelled in the end to ask this question because we flash back to when Dawn was a little girl. She is cute, innocent, full of life, performing like a red-haired Shirley Temple. She is a far cry from the naked, painted-black, barking, overweight woman who falls out of a tree and dies. How did she get from here to there? And, although we are not offered a flashback of Kay's early life, asking the question about Sweetie prompts the same question about her: how did she get from a happy childhood to living in deathly fear? In Kay's case, the answer may be that society cannot tolerate her sensitivity; oddly, the answer in Sweetie's case is the same.

The word "sensitivity" denotes being overly responsive to one's environment. One tending to the shy, if sensitive, will be driven into safe quarters: one tending to the flamboyant, if sensitive, will be driven over the edge. As the force that drives Kay and Dawn in these different ways, the Australian culture is insensitive. It sends out its rolling roots, full of life, not aware that those who are overly sensitive could be damaged by it. What we see in the story of two very different sisters is not unlike what we have seen in other characters discussed in this chapter. Kay seems much like Paul Cox's characters Peter and Patricia in *Lonely Hearts* and Charles in *Man of Flowers*. All are the shy, sensitive types for whom the prevailing culture poses problems in its brashness. Sweetie seems a bit like Lou in *Winter of Our Dreams*, the flamboyant, sensitive type for whom the prevailing culture can lead to a high from which one can only crash. The closest match to Sweetie, however, is yet to be discussed.

AN ANGEL AT MY TABLE (JANE CAMPION, DIRECTOR, 1990)

The picture of Sweetie as a little girl is, in an eerie way, an anticipation of the youngest of the three actresses who play New Zealand author Janet Frame in Campion's adaptation of Frame's autobiography. And since the actresses were chosen, at least partially, because they resemble Frame, if young Sweetie resembles Alexia Keogh, then young Sweetie also resembles Janet Frame. This link is instructive because it is flamboyant sensitivity that will lead young Frame, supposedly, over the edge. The role that society plays, however, in Frame's story is somewhat different, as is, of course, the ending. Janet Frame does not end up naked and painted black, dead on the ground beside a big tree.

Author Janet Frame is an eccentric from her very early years. She exhibited a fascination with words and a love of solitude that separated her from the more social norms of New Zealand society. Within the family context and within the school context, she was on the margins, in her own world. She also developed through those years a rather debilitating shyness that impeded, for example, her effectiveness as a schoolteacher. Meanwhile, she worked on her writing.

To be a writer in New Zealand in the first half of the twentieth century was just as fanciful a notion as being a writer in Australia a few decades earlier. Thus, Janet's aspirations were treated no more seriously than Sybylla Melvyn's in *My Brilliant Career* (1979). In fact, one might argue that Sybylla's were treated more seriously because her personality was so strong that it compelled such treatment. Janet, on the other hand, was standoffish, a tendency reinforced by the prejudice she experienced growing up because she was not thin and was not "pretty." Since young Janet's aspirations were not taken seriously, her behavior was not labeled that of an artist in the making and tolerated; rather, it was labeled that of someone who is mentally disturbed and treated as such.

Frame's novel *Faces in the Water* is very autobiographical. In both it and the autobiography Campion is working from, we get vivid depictions of the horrors of New Zealand's mental asylums at this time. Among the worst of these horrors was the electric shock therapy. In both novel and autobiography and on the screen, we view them because young Janet is faced with shock therapy as well as many other indignities during her institutionalization.

Even after she was judged sufficiently "sane" to leave and live on her own, she carries the stigma with her. It affects how people view her if they know:

they push her outside the circle of normality. It affects how she views herself: she pushes herself outside that circle. Thus, once an eccentric, always an eccentric. The result is that Frame's writing very much emerges from that external perspective. Later in life, residing in England, Frame commits herself to a very reputable mental institution. She is not suffering a relapse; rather she feels she must know if the label of schizophrenic that had been stamped on her was valid. She finds out that it was invalid, that—in the judgment of the psychiatrists at this "better" institution—she was simply an overly sensitive child and young woman and, therefore, a potentially creative one.

We imagine that this final verdict improves Janet's self-image considerably. The point of the film, however, is not just to bring us to this "happy" ending, but to confront us with what Janet had to suffer because her society had declared her "abnormal." Given the film's length—three hours because it was produced simultaneously as a television miniseries and a feature film—we are exposed to a great deal of that suffering. What then does the society's judgment that Jane was outside its norms say about those norms? It implies that shy people, private people, introspective people, and creative people "need not apply." The society, in other words, so privileges certain social behaviors that it labels those who are antisocial as insane rather than trying to understand what such people are up to. Not all antisocial people are artistic, and not all artists are antisocial. That said, there is a tendency for those who create to be loners, at least at times, and to seek ideas and words from within themselves. The society depicted in this film just cannot grasp that situation and that necessity. Therefore, the would-be artist is declared schizophrenic, not creative. Not finding room for creativity, and its quirks within the circle, the society is much diminished. Janet Frame is probably contemporary New Zealand's most noteworthy writer. Because there was not room for her, she was almost lost. And that would have been her country's loss.

Australia and New Zealand are often conflated. The fact that the new nations fought together as one unit (Anzac) in both world wars is one cause of the merging, as is the fact that many New Zealanders have received their higher education in Australia and even work there. Actor Sam Neill, who has appeared in many Australian films that we have discussed, is an example, as is Jane Campion who received her training in fillmmaking at the new Australian film school in the Sydney suburbs and did her initial work in Australia. *Sweetie* is generally considered an Australian film; *An Angel at my Table* and *The Piano* (1993) are a bit more problematic (O'Regan, *Australian 72*) although I am treating both as Australian. This merging of the two nations should not obscure the fact that there are cultural differences, as well as geographical and demographic ones. That said, there are also similarities. And in the case of *An Angel at My Table*'s depiction of a culture that marginalizes creativity and, more generally, sensitivity, I would suggest that there are very definite similarities. Characters such as Charles Brenner in *Man of Flowers*, Malcolm and Pete in Nadia Tass' two films, and Dawn in *Sweetie* are examples of the creative and sensitive pushed aside by Australian norms, as are Danny Embling in John Duigan's *Flirting* (1991), Scott Hastings in Baz Luhrman's *Strictly Ballroom* (1992), Antoinette Cosway Rochester in John Duigan's *Wide Sargasso Sea* (1993), and David Helfgott in Scott Hicks' *Shine* (1997)—all of which will be discussed later in this chapter.

PROOF (JOCELYN MOORHOUSE, DIRECTOR, 1991)

In some ways, *An Angel at My Table* seems more Australian than the film *Proof.* In Campion's film, it is clearly a society with certain attitudes that drives young Janet Frame into a mental institution: in film-school-graduate Jocelyn Moorhouse's film, it is less a society that "puts off" the main character than simply the way humans, as flawed beings, are.

The central character, Martin, is blind. That in and of itself makes him eccentric (i.e., outside the circle of normality). The blindness, however, is both a medical condition and an emblem of his disconnection with the rest of humanity. Why is he so disconnected? Because, as a young boy, he was scolded for touching people and, then, once blind, he was also psychologically punished for his condition by an embarrassed mother. He quickly began to resent his mother's attitude, and as a result, he began distrusting her and other adults. This distrust distanced him. Furthermore, he could not trust enough to love, and the absence of love in his life further distanced him.

He very much lives on the fringes of society. He feels he must rely on his own flawed senses to deal with the world. Thus, he takes photographs and asks others to tell him what is in them. If their rendition matches what his senses told him was there, he has "proof" that the world is as he thinks and he can rest comfortably. Of course, the flaw in his procedure for maintaining this control is that he must trust that these others are telling him truthfully what is in the photographs. He developed this habit early in life, and he is convinced that his first "verifier," his mother, actually lied to him about the photographs' contents.

Martin's housekeeper is Celia. One would think he might turn to her to read his photographs. However, from the film's beginning, we pick up on his distrust of her. We also find that he is right to distrust her because she frequently plays tricks on him. Her tendency to do so validates his general distrust of others and his particular distrust of his now deceased mother.

Celia is, like Martin, a marginal character. We are not provided with much information about her, but we do know that she is a very lonely woman. We also know that she has fallen in love with Martin. Later in the film, we discover that this love is more of an obsession since she has been taking her own pictures—of Martin—and she has them plastered all over the walls of her flat. Martin realizes that Celia is interested in being more than a housekeeper, but he does not respond. So, pushed, Celia takes embarrassing pictures of Martin and threatens to "publish" them if he does not take her out for a night on the town. He has a wonderful time, but not because of Celia's presence, rather, because she has taken him to hear a symphonic orchestra, something he has never experienced. The experience is heightened by the fact that his sense of hearing has become especially acute with the dimming of his eyes. Once back at Martin's apartment Celia attempts to seduce him. He runs away when faced with touching her and being touched. (Recall that he was taught as a child that touching is bad).

Celia becomes jealous of the third character in the story, a young man named Andy (Russell Crowe). Andy becomes Martin's trusted friend, the person he relies on to "read" the photographs. They gradually become mates, even going to a drive-in movie together where, of course, Andy must narrate the movie. There also seems to be homoerotic tension beneath the surface of the relationship (Karl Quinn in Murray, *Australian Film* 322; O'Regan, *Australian* 199). Andy eventually betrays Martin by lying to him about one photograph. If Andy had told the truth, he would have exposed one of Celia's games. He chose to protect Celia rather than be totally honest with Martin. Taking advantage of this crack in the Martin–Andy relationship, Celia decides to tear it down by seducing Andy.

Celia then makes sure that Martin discovers Andy's lie about the photograph and that Martin discovers Andy and her in bed in his house. Andy, totally duped by Celia, protests that they are in love. Celia is glumly satisfied when Martin throws both Andy and her out. Martin's trust in humanity is further dented by these events—so much so that he visits his mother's grave and wonders if she is really there in the coffin. He thinks that, perhaps, her death was a lie too—constructed so that she could finally be rid of the embarrassing responsibility of taking care of her blind son Martin.

Martin also realizes that he has been dishonest too. He knew Celia was in love with him and deliberately ignored her to torment her. His attitude was that if he could not touch and love, then she would not touch and love either. He realizes that he was as dishonest as Andy and Celia. He also realizes that, although to be human might mean to be occasionally dishonest, there were good people who weaken under straining circumstances and bad people who rarely are honest, even with themselves. He commits himself to being the former and shunning the latter. Thus, he, in honesty, apologizes to Celia (who has returned as housekeeper) and then dismisses her. Thus, he re-embraces Andy's friendship. In the end, he asks Andy to read a photograph that he has been positive his mother lied to him about. Andy describes the picture much as Martin's mother had, convincing Martin that his mother was also a good person who weakened under the strain of having a blind child and, then, fell very ill.

Martin in the end moves back toward the center of things. He does so by redefining that center. He discovers that rather than being full of deceit, the center features goodness and weakness alongside some of the deceit he feared and detested. Redefining the center allows Martin to chart a course for himself in that society rather than live forever on its fringes.

FLIRTING (JOHN DUIGAN, DIRECTOR, 1991)

Athough written earlier, *Flirting* is a sequel to *The Year My Voice Broke* (1987). However, one does not need to know the earlier film to appreciate the latter. In the earlier film, two young people, neither of whom fit in their small outback town, part company at the train station. Freya heads for the city and we feel good for her. The other young person, Danny, is still stuck in the town. In *Flirting*, we find that Danny, three years later, has left to attend a rather posh boarding school for boys—St. Alban's in Canberra. He does not fit in there either. He is not athletic: he is not "one of the guys;" rather, he is a tad intellectual, has developed a nervous stutter, and is more than a bit iconoclastic. In fact, the only characteristic Danny may have in common with the other boys at the school is an interest in sex. But, whereas for the others the interest leads to crude remarks, which are quickly quashed in a rather repressive atmosphere, for Danny the interest melds with genuine affection for a soul mate at the magical place he stares at across the lake: the private girls' school Cirencester College.

The girl's name is Thandiwe Adjewa. She is African. Her father is posted at his nation's embassy in the Australian federal capital. Thandiwe is also eccentric. She is not Australian, and she has had a range of experiences in her life that not only distinguish her from the other girls but make her more mature. She is also more mature in her understanding of sexuality. She, like Danny, sees sexuality as a dimension of a relationship built on connections that are other than physical. Like Danny, she sees sexuality as beautiful. Unfortunately, both the boys at St. Alban's and the girls at Cirencester see sex as part of the games young boys and girls play, while the adults at the two schools see it as something to be suppressed.

Life could be worse for Danny at St. Alban's. He has friends; he seems respected for his academic ability and some of his antiauthoritarian stances. However, he is mocked by some of the boys who are more a part of the dominant culture at the school, which is but a youthful version of the macho Australian culture. Thandiwe similarly has some friends and is also respected for certain achievements. However, she is mocked by some of the girls because she is Black. In doing so, these girls embody the racism that is an ugly part of the Australian culture.

Danny and Thandiwe come to see the world differently. His interest in Africa opens him up to the entire world; her interest in Danny engages her in Australia and expands her already broad sense. They see the whole world, not just parts, his or hers. They see that the boundaries that separate people are artificial, that people have the same thoughts and same yearnings no matter which side of which ocean they are from. They find that people can be beautiful. These realizations are quite alien to the Australian world they are in. When their tryst in a nearby motel room is interrupted, we see the Australian world asserting its primacy over this aberrant global perspective. When Danny and Thandiwe must go their separate ways in the end, we see that different perspective—that better perspective—fade. We realize how less beautiful the Australian perspective and the Australian world are from this eccentric couple and the eccentric view of life they embody in their relationship.

STRICTLY BALLROOM (BAZ LUHRMAN, DIRECTOR, 1992)

Luhrman's film received mixed reviews. Some, such as Tom O'Regan, thought it reverently campy and fill of energy *(Australian 50)*; others, like Pat Gillespie, thought the characters and situations clichés and the musical numbers not even all that good (in Murray, *Australian Film* 349). It is some viewers' favorite Australian film, whereas others saw it as pandering to Hollywood tastes. From the point of view of this study, it is a very good example of an eccentricity that is positive and that thereby casts Australian culture in a negative light

The film's eccentric is Scott Hastings (Paul Mercurio). He is a competitive ballroom dancer and so very talented that many, including his very pushy parents, assume he will be the next Pan Pacific Grand Prix champion. Scott, however, is a rebel. He wants to win, but he wants to win on his own terms. Those terms would have him dancing steps that are not "strictly ballroom" and, therefore, not allowed. His rebellion angers his parents. It also costs him partners who now see Scott as a risk, not an opportunity.

The film does present this rebel versus the establishment drama in rather stereotypical terms. He is noble; the establishment is comically rigid, comically self-important. To enhance Scott's nobility, the film finally gives him a partner: the rather awkward, rather plain-looking newcomer Fran (Tara Morice). Initially, Scott is reluctant to dance with her because she lacks experience. Once they start dancing, however, she progresses rapidly and the sparks of love begin to fly between the two. Of course, she will, in the end, not only prove to be a good dancer, but beautiful as well. If the story sounds like a suburban Australian fairy tale, it is one with an ethnic twist in a nation that had become much less Anglo–Irish than once upon a time (O'Regan, *Australian* 20, 54, 75, 148, 307–8, 319). Fran is Spanish, the illegal dance steps Scott wants to perform are Spanish, and Fran's father is a master of them. After initially acting coolly toward Scott, he warms up to the boy once he realizes that the boy's interest in Spanish dancing—forget the girl—is sincere. So, Scott, rebel Prince Charming with an ethnic cheering section, "goes for the gold" at the film's conclusion. Yes, cliched formulas are being invoked here, but the film's saving grace is that Luhrman is just as aware that he is using these formulas (with a campy bravado) as he is that is he is overdoing the makeup, the hairstyles, the dress, and the self-important behavior of those who are so very seriously committed to ballroom and to doing ballroom the "right" (i.e. traditional) way (Gillespie in Murray, *Australian Film* 349).

Not done with clichés yet, Luhrnan in the finale reveals that Scott's adulterous mother is really the villain: she so wants to win vicariously through Scott

Scott Hastings (Paul Mercurio) practices his "illegal" dance steps in *Strictly Ballroom* (1992). Photo: ScreenSound Australia. Permission granted by M & A Film Corporation.

that she feeds him lies about his father's defeat years earlier. Scott's father, however, saves the day by telling his son the truth—that he had never been allowed to dance his own steps—and by encouraging Scott to do "his own thing." And Scott and Fran do. They do not win the trophy, so they do not technically defeat the "evil" ballroom forces that are arrayed against them. However, in the eyes of all watching, they are the winners and those in the "strictly ballroom" crowd are revealed to be ridiculously self-important and pathetically afraid of anything new.

Luhrman's film makes it clear what is being celebrated. But what is being satirized? If it is the ballroom dancing establishment, then that would seem to be a rather small target even given the fact the ballroom dancing is taken fairly seriously. Luhrman has larger targets in mind (Taylor). What Luhrnan seems to be targeting is competitition more generally as well as a society that has its "in's" its "out's," and its "rules." The Australian culture is a competitive one, with sports the more usual venue. But everything that one might say of those who fight at rugby or footy could be said of these dancers. The competitive spirit is then satirized as all-consuming. People live and breathe their sport, be it athletic or more decorous; people go overboard—to the point of taking unfair advantage if they can—to win at their sport.

The Australian culture also has historically featured exclusions. Way back, the English were in; the Irish out. Then, the Anglo–Irish were in; other Europeans out. Then, Whites were in; Asians out. All along, until recently, aborigines have been out. And, in a culture that is as male-defined as that of Australia, women have always been in their inferior place within and therefore really out. Luhrman might be glancing at this history of exclusion through the comic lens of ballroom dancing because the world of ballroom dancing has its hierarchical class structure as well as a very "blonde" feel. (Even brunette Gia Carides is a blonde.) Scott's "new steps" embrace a non-blonde culture, relegated to a lower social class because of ethnicity. His challenge, then, highlights the extent to which ballroom dancing and Australian society exclude the "other."

The film also satirizes the conservative, rule-bound nature of the Australian culture. Ballroom dancing has its rules—for example, that only certain steps are allowed, and the basis for this rule, we gradually find out, is fear. Should innovative steps be allowed, Barry Fife (Bill Hunter) and the dance schools such as that run by Scott's mother and Les Kendall would quickly be out of business. Fearing for their livelihood, they admit neither changes nor exceptions. As the film's final scene makes clear, new steps add excitement: new steps keep the activity alive. As the crowd cheers Scott and Fran, Barry Fife, Shirley Hastings, and Les Kendall perhaps realize that new ideas need not be feared. Luhrman is suggesting that this fear characterizes Australian society in general. His call, then, is for a more open society that tolerates "new steps" of whatever kind.

Strictly Ballroom is a comic film. Its many dance numbers also give it a high energy level. One should not, therefore, take it too seriously. It clearly sends up a popular competitive art form and suggests that those who are enthralled by it have, perhaps, overindulged. The film, though, seems to get at something more basic. One not familiar with ballroom dancing has to wonder about its competitiveness and its hierarchies and its unwillingness to accept innovation. Furthermore, one has to wonder if the Australian society's more general competitiveness, its social stratifications based on skin color and gender, and its fear of change are not lurking beyond the comic lens.

WIDE SARGASSO SEA (JOHN DUIGAN, DIRECTOR, 1993)

Duigan's film is, like *Strictly Ballroom*, a film with foes and friends. Duigan's film is, of course, an adaptation of Jean Rhys' now-venerated 1964 novel, one that tells the story of Bertha, the madwoman in the attic in Charlotte Brontë's *Jane Eyre*. Thus, Rhys' book is a prequel to Brontë's. Rhys novel is masterful in many ways, and it is always difficult for a director to satisfy everyone when dealing with sources thought to be masterful. Rhys' novel, in addition, delivers strong postcolonial and feminist messages. Therefore, everyone who appreciates those messages is going to be watching Duigan's film to see to what extent those messages come through. In other words, many viewers of the film begin watching it, waiting to see evidence of its failure. Not surprisingly, many of these viewers find evidence. I would argue, however, that Duigan does a good job establishing the mood of the film and a good job presenting Antoinette Cosway Rochester's part of the story. Thus, the postcolonial and feminist messages are at least implicit in the film. Where I think Duigan fails is in giving sufficient depth to Edward Rochester's character. If one knows the composition history of Rhys' novel, she had the same problem. She solved it by allowing Rochester to narrate some of the book. Since movies do not typically have narrators (let alone two of them), Duigan could not bring viewers Rochester's thoughts and feelings by offering his perspective. And Duigan found no substitute for Rhys' solution.

To fully understand the book, one needs to see how both Antoinette and Edward are victims. Since the film does not sketch his victimization very fully, we can be true to the film and focus on her story. She is, from shortly after her birth, a character on the margins of two societies. Her mother is a quadroon; her father English. Antoinette is, therefore, one-eighth Black. That is enough to marginalize her in the English-dominated high society of her Caribbean island. In addition to this mark against her, there is her mother's madness. It is thought to be hereditary, although anyone who considers her mother's life will understand why she went mad. She lost her home and her son in racial violence directed at her husband's rather imperious management of the plantation. Then, when she did not recover from the shocks, he placed her in the care of men who raped her further into insanity while he simply forgot she existed. To think that Antoinette would necessarily follow in Annette's path is to misunderstand the nature of insanity and totally overlook how Annette was driven mad. Nonetheless, the English on the island, already suspicious because of Antoinette's Black blood, further marginalize her because she is thought to be very much her mother's daughter.

The Black community on the island also pushes her away. She is too White. They are deferential when they have to be, but behind her back there are glances. Only Christophine, who took care of Antoinette when she was little, remains loyal. The others are waiting to taunt her as a "White cockroach."

The Black community's rejection of her means she has no people to rely on should she need them. And she does need them because her new husband Edward turns on her. He had not been told everything about her background in an arranged marriage designed to help his father and older brother back in England more than himself. When he finds out about the madness, he is distressed. He sees evidence of it in Antoinette's passion, whereas the passion was just part of her nature, a positive part if he could have allowed himself to embrace it without guilt. But guilt there was. Such passion is not right, is not natural, he thought, when, in reality, it was very natural. Being a member of his English culture, he just could not be as open, as natural, and as passionate as his beautiful young wife. So, rather than blame himself, he perverted what was so very beautiful in Antoinette into evidence of incipient madness. Then, to prove his point, he drove her into madness through unloving sex, the betrayal of her love, and the withdrawal of his love. Then, Edward Rochester ripped her from the Caribbean island, in whose nature she was rooted, and took her back to the cold, windswept moors, where he confined her in the attic.

Antoinette is pushed away by the island's English population, by its Black population, and by her husband Edward. At the root of her exclusion is a history of racism: enslavement followed by Black resentment and lingering English feelings of superiority. Also at the root is the English culture's repression of the sexual and rejection of the natural.

But what does Antoinette's story have to do with Australia? After all it takes place in the Caribbean. The history and the culture at fault are not Australian. Another way to put this same question is to ask why an Australian director would choose this story. My suspicion is that Duigan saw in the colonial situation in the Caribbean, one that could be generalized throughout the former Empire. England's history in dealing with Blacks is not a positive one. In Africa, England participated in the slave trade, bringing Africans from West Africa to the Caribbean to work on sugar plantations. In Australia, there was no such lucrative use for the Black population, so England tolerated its annihilation. Time has passed on both the islands and in Australia, but Black resentment and White racism continue. Furthermore, England's movement into lands more lush and cultures more sexually open necessarily created discomfort. The jungle and the bush were dangerously wild and to be tamed, certainly not luxuriated in. The near-naked were to be clothed, and the sexual was to be regulated along more "polite" lines. The discomfort never caused the colonizer to look at his (pronoun deliberate) culture because that culture was the presumed norm against which all others were to be judged. What a postcolonial perspective allows us to see as European repression and African and aborigine comfort with the body were consistently seen as propriety on the one hand and indecency (reflective of inferiority and amorality) on the other.

Wide Sargasso Sea as an Australian film offers the nation a fable about colonialism. The victimization of those eccentric to the colonial norms, such as Antoinette Cosway Rochester, causes one to question those norms. The next question, then, is whether those norms still exist. Is there still racism in Australia? Is there Black resentment at how aborigines have been treated through the years? Does a repressive attitude toward sexuality and the body still exist? I think Duigan's answer to all of these questions would be Yes. Thus, the film as fable is still relevant in 1993.

THE ADVENTURES OF PRISCILLA, QUEEN OF THE DESERT (STEPHAN ELLIOTT, DIRECTOR, 1994)

Elliott's film was a campy affront to both repressed sexuality and expressed or unexpressed homophobia. The in-your-face film takes us on a long journey—from Sydney to Alice Springs—with one transexual and two gay transvestites.

One might almost automatically assume that such characters are eccentrics. Within the context of Sydney, with its very popular Gay and Lesbian Mardi Gras celebration and its large gay and lesbian conununity in the sections of the city just west of King's Cross, they might not be that eccentric. The film, however, only begins in Sydney. Sydney is the relatively safe haven the three inhabit before they begin their journey into the outback, into the "real" Australia. If their eccentricity was questionable in the context of Sydney, it is undeniable in the context of outback towns such as Broken Hill and Alice Springs.

Priscilla, it is important to note, is not just about the clash between the transexual–transvestite lifestyles on parade and the mainstream Australian society. In the course of the film, we get to know the three central characters well. We know their very different stories, and we watch their sometimes brutal, sometimes sensitive interactions. I am not going to explore this aspect of the film because such an exploration would take me away from this book's focus. However, it is an important aspect. I stress this because *Priscilla* has in some quarters—more so in the United States than in Australia—been too quickly labeled a pro-gay film (Epstein, 4–5; O'Regan, *Australian* 60). It is that, but that message is in many ways subordinate to the human stories that develop as we travel down the road to Alice Springs with the trio.

The best place to see their eccentricity and the reactions it evokes from the mainstream is Broken Hill, where the trio stops for the night. Their presence walking along the main street elicits curious stares; their initial appearance in the pub, hostility. However they manage to overcome that hostility. By the end of the evening, they are acting like mates with their fellow drinkers at the bar. As they crawl back to their hotel room, one feels good about how they have won tolerance in a rather unlikely spot. Then, the next morning, they discover that Priscilla—the bus—has been defaced with anti-gay graffiti. The good feelings evoked by the previous night's drunken harmony disappear.

In many ways, the rhythm of the Broken Hill stop is the rhythm of their outback journey. Everytime they seem to gain against prejudice, the next minute they are again assaulted by it. That they can overcome it once they become known as individual people is a hopeful note. However, the film leaves the undeniable impression that prejudice runs deep in the land.

There are some pleasant surprises along the way. In a small mining town between Broken Hill and Alice Springs, they meet a middle-aged man (Bill Hunter), who is unhappily married to mail-order bride Cynthia. He and transexual Bernadette become good friends. Out of that a deeper relationship develops. Surprisingly, he seems without the prejudice of his small-town fellows. This lack is evident in his asking the trio to perform at the pub. He is convinced that female impersonators will be a big hit. He is very wrong in his guess. The men are quite hostile. If it were not for the intervention of Cynthia, who strips and fires Ping-Pong balls from out of her vagina, the trio probably would have been beaten. That he is so wrong is proof that the prejudices of the other men are not at all a part of his being. His freedom from prejudice allows him to go along with Bernadette to Alice Springs. As the film ends, they are going to stay together and see how their relationship evolves. Another pleasant surprise is "Mitzi"'s wife, who runs a casino–nightclub in Alice Springs One might expect the ex-wife of a man who "turns" gay and bails out to be quite hostile. She is not. She is still very much his friend, and the two of them are good parents to their son. She has even had a lesbian lover; she is that open to the lifestyle her husband has chosen. Finally, their son is similarly open. He seems aware—as aware as possible for a relatively small child—of his father's sexual orientation. He is very aware of what his father does for a living; in fact, he is proud of his father's work and wants to see his father perform. These three pleasant surprises in the film are notes of hope that prejudice is not universal. The son's freedom from prejudice is especially hopeful because he represents the generation to come.

Unfortunately, one must note that the film itself exhibits prejudice in the scenes involving Cynthia, the Fillipino mail-order bride. Her portrayal struck many as confirming a negative stereotype of Fillipino women. It drew an angry response from Fillipino groups and scolding editorials from the Australian press (Cafarella; "Priscilla Puts Down"). This portrayal is doubly unfortunate because it undermines one of the film's overall messages. The film is about tolerance and intolerance. It depicts a society that is characterized largely by the latter, but offers some notes of hope. But if the filmmakers themselves can unwittingly stumble into a display of prejudice, then those notes are considerably softened. Director Elliott claims that Cynthia is no different from the transvestites: quirky, easily stereotyped, but ultimately human. He argues that Cynthia is no more mocked than the transvestites (O'Regan, *Australian* 154–56).

Elliott's response makes some sense: however, perhaps Cynthia is not on the screen enough for the human dimensions of the character to emerge fully.

OSCAR AND LUCINDA (GILLIAN ARMSTRONG, DIRECTOR, 1997)

Like Ray Lawrence (*Bliss* [1985]) and Brian Trenchard-Smith (*Dead-End Drive-In* [1986]) Gillian Armstrong faced the problem of transforming a work of Peter Carey's fiction that resembles formal realism, but really is not, into a film that, because it is visually before the audience, probably has to be pushed to either the realistic or the fantastic extreme. *Bliss* the film seems more tied to a here-and-now reality than Carey's novel; *Dead-End Drive-In*, because of its generic ties with science fiction and horror movies, seems more consistently fantastic than Carey's short story "Crabs." Armstrong's solution to the problem is more like Lawrence's than Trenchard-Smith's. She had to go one step further than Lawrence, however. She had to offer a there-and-then reality complete with appropriate sets and costumes because the temporal jumping-off point for Carey's story is back in the nineteenth century. As a result, Armstrong's decision to push the story in the realistic direction caused her to create a film that resembles period pieces such as Bruce Beresford's *The Getting of Wisdom* (1977) or her own *My Brilliant Career* (1979) that were very popular in the late 1970s and early 1980s.

This decision also mutes the eccentricity of the film's two major characters. Oscar's obsessions become less fantastic and more truly problematic. His gambling is not just a metaphysical state but an addiction with very real consequences. Lucinda's fascination with glass becomes less fantastic and more the springboard for business with the opposed prospects of financial success or financial ruin being more "real" than in the book. And her dream of a glass chapel in the outback also becomes less a shared fantasy and more a real task and a real testament to real love. The eccentricities then become less resonant with philosophical implications and more genuine quirks.

Quirks or something more profound, these eccentricities do distinguish Oscar and Lucinda from the norm. That norm is provided in book and movie alike by establishments. In Oscar's case, it is the church, of which he is an ordained minister. In Lucinda's, it is the world of business, which expects productivity and profits. Both establishments try, largely in vain, to regulate the behavior of the whimsical couple. The question to ask, then, is: Is there anything wrong with such regulation? Put another way: Does the film in any way criticize these establishments for acting as they do?

To have populated either the church or industry with stereotypes of pomposity or greed would have offered a quick answer. The film does not do that. Rather, both religion and commerce come across as mixed bags, with good people and hypocritical people and rigid people and money- and power-grubbing people. Religion and commerce, then, would probably tolerate a degree of deviation, but just a degree. Oscar and Lucinda exceed this permitted degree. Thus, the establishments act against them and in a manner that does seem unduly severe.

Armstrong, then, depicts a world in which the characteristics Oscar and Lucinda embody are only tolerated a tiny bit. This lack of toleration is being criticized by the film because, on principle, tolerance is good, intolerance bad. It is also being criticized because of what the world can lose by being so "narrow." Above all else, Oscar and Lucinda are dreamers and chance-takers. The mundane and the safe are without much appeal to them. They want to exceed the mundane, and they take risks to do so. Given their personalities, the risks they take sometimes seem focused on their dreams, sometimes not. They prove by example that asking creative people to maintain focus and discipline (and other good Victorian values) is asking them to be other than themselves.

There are sad moments and there are happy moments in these two characters' lives. Many of those are tied to their crisscrossed love lives, a dimension of the film heightened by Armstrong (and screenplay writer Laura Jones). Overall, however, the effect of the film on the audience is disappointment that these two could not have found a way to make all of their dreams work. It is worth noting that novel and film end differently and that the novel's ending is far bleaker than the film's. For example, in the novel Lucinda is penniless, whereas in the film she still has the money she wagered Oscar. Despite these changes—intended, one imagines, to make the film more appealing to an audience—the audience still feels as if something that could have been achieved was not achieved and that the world is somehow at fault for thwarting dreams.

By offering a period piece, Armstrong runs the risk of having her late twentieth-century audience dismiss this criticism of the world as criticism of Victorian mores and Victorian intolerance A postmodern work of fiction such as Carey's, because it is not as firmly rooted in time and place, runs this risk less. But with either medium, one needs to ask why the artist would bother to criticize times more than a century old. The almost inevitable answer is that the artist—be he or she novelist or director—is trying to make a point (indirectly) about the time and place the novel or film is being "consumed" in. Thus, Armstrong is suggesting that the establishment forces that denied Oscar and Lucinda all of their dreams are still with us, in Australia and beyond, quashing eccentrics such as these two and thwarting their attempts to make their visions realities.

SHINE (SCOTT HICKS, DIRECTOR, 1997)

Hicks' film is a study of genius, and, as we all know, genius is near-allied to madness. Thus, gifted pianist David Helfgott (Geoffrey Rush) is not surprisingly on the edge. Both his musical genius and his near-madness make him an eccentric. The essence of the film's story is determining whether David will exist on that circle, creating music for his and others' pleasure, or fall away from the circle entirely and share nothing.

The film is very similar to Campion's *An Angel at My Table*. The question in that film is whether writer Janet Frame will live to write or be forever labeled schizophrenic and not have the opportunity to share her vision. We know the answer because the film is successful writer Janet Frame's true story, but that does not detract from the poignancy of her struggle. The same is true for *Shine*. We know the answer because the film is based on another true story. Nonetheless, the film depicts a poignant struggle to survive as an artist.

Pianist David's struggle is within himself, but his father Peter played a major role in creating that struggle. Peter survived the Holocaust in Poland but lost all of his family except his four children. He is, therefore, overly devoted to them. Recognizing David's talent, Peter pushes him. Then, David's teacher pushes him. The culmination is David being offered a scholarship by Isaac Stern to study music in the United States. At this point, Peter fears losing David, as he had lost others, and forbids the trip. David is understandably upset. A friendship he develops with an older Australian writer helps him get through this trying time. That friendship, however, becomes a much more sustaining force in David's life than his relationship with his father. David is then offered another scholarship—this one to study in London. He defies his father and accepts it, pretty much severing that relationship. The loss of his father's support and love, however, will haunt David.

In London David excels under the guidance of an equally eccentric teacher. David's behavior, however, becomes obsessive. His dear author friend Katherine dies, and, after performing the emotionally- and psychologically-draining Concerto No. 3 by Rachmaninoff, David suffers a complete breakdown. Years go by, years that feature institutionalization and treatment that deny him the piano. His journey back begins when he plays successfully at a Sydney bar and has a liberating romance with a middle-aged astrologer. His father's death then frees him from the ghost that is haunting him and he can take to the stage once again, playing in an emotional style that attracts popular acclaim.

The opportunity to listen to Helfgott's music would convince one that he is on the edge when he plays. What, during his London sojourn, pushed him over? Put simply, the answer is the loss of his father's support. That loss seems to be what drives him in London: he pushes himself to prove to his father that going away was the right decision. That loss also makes his attachment to Katherine so much more important and her death so devastating. She, as a surrogate parent, kept him propped up. When she dies, there is neither father nor father-substitute.

An audience's applause and a woman's love help David regain his footing on the circle's edge, but what really reconnects him to his musical artistry is realizing that the task he had set for himself—proving something to his father—was no longer important, if it ever had been. His father's death, of course, plays a role in this realization, but more important is David's recognition that, in the final analysis, the only person he has to answer to is himself. His finding himself is a necessary prelude to his stepping back onto the stage and performing at the film's end.

David's father Peter is trapped by the past. He wants to get beyond the past, but, ironically, the past is what prevents him from doing so. Much of the film takes place in Australia, but one is hard-pressed to link much of its drama to any particular nation. That Peter is an immigrant, not a native Australian, also makes the drawing of a link tenuous. There does, however, seem to be a way in which Peter's situation is very Australian. Australia also wants to get beyond the past because the past is somewhat embarrassing. The convict past one can very readily get beyond. There are other pasts, however, that are not as easy to ignore. The Australians' past behavior toward the country's indigenous people is difficult to dismiss, as is the "White Australia" policy of the mid-twentieth century. Also strong are the people's historical ties to Great Britain and more recent ties to the United States. The Queen is still on Australian currency, American policies are still front-page news, and American popular culture is still dominant in music, on television, and in motion picture theaters. These intrusions from abroad are as difficult to escape as the Australians' past behavior. Finding out what one's national identity is, like David finding himself, requires getting beyond the past and, maybe, the intruding present. Peter, understandably, has a difficult time doing so. (So must David, who must get beyond his soured relationship with his father.) Before he dies, Peter seems to have, at least in his heart, dealt with the damage his past caused him to inflict on his son. David's case is the more optimistic one. He focuses less on the past and more on his present, and he is thereby able to create again.

Chapter 9

Conclusion

Studies that have a chronological framework, as this one does within each chapter, end strongly or weakly, depending on the last items in the chronology. Australian film becomes, during the thirty-year period chronicled in this book, increasingly international. What happens to it is, in some ways, what happens to economic enterprises in general. Economic forces of various sorts make globalization an attractive, perhaps even a necessary, strategy. Since this study focuses on how film reveals the Australian culture, the discussion then may become less compelling as each chapter reaches its end. Therefore, it strikes me as necessary to end not with the last films but, rather, with an overview of the entire 1970–2000 enterprise.

This study has simultaneously looked at thirty years of Australian film as a cultural project and as a cultural expression. The first presupposes that many people, among them producers and directors as well as funders, saw Australian film as an opportunity to define and promote the nation's culture. The second presupposes that Australian culture, for good or for ill, finds its way into the nation's artifacts, even when, as in the 1980s, there is a strong Hollywood influence. These two perspectives on Australian film are not, however, easy to separate, because, in some films, an attempt to define and promote Australia is evident, as are other elements of the national culture that, perhaps, the definers and promoters would rather have excluded from the pictures.

As a merged cultural project and cultural expression, Australian cinema is a more coherent body of films than previous studies have suggested. Some early films present a very traditional Australian heroism. Whether in the bush or in the cities, whether set in the nineteenth century or the twentieth, this heroism is both appealing and unappealing. Many films, both early and later, transform this traditional heroism somewhat so as to make it more appealing. These films sand off the unappealing rough edges; these films sanitize a bit that which is crude or criminal in the traditional heroism. The films that present traditional heroism and the films that revise it a bit are at the core of this study.

This heroism, traditional and revised, is male and White. Yet, there are many very fine Australian films of the 1970–2000 period that focus on women, and there are a few that focus on the nation's aboriginal population. These films, rather than being strikingly different, actually present this heroism, but with twists. The films that deal primarily with women show how many barriers are placed in their heroic paths. They also suggest that, perhaps, the heroism that emerges out of the dominant patriarchal culture needs to be revised somewhat to fit the different life stories of women. The films that deal primarily with aborigines do, at times, show how this heroism might be embodied by aboriginal men and women. However, the fact of their victimization often prevents filmmakers, especially White filmmakers, from depicting the heroic. Nagging stereotypes of aborigines also intrude into these films.

There are other kinds of films that were produced in Australia during the thirty-year period. I would suggest that they too can be related to the cultural picture sketched in this book's earlier chapters.

Many films deal with youth. They seem, in one way or another, to ask if the next generation will be like the traditional or revised heroes seen in the "classic" Australian films. Not surprisingly, almost all of the youth are in one way or another rebellious. Will this adolescent rebellion prove to be the irreverence and iconoclasm of the Australian hero? Has the culture the young people inhabit changed in ways that make the ground no longer fertile for this heroism? Will the excesses often depicted in these youth films result in a "lost generation" instead? The films of 1970–2000 do not offer a univocal answer to these questions.

Many Australian films speculate about the future in another way: by spinning scenarios such as alien contact or nuclear holocaust and then asking "what if." One of the crucial questions these films ask is what will happen to heroism if these scenarios unfold. Again, the answers are not univocal. Directors' speculations offer bleak assessments and optimistic assessments, and no clear chronological pattern emerges.

Many other Australian films focus on eccentric characters—that is, characters who are outside the culture that the films, in general, inscribe. These characters offer filmmakers an opportunity to offer satirical commentary on the heroism characteristic of that culture. Some films show an Australian trait taken to an eccentric extreme, the point being to satirize that trait by exaggeration. Other films show a trait that is lacking in the Australian character. In these films, it is the possession of that unusual trait that makes the characters eccentric. The absence of the trait in the Australian hero is what is being satirized in these films. As is true with satire in general, sometimes the satire in these films is strong; sometimes it is more gentle.

As a body of films that are sometimes a cultural project and almost always a cultural expression, Australian cinema during the 1970–2000 period is coherent. Whether it is accurate is a topic for the social sciences. Its success, however, cannot be denied. Australia is a rather small nation: its 30 million people cling to the ocean-bound edges of an otherwise sparsely populated land. Its global impact in film circles exceeds what its size would suggest as being likely. A large part of this impact has been its abilty to project (usually positively) the Australian culture so that global audiences know the heroism described in this study as Australian. These audiences might not be able to list quickly the heroism's characteristics. These audiences might be quick to note how this heroism is in some or in many ways like that evident in their own artifacts as well as different. These audience would nonetheless, grasp that there is a distinct Australian quality to the stories the films present.

Viewing film through a cultural lens is, of course, not the only way to study cinema. However, doing so answers an important question: What is Australian film as opposed to French or German or any other national cinema? Using this cultural lens should not obscure three observations I wish to offer in concluding this study.

First, there were many noteworthy films produced in Australia during the 1970–2000 period. The films are not interesting solely as cultural phenomenal; every critic probably has his or her own favorites. "Classics" such as *Picnic at Hanging Rock* (1975), *Breaker Morant* (1980), *My Brilliant Career* (1979), and *Gallipoli* (1981) would make most lists. Films such as *Sunday Too Far Away* (1975), *Wake in Fright* (1971), *Far East* (1982), *High Tide* (1987), *Radiance* (1997), *Puberty Blues* (1981), *Mad Max II* (1981), and *Winter of Our Dreams* (1981) would make mine. These films are outstanding because of what they "say"; they, and others, are also outstanding because of the talent they reveal. And that's my second observation: there is a great deal of talent evident in the films of this period. Talented directors and talented performers have worked in Australian film, so have talented cinematographers and film musicians. I have tried to note this work as I have discussed the heroism in the films. However, this work has not been my focus. So to highlight this talent, I have appended a list of the people behind Australian film and the films in this book they contributed to. Using that list, one might, for example, choose to consider photographer Don McAlpine's contribution to 1970–2000 Australian film or director John Duigan's or writer David Williamson's or musician Brian May's.

The third observation grows out of the response of some of my colleagues to the fact that I teach and write on Australian film. These colleagues, initially, do not see the films from Down Under as worthy of serious scholarly attention the way European film is. The reason is because Australian films are, in general, so very highly entertaining. "You don't teach *Crocodile Dundee,* do you?" they ask. Well, I do, as well as other "more serious" films such as the classics listed earlier that are nonetheless quite entertaining. The point to extract from this anecdote is that Australian film has managed to merge the serious and the entertaining. Some insist on talking about the "art film" and "Hollywood film" traditions in Australia, but the fact is that in the best films the two traditions are merged.

This merging is perhaps a final cultural note to close with. Australians—heroes and those who watch them—do not *seem* to take "matters" all that seriously. I say "seem" because I am convinced that the Aussie as beer-guzzling, sports-loving, anti-intellectual is a stereotype based on the facade one does indeed see Down Under. This facade masks serious questioning, serious reflecting. Australian films, then, mirror this characteristic of the culture quite well. Beneath their very entertaining facade is oftentimes very serious, very significant substance. That cinema does indeed seem intent on defining the nation and its people, but it also seems intent on raising issues that matter well beyond Australia and raising them within the context of entertaining films.

Appendix: The People behind Australian Film, 1970–2000

When studying this body of film, one is struck by the recurrence of names. Because I want to be sure these people, who played an important role in Australian filmmaking during this period, receive their due, this appendix lists the directors, producers, writers, cinematographers, musicians, and performers who played major roles in at least three of the films discussed in this book. In some instances, those who worked on two are also included. These are cases where the artist has had considerable impact.

DIRECTORS

Gillian Armstrong
My Brilliant Career, 1979
Starstruck, 1982
High Tide, 1987
The Last Days of Chez Nous, 1992
Oscar and Lucinda, 1997

Bruce Beresford
The Adventures of Barry McKenzie, 1972
Don's Party, 1976
The Getting of Wisdom, 1977
Breaker Morant, 1980
Puberty Blues, 1981
The Fringe Dwellers, 1986

Tim Burstall
Stork, 1971

Petersen, 1974
Eliza Fraser, 1976
The Last of the Knucklemen, 1979
Attack Force Z, 1982

Jane Campion
Sweetie, 1989
An Angel at My Table, 1990
The Piano, 1993

Paul Cox
Lonely Hearts, 1982
Man of Flowers, 1983

Donald Crombie
Caddie, 1976
The Irishman, 1978
The Killing of Angel Street, 1981
Robbery under Arms, 1985 (with Ken Hannam)

John Duigan
Mouth to Mouth, 1978
Winter of Our Dreams, 1981
Far East, 1982
The Year My Voice Broke, 1987
Flirting, 1991
Wide Sargasso Sea, 1993

Don McLennan
Hard Knocks, 1980
Slate, Wyn & Me, 1987
Mull, 1989

George Miller
The Man from Snowy River, 1982
Cool Change, 1986

Dr. George Miller
Mad Max, 1979
Mad Max II, 1981
Mad Max beyond Thunderdome, 1985 (with George Ogilvie)

Phillip Noyce
Heatwave, 1982
Echoes of Paradise, 1988

Fred Schepisi
The Devil's Playground, 1976
The Chant of Jimmie Blacksmith, 1978

Carl Schultz
Goodbye Paradise, 1983
Travelling North, 1987

Peter Weir
: *The Cars That Ate Paris*, 1974
: *Picnic at Hanging Rock*, 1975
: *The Last Wave*, 1977
: *Gallipoli*, 1981
: *The Year of Living Dangerously*, 1982

Simon Wincer
: *Phar Lap*, 1983
: *The Lighthorsemen*, 1987
: *Quigley*, 1991

PRODUCERS

Philip Adams
: *The Adventures of Barry McKenzie*, 1972
: *Don's Party*, 1976
: *The Getting of Wisdom*, 1977

Anthony Buckley
: *Caddie*, 1976
: *The Irishman*, 1978
: *The Killing of Angel Street*, 1981
: *Bliss*, 1985

Tim Burstall
: *Stork*, 1971
: *Petersen*, 1974
: *Eliza Fraser*, 1976
: *The Last of the Knucklemen*, 1979

Matt Carroll
: *Sunday Too Far Away*, 1975
: *Breaker Morant*, 1980

Jan Chapman
: *The Last Days of Chez Nous*, 1992
: *The Piano*, 1993

Margaret Fink
: *My Brilliant Career*, 1979
: *For Love Alone*, 1986

Byron Kennedy
: *Mad Max*, 1979
: *Mad Max II*, 1981

Patricia Lovell
: *Picnic at Hanging Rock*, 1975 (with Hal McElroy and Jim McElroy)
: *Gallipoli*, 1981 (with Robert Stigwood)
: *Monkey Grip*, 1982

Hal McElroy and Jim McElroy
- *The Cars That Ate Paris*, 1974
- *Picnic at Hanging Rock*, 1975 (with Pat Lovell)
- *The Last Wave*, 1977
- *The Year of Living Dangerously*, 1982 (without Hal McElroy)
- *Razorback*, 1984 (without Jim McElroy)

George Miller
- *The Year My Voice Broke*, 1987 (with Terry Hayes and Doug Mitchell)
- *Flirting*, 1991 (with Terry Hayes and Doug Mitchell)

Jane Scott
- *Goodbye Paradise*, 1983
- *Echoes of Paradise*, 1988
- *Shine*, 1996

Fred Schepisi
- *The Devil's Playground*, 1976
- *The Chant of Jimmie Blacksmith*, 1978

WRITERS

Bruce Beresford
- *Breaker Morant*, 1980 (with Jonathan Hardy and David Stephens)
- *The Fringe Dwellers*, 1986 (with Rhoisin Beresford)

John Duigan
- *Mouth to Mouth*, 1978
- *Winter of Our Dreams*, 1981
- *Far East*, 1982
- *The Year My Voice Broke*, 1987
- *Flirting*, 1991
- *Wide Sargasso Sea*, 1993 (with Bronwyn Murray)

Laura Jones
- *High Tide*, 1987
- *An Angel at My Table*, 1990
- *Oscar and Lucinda*, 1997 (with Peter Carey)

Dr. George Miller
- *Mad Max*, 1979 (with James McCausland)
- *Mad Max II*, 1981 (with Terry Hayes and Brian Hannant)
- *Mad Max beyond Thunderdome*, 1985 (with Terry Hayes)

Fred Schepisi
- *The Devil's Playground*, 1976
- *The Chant of Jimmie Blacksmith*, 1978

Peter Weir
- *The Cars That Ate Paris*, 1974
- *The Last Wave*, 1977 (with Tony Morphett and Petru Popescu)
- *The Year of Living Dangerously*, 1982 (with David Williamson and C. J. Koch)

Eleanor Whitcombe
The Getting of Wisdom, 1977
My Brilliant Career, 1979

David Williamson
Stork, 1971
Petersen, 1974
Don's Party, 1976
Eliza Fraser, 1976
Gallipoli, 1981
The Year of Living Dangerously, 1982 (with Peter Weir and C. J. Koch)
Phar Lap, 1983
Travelling North, 1987

CINEMATOGRAPHERS

Russell Boyd
Picnic at Hanging Rock, 1975
The Last Wave, 1977
Gallipoli, 1981
A Town Like Alice, 1981
Starstruck, 1982
The Year of Living Dangerously, 1982
Phar Lap, 1983
Crocodile Dundee, 1986
High Tide, 1987

Geoff Burton
Sunday Too Far Away, 1975
The Year My Voice Broke, 1987
Flirting, 1991
Wide Sargasso Sea, 1993

Robin Copping
Stork, 1971
Petersen, 1974
Eliza Fraser, 1976

Tom Cowan
Journey among Women, 1977
Mouth to Mouth, 1978
Winter of Our Dreams, 1981

Peter James
Caddie, 1976
The Irishman, 1978
The Killing of Angel Street, 1981
Echoes of Paradise, 1988

Don McAlpine
The Adventures of Barry McKenzie, 1972
Surrender in Paradise, 1976

Don's Party, 1976
The Getting of Wisdom, 1977
Patrick, 1978
My Brilliant Career, 1979
Breaker Morant, 1980
Puberty Blues, 1981
The Fringe Dwellers, 1986

Vincent Monton
Heatwave, 1982
Moving Out, 1983
Lucky Break, 1994

Paul Murphy
Bliss, 1985
Dead-End Drive-In, 1986
Dallas Doll, 1993

Dean Semler
Mad Max II, 1981
Razorback, 1984
Mad Max beyond Thunderdome, 1985
The Lighthorsemen, 1987

Geoffrey Simpson
The Last Days of Chez Nous, 1992
Shine, 1996
Oscar and Lucinda, 1997

Yuri Sokol
Lonely Hearts, 1982
Man of Flowers, 1983

MUSICIANS

Cameron Allan
Heatwave, 1982
Emoh Ruo, 1985
The Umbrella Woman, 1987

Peter Best
The Adventures of Barry McKenzie, 1972
Petersen, 1974
We of the Never Never, 1982
Goodbye Paradise, 1983
Bliss, 1985
Crocodile Dundee, 1986
High Tide, 1987
Muriel's Wedding, 1994

Patrick Flynn
Sunday Too Far Away, 1975

Caddie, 1976
Mad Dog Morgan, 1976

Brian May
Patrick, 1978
Mad Max, 1979
Gallipoli, 1981
The Killing of Angel Street, 1981
Mad Max II, 1981

Bruce Rowland
The Man from Snowy River, 1982
Phar Lap, 1983
Cool Change, 1986

Bruce Smeaton
The Cars That Ate Paris, 1974
Picnic at Hanging Rock, 1975
The Devil's Playground, 1976
Eliza Fraser, 1976
The Chant of Jimmie Blacksmith, 1978
The Last of the Knucklemen, 1979
A Town Like Alice, 1981
Monkey Grip, 1982
Squizzy Taylor, 1982

Nathan Waks
My Brilliant Career, 1979
For Love Alone, 1986

PERFORMERS

David Argue
Gallipoli, 1981
Razorback, 1984
Backlash, 1986

Ray Barrett
Don's Party, 1976
Goodbye Paradise, 1983

Bryan Brown
The Irishman, 1978
Breaker Morant, 1980
Winter of Our Dreams, 1981
A Town Like Alice, 1981
Far East, 1982
The Umbrella Woman, 1987

Tom Burlinson
The Man from Snowy River, 1982
Phar Lap, 1983

Gia Carides
    Bliss, 1985
    Backlash, 1986
    Strictly Ballroom, 1992
    Lucky Break, 1994

Russell Crowe
    Proof, 1991
    Romper Stomper, 1992

Judy Davis
    My Brilliant Career, 1979
    Winter of Our Dreams, 1981
    Heatwave, 1982
    High Tide, 1987

Arthur Dignam
    Petersen, 1974
    The Devil's Playground, 1976
    We of the Never Never, 1982

Colin Friels
    Monkey Grip, 1982
    Malcolm, 1986
    Ground Zero, 1987

Mel Gibson
    Tim, 1979
    Mad Max, 1979
    Gallipoli, 1981
    Mad Max II, 1981
    Attack Force Z, 1982
    The Year of Living Dangerously, 1982
    Mad Max beyond Thunderdome, 1985

David Gulpilil
    Walkabout, 1971
    Mad Dog Morgan, 1976
    The Last Wave, 1977
    Crocodile Dundee, 1986

John Hargreaves
    Don's Party, 1976
    The Killing of Angel Street, 1981
    Malcolm, 1986

Chris Haywood
    Attack Force Z, 1982
    Man of Flowers, 1983
    Razorback, 1984
    The Tale of Ruby Rose, 1988

Noni Hazlehurst
   Monkey Grip, 1982
   Fran, 1985
   Australian Dream, 1987

Wendy Hughes
   Petersen, 1974
   My Brilliant Career, 1979
   Lonely Hearts, 1982
   Echoes of Paradise, 1988

Bill Hunter
   Strictly Ballroom, 1992
   Muriel's Wedding, 1994
   The Adventures of Priscilla, Queen of the Desert, 1994

Norman Kaye
   Lonely Hearts, 1982
   Man of Flowers, 1983

Tommy Lewis
   The Chant of Jimmie Blacksmith, 1978
   Robbery under Arms, 1985

Sam Neill
   My Brilliant Career, 1979
   Attack Force Z, 1982
   Robbery Under Arms, 1985
   For Love Alone, 1986
   The Umbrella Woman, 1987
   The Piano, 1993

Helen Morse
   Petersen, 1974
   Picnic at Hanging Rock, 1975
   Caddie, 1976
   A Town Like Alice, 1981
   Far East, 1982

Bruce Spence
   Stork, 1971
   Mad Max II, 1981
   Mad Max beyond Thunderdome, 1985

Jack Thompson
   Wake in Fright, 1971
   Petersen, 1974
   Sunday Too Far Away, 1975
   Mad Dog Morgan, 1976
   The Chant of Jimmie Blacksmith, 1978
   Breaker Morant, 1980
   The Man from Snowy River, 1982

Sigrid Thornton
- *The Man from Snowy River*, 1982
- *The Lighthorsemen*, 1987
- *Slate, Wyn & Me*, 1987

Jacki Weaver
- *Stork*, 1971
- *Petersen*, 1974
- *Caddie*, 1976
- *Picnic at Hanging Rock*, 1976
- *Squizzy Taylor*, 1982

Hugo Weaving
- *For Love Alone*, 1986
- *Proof*, 1991
- *The Adventures of Priscilla, Queen of the Desert*, 1994

Bibliography

Abbey, Ruth, and Jo Crawford. "Crocodile Dundee or Davy Crockett?: What *Crocodile Dundee* Doesn't Say about Australia." *Meanjin* 2 (1987): 145–53.
Bell, Philip, and Roger Bell. *Implicated: The United States in Australia*. Melbourne: Oxford University Press, 1993.
Brown, Miranda. "*Puberty Blues*" (Interview with Margaret Kelly and Joan Long). *Cinema Papers* 35 (1982): 433–37.
Burstall, Tim. "Twelve Genres of Australian Film." *An Australian Film Reader*. Ed. Albert Moran and Tom O'Regan. Sydney: Currency Press, 1985. 215–22.
Cafarella, Jane. "Fillipino Women Blast 'Priscilla' for Portrayal of 'Worst Stereotype'." *The Age* (October 7, 1994). Rpt. *Cinedossier* 654 (October 11, 1994): 20.
Carey, Peter. *True History of the Kelly Gang*. New York: Alfred A. Knopf, 2000.
Carroll, John, ed. *Intruders in the Bush: The Australian Quest for Identity*. Melbourne: Oxford University Press, 1982.
Clancy, Jack. "Film: The Renaissance of the Seventies." *Intruders in the Bush: The Australian Quest for Identity*. Ed. John Carroll. Melbourne: Oxford University Press, 1982. 168–79.
Collins, Diane. *Hollywood Down Under: Australians at the Movies, 1896 to the Present Day*. Sydney: Angus and Robertson, 1987.
Crofts, Stephen. "*Breaker Morant* Rethought or Eighty Years On, the Culture Still Cringes." *Cinema Papers* 30 (1980): 420–21.
———. *Identification, Gender, and Genre in Film: The Case of* Shame. South Melbourne: Australian Film Institute, 1993.
Cunningham, Stuart. "Hollywood Genres, Australian Movies." *An Australian Film Reader*. Ed. Albert Moran and Tom O'Regan. Sydney: Currency Press, 1985. 235–41.

Dermody, Susan, and Elizabeth Jacka, eds. *The Imagining Industry: Australian Film in the Late '80s.* North Ryde: AFTRS Publications, 1988.
———. *The Screening of Australia.* 2nd vol. Sydney: Currency Press, 1987, 1988.
Enker, Debi. "Cross-Over and Collaboration: Kennedy Miller." *Back of Beyond: Discovery Australian Film and Television.* Ed. Scott Miller. North Sydney: Australian Film Commission, 1988. 52–67.
Epstein, Jan. "Stephan Elliot: *The Adventures of Priscilla, Queen of the Desert.*" (Interview). *Cinema Papers* 101 (1994): 4–10, 86.
Gibson, Ross. "Formative Landscapes." *Back of Beyond: Discovering Australian Film and Television.* Ed. Scott Murray. North Sydney: Australian Film Commission, 1988. 20–33.
Gillespie, Pat. "*Strictly Ballroom.*" *Cinema Papers* 91(1993): 52.
Grunberg, Serge. "Australia: From the Desert to Hollywood." *Metro* 100 (1994): 27–31.
Hall, Ken G. *Australian Film: The Inside Story.* Sydney: Summit Books, 1993.
Hamilton, Peter, and Sue Mathews, eds. *American Dreams: Australian Movies.* Sydney: Currency Press, 1986.
Hinde, John. "*Barry McKenzie* and *Alvin*, Ten Years Later." *An Australian Film Reader.* Ed. Albert Moran and Tom O'Regan. Sydney: Currency Press, 1985. 184–87.
Hodge, Bob, and Vijay Mishra. *Dark Side of the Dream: Australian Literature and the Postcolonial Mind.* Sydney: Allen and Unwin, 1991.
Hodsdon, Barrett. "The Avant-Garde Impulse and Australian Narrative: *Palm Beach* in Context." *An Australian Film Reader.* Ed. Albert Moran and Tom O'Regan. Sydney: Currency Press, 1985. 288–95.
———. "Flagship Culture and Commercial Chimera: Government Involvement in Australian Film." *A Century of Australian Cinema.* Ed. James Sabine. Melbourne: William Heinemann, 1995. 154–71.
Jacka, Elizabeth. "Australian Cinema." *The Oxford Guide to Film Studies.* Ed. John Hill and Pamela Church Gibson. Oxford: Oxford University Press, 1998. 516–22.
Jakubowicz, Andrew. "Australian (dis)Contents: Film, Mass Media, and Multiculturalism." *Culture, Difference, and the Arts.* Ed. Sneja Gunew and Fazal Rivi. Sydney: Allen and Unwin, 1994. 86–107.
Kael, Pauline. "A Dreamlike Requiem Mass for a Nation's Lost Honour." *An Australian Film Reader.* Ed. Albert Moran and Tom O'Regan. Sydney: Currency Press, 1985. 204–10.
Kemp, Peter. "Developing Pictures: Australian Cinema (1970–1995)." *A Century of Australian Cinema.* Ed. James Sabine. Melbourne: William Heinemann, 1995. 172–97.
Langton, Marcia. *Well, I Heard It on the Radio and I Saw It on the Television. . . .* Woolloomooloo, NSW: Australian Film Commission, 1993.
Laseur, Carol. "Australian Exploitation Film: The Politics of Bad Taste." *Continuum* 5 (1992): 366–77.
Leigh, Michael. "Curiouser and Curiouser." *Back of Beyond. Discovering Australian Film and Television.* Ed. Scott Murray. North Sydney: Australian Film Commission, 1988. 78–89.

Lewis, Glenn. *Australian Movies and the American Dream.* New York: Praeger, 1987.

Lohrey, Amanda "*Gallipoli:* Male Innocence as a Marketable Commodity." *Island Magazine* 9/10 (March 1981): 29–34

Martin, Adrian. "Double Trouble: Women's Films." *The Australian Screen.* Ed. Albert Moran and Tom O'Regan. Ringwood, Victoria: Penguin, 1989. 191–215.

———. "Nurturing the Next Wave." *Back of Beyond. Discovering Australian Film and Television.* Ed. Scott Murray. North Sydney: Australian Film Commission, 1988. 90–105.

Maynard, Sean. "Black (and White) Images: Aborigines and Film." *The Australian Screen.* Ed. Albert Moran and Tom O'Regan. Ringwood, Victoria: Penguin, 1989. 216–35.

McFarlane, Brian. *Australian Cinema.* New York: Columbia University Press, 1988.

Moran, Albert. "A State Government Business Venture: The South Australian Film Corporation." *An Australian Film Reader.* Ed. Albert Moran and Tom O'Regan. Sydney: Currency Press, 1985. 252–63.

Morris, Meaghan. *The Pirate's Fiancée: Feminism, Reading, Postmodernism.* London: Verso, 1988.

———. "The Very Idea of a Popular Debate." *Communal/Plural* 2 (1992): 153–67.

Murray, Scott. "Australian Cinema in the 1970s and 1980s." *Australian Cinema.* Ed. Scott Murray. Sydney: Allen and Unwin, 1993. 71–146.

———, ed. *Australian Film, 1978–1992: A Survey of Theatrical Features.* Melbourne: Oxford University Press, 1993.

———, ed. *The New Australian Cinema.* London: Elm Tree Books, 1980.

———. "*Starstruck:* Scott Murray Talks to Scriptwriter Stephen Maclean." *Cinema Papers* 37 (1983): 111–16.

———. "Tracey Moffatt: *Night Cries*, A Rural Tragedy." *Cinema Papers* 79 (1990): 18–22.

O'Regan, Tom. *Australian National Cinema.* London: Routledge, 1996.

———. "Cinema Oz: The Ocker Films." *The Australian Screen.* Ed. Albert Moran and Tom O'Regan. Ringwood, Victoria: Penguin, 1989. 75–98.

———. "The Enchantment with Cinema: Film in the 1980s." *The Australian Screen.* Ed. Albert Moran and Tom O'Regan. Ringwood, Victoria: Penguin, 1989. 118–46.

———. "*The Man from Snowy River* and Australian Popular Culture." *An Australian Film Reader.* Ed. Albert Moran and Tom O'Regan. Sydney: Currency Press, 1985. 242–51.

Partridge, Dinah. "*Shame:* Radical Change in the Representation of Women." *Filmviews* 33 (1988): 136–37.

Pike, Andrew, and Ross Cooper. *Australian Film, 1900–1977: A Guide to Feature Film Production.* 1980. Melbourne: Oxford University Press, 1998.

Pip, Chris, Marion Marsh, and Eva Cox. *Women in Australian Film, Video, and Television Production.* Sydney: Australian Film Commission, 1987.

"Priscilla Puts Down." *The Age* (October 10, 1994). Rpt. *Cinedossier* 654 (October 11, 1994): 21.

Rattigan, Neil. *Images of Australia: 100 Films of the New Australian Cinema.* Dallas: Southern Methodist University Press, 1991.

Ricketson, James. "Poor Movies, Rich Movies." *An Australian Film Reader*. Ed. Albert Moran and Tom O'Regan. Sydney: Currency Press, 1985. 223–27.
Robson, Jocelyn, and Beverley Zalcock. *Girls' Own Stories: Australian and New Zealand Women's Films*. London: Scarlet Press, 1997.
Rohdie, Sam. "The Australian State, A National Cinema." *An Australian Film Reader*. Ed. Albert Moran and Tom O'Regan. Sydney: Currency Press, 1985. 264–78.
———. "*Gallipoli* as World Camera Fodder." *Arena* 60 (1982): 36–42.
———. "*Gallipoli*, Peter Weir, and an Australian Art Cinema." *An Australian Film Reader*. Ed. Albert Moran and Tom O'Regan. Sydney: Currency Press, 1985. 194–97.
Rowse, Tim, and Albert Moran. " 'Peculiarly Australian': The Political Construction of Cultural Identity." *Australian Society*. 4th ed. Ed. S. Encel and L. Bryson. Melbourne: Longman Cheshire, 1984. 229–78.
Ryan, Penn, Margaret Eliot, and Gil Appleton. *Women in Australian Film Production*. Sydney: Women's Film Fund, Australian Film and Television School, 1983.
Sands, Kate. "Women of the Wave." *Back of Beyond: Discovering Australian Film and Television*. Ed. Scott Murray. North Sydney: Australian Film Commission, 1988. 2–19.
Sheckels, Theodore F. "Filming Peter Carey: From the Adequate to the Distorted." *Antipodes* 13 (1999): 91–94.
———. " 'New Wave' Cinema's Definition of Australian Heroism." *Antipodes* 12 (1998): 29–36.
Stratton, David. *The Avocado Plantation: Boom and Bust in the Australian Film Industry*. Sydney: Pan Macmillan, 1990.
———. *The Last New Wave: The Australian Film Revival*. Sydney: Angus and Robertson, 1980.
Taylor, Ronnie. "*Strictly Ballroom*." (Interview with Baz Luhrman and Paul Mercurio) *Cinema Papers* 88 (1992): 6–10.
Tosi, George. "Geoff Burrowes and George Miller: Two Men Behind *Snowy River*," (Interview). *Cinema Papers* 38 (1983): 207–12, 283.
Tudor, Andrew. "The Aussie Picture Show." *An Australian Film Reader*. Ed. Albert Moran and Tom O'Regan. Sydney: Currency Press, 1985. 211–14.
Tulloch, John. *Australian Cinema: Industry, Narrative, and Meaning*. Sydney: Allen and Unwin, 1982.
Turner, Graeme. "Art Directing History: The Period Film." *The Australian Screen*. Ed. Albert Moran and Tom O'Regan. Ringwood, Victoria: Penguin, 1989. 99–117.
———. *Making It National: Nationalism and Australian Popular Culture*. Sydney: Allen and Unwin, 1994.
———. "Mixing Fact and Fiction." *Back of Beyond: Discovering Australian Film and Television*. Ed. Scott Murray. North Sydney: Australian Film Commission, 1988. 68–77.
———. *National Fictions: Literature, Film, and the Construction of Australian Narrative*. 2nd ed. Sydney: Allen and Unwin, 1993.
Ward, Russel. *The Australian Legend*. 2nd ed. Melbourne: Oxford University Press, 1965.

Wark, McKenzie. "Cinema II: The Next Hundred Years." *A Century of Australian Cinema*. Ed. James Sabine. Melbourne: William Heinemann, 1995. 198–211.

White, David. *Australian Movies to the World: The International Success of Australian Films since 1970.* Melbourne: Fontana Australia and Cinema Papers, 1984.

Wignall, Louise. "The Extraordinary in the Ordinary: P. J. Hogan Talks about *Muriel's Wedding.*" (Interview). *Metro* 99 (1994): 31–34.

Wood, Robin. "Quo Vadis Bruce Beresford?" *An Australian Film Reader*. Ed. Albert Moran and Tom O'Regan. Sydney: Currency Press, 1985. 198–203.

Wright, Andree. *Brilliant Careers.* Sydney: Pan Books, 1986.

Index

ABBA, 111–12, 114–15
Abbey, Ruth, 64
Aboriginal land rights, 39, 65, 67, 73
Adams, Phillip, 176, 227
The Adventures of Barry McKenzie, 6, 12, 14–16, 31, 36, 40, 225, 227, 229–30
The Adventures of Priscilla, Queen of the Desert, 7, 215–17, 233–34
Agutter, Jenny, 120
Alexander, Elizabeth, 85
Allan, Cameron, 230
Alvin Purple, 6, 14
Amagula, Nandjiwarra, 123
An Angel at My Table, x, 205–7, 219, 226, 228
Anzac, 8, 46–47, 69, 206
Appleton, Gil, 75–76
Argue, David, 38, 126, 231
Arkin, Alan, 178
Armstrong, Gillian, vii, ix–x, 6, 80–81, 98, 100–101, 104, 109, 153, 158, 179, 217–18, 225
Armytage, Lisa, 62
Atkins, David, 26

Attack Force Z, 50–52, 226, 232–33
Australian Dream, 98–100, 103, 114, 233
Australian Film Commission, 5–6, 14–15, 21, 23, 92
Australian Film, Radio, and Television School, ix–x, 2
Auzins, Igor, 5, 88

Backlash, 125–27, 130, 134, 231–32
Barbarosa, x
Barlow, Helen, 37, 95, 126
Barrett, Ray, 176, 231
Bennett, Bill, 125–27, 130
Beresford, Bruce, ix–x, 4–6, 12, 14, 31, 35, 40, 43, 46, 66, 119, 127, 143–44, 149–51, 217, 225, 228
Beresford, Rhoisin, 228
Bernhard, Sandra, 185
Berry, Chuck, 161
Bertrand, Ian, 105
Best, Peter, 42, 230
Blake, Jon, 62
Bliss, 179–81, 217, 227, 230
BMX Bandits, 155–58

Bond, Gary, 32–33
Boyd, Russell, 46, 48, 51, 58, 100, 139, 154, 229
Brannigan, Laura, 158
Breaker Morant, vii, 6, 9, 14, 31, 43–46, 52, 59, 66, 78, 149, 199, 223, 225, 227–28, 230–31, 233
Brontë, Charlotte, 213
Brown, Bryan, 22, 43–44, 49, 53, 97, 194, 231
Brown, Lou, 22
Brown, Miranda, 150
Buchanan, Miles, 180
Buckley, Anthony, 227
Buday, Helen, 94
Burke, Simon, 22
Burke & Wills, 14
Burlinson, Tom, 55, 58–60, 231
Burrowes, Geoff, 57
Burstall, Tim, 5–6, 12, 14, 23–25, 31, 40–42, 50–51, 78, 190–91, 225–27
Burton, Geoff, 229

Caddie, 76–78, 94, 226–27, 229, 231, 233–34
Cafarella, Jane, 216
Cameron, Ken, 90–92, 96
Camilleri, Terry, 171
Campion, Jane, ix–x, 6, 110, 112, 203, 205–7, 219, 226
Cannes Film Festival, 16, 92
Capelja, Jad, 151
Caputo, Raffael, 164
Carey, Gabrielle, 149
Carey, Peter, 12, 179–80, 183, 185, 217, 228
Carides, Gia, 126, 180, 212, 232
Carmen, Loene, 162
Carroll, John, 6, 8
Carroll, Matt, 227
The Cars that Ate Paris, 4, 171–73, 226, 228, 231
The Castle, 31, 72–74
Castle, John, 78
Chamberlain, Richard, 123
Chandler, Jan, 105
Chandler, Raymond, 176

The Chant of Jimmie Blacksmith, vii, 14, 123–27, 130, 132, 134, 226, 228, 231, 233
Chapman, Jan, 227
Chauvel, Charles, 131
Clancy, Jack, 6
Clifford, Graeme, 14
Colette, Toni, 113–14
Collins, Diane, 3
Colston, Karen, 203
Cool Change, 62–64, 66, 70, 75, 181, 226, 231
Cooper, Ross, 3, 12, 14, 18–19, 34, 43, 122–23, 138, 146, 170–71
Copping, Robin, 229
Couzens, Paul, 146
Cowan, Tim, 79
Cowan, Tom, 148, 229
Cox, Eva, 75–76
Cox, Paul, 189, 195–96, 199, 205, 226
Cox, Peter, 34
Craig, Michael, 21–22
Crawford, Jo, 64
Crocker, Barry, 15
Crocodile Dundee, ix, 6, 9, 39, 64–67, 70, 181, 223–34, 229–30, 232
Crofts, Stephen, 43, 45, 108
Crombie, Donald, 11–13, 21, 25, 27, 76, 85, 226
Crowe, Russell, 166, 208, 232
Cullen, Fred, 56
Cummins, Christopher, 28
Cunningham, Stuart, 7
Curran, Lynette, 180

Dallas Doll, 9, 185–87, 230
Davies, Lindy, 199
Davis, Judy, 81, 86, 100–101, 194, 232
Dead-End Drive-In, 9, 179, 183–85, 217, 238
Dead Poets' Society, x
Dermody, Susan, 5–6, 14, 189
The Devil's Playground, 141–44, 226, 228, 231–32
Diamond, Neil, 35
Dickinson, Eva, 146
Dignam, Arthur, 42, 50, 89, 142, 232
Dimboola, 14

Dirty Harry, 35
Dixon, John, 56
Dobson, Kevin, 12, 25–26
Dogs in Space, 9, 157–58, 163–64
Don's Party, 35–37, 39, 225, 227, 229–32
Douglas, Kirk, 55
Dreyfuss, Richard, 37
Driving Miss Daisy, x
Duigan, John, 14, 53, 147, 149, 161, 193, 195, 206–7, 209, 213–15, 223, 226, 228
Dzenis, Anne, 93

Eastway, John, 14
Eastwood, Clint, 173
Echoes of Paradise, 103–4, 106, 226, 228–29, 233
Edgeworth, Patrick, 63, 157
Eliot, Margaret, 75–76
Eliza Fraser, 78–79, 226–27, 229, 231
Elliott, Stephan, 215–16
Ellis, Bob, 177
Emoh Ruo, 60–62, 75, 128, 230
Enker, Debi, 54
Epstein, Jan, 215
Erin Brockovich, 73

Faiman, Peter, 6, 39, 64–65
Far East, ix, 4, 53–55, 223, 226, 228, 231, 233
Ferrier, Noel, 78
Fink, Margaret, 82, 94–95, 227
Fits-Gerald, Lewis, 44
The F. J. Holden, 145–47, 149, 156
Flirting, 207, 209–10, 226, 228–29
Flynn, Patrick, 230
For Love Alone, 94–96, 227, 231, 233–34
Fowle, Susannah, 144
Fox Studios, Sydney, 2
Frame, Janet, 205–207, 219
Fran, 92–94, 98, 233
Franklin, Miles, vii, 81–83, 94–95
Franklin, Richard, 191–92
Friels, Colin, 67, 91, 198, 232
The Fringe Dwellers, 4–5, 119, 127–28, 225, 228, 230

Gallipoli, vii–viii, 5–6, 9, 46–48, 51–52, 55, 59–60, 66, 68, 70, 78, 147, 223, 226–27, 229, 231–32
Gardner, Geoff, 68, 98
Gare, Nene, 127
Garner, Helen, 90–92, 109
Garner, Nadine, 164
Gaty, Andrew, 178
The Getting of Wisdom, x, 3, 143–45, 217, 225, 227, 229–30
Gibson, Mel, 43, 46, 50–52, 172–74, 192, 232
Gibson, Ross, 8
Gildbert, Ross, 34
Gillespie, Pat, 210
Going Down, 159–60
Goodbye Paradise, 176–78, 226, 228, 230–31
Griffiths, Rachel, 114
Ground Zero, 67–68, 232
Grunberg, Serge, 167
Gul, Anna, 152
Gulpilil, David, 20, 65, 120–21, 123, 232
Gunn, Jeannie, 88–89

Hagg, Russell, 157
Hambly, Glenda, 92, 98
Hamilton, Peter, 55
Hannam, Ken, 6, 11–12, 16, 27, 226
Hannant, Brian, 228
Harbutt, Sandy, 138
Harders, Jane, 170
Hard Knocks, 4–5, 84–85, 94, 226
Hardy, Jonathan, 228
Hargreaves, John, 36, 86, 199, 232
Harrison, Gregory, 37
Hawler, Philippa, 184
Hayes, Terry, 228
Haywood, Chris, 38, 50, 105, 232
Hazlehurst, Noni, 91, 98, 233
Heatwave, 5, 86–88, 226, 230, 232
Hicks, Scott, 207, 218
High Tide, 6, 100–104, 223, 225, 228–30, 232
Hill, John, 129
Hinde, John, 15
Hitchcock, Alfred, 191

Hodge, Bob, 8
Hogan, Paul, 39, 64–66
Hogan, P. J., 112, 115
Hopper, Dennis, 11, 19, 21
Howard, Marcia, 165
Howard, Trevor, 78
Hughes, Wendy, 42–43, 50, 82, 103, 195, 233
Humphries, Barry, 15
Hunt, Linda, 51
Hunter, Bill, 212, 216, 233
Hunter, Holly, 110
Hutchence, Michael, 163

The Irishman, 12, 21–23, 25, 226–27, 229, 231

Jacka, Elizabeth, 3, 5–6, 14, 189
Jacquard, Susan, 191
Jagger, Mick, 12
Jakubowicz, Andrew, 119
James, Peter, 21, 229
Jaws, 37–38
Jedda, 131
Joddrell, Steve, 43, 106, 109
John, Lucien, 120
Jones, Helen, 180
Jones, Laura, 100, 218, 228
Journey among Women, 79–80, 82, 229
Jupp, Eric, 192
Jurisic, Melita, 104

Kael, Pauline, 125
Karr, Bill, 52
Kaye, Norman, 195, 233
Kearney, Stephen, 202
Keenan, Haydn, 159
Keitel, Harvey, 111
Kelly, Margaret, 149
Kemp, Peter, 3–4
Keneally, Thomas, vii, 123, 142
Kenna, Peter, 96
Kennedy, Byron, 227
Kennedy, Gerard, 24
Kennedy, Jo, 154
Kenny, Jan, 93–94
Keogh, Alexia, 205
Kerr, Bill, 37

Kerr, Greg, 185
Kidman, Nicole, 156
The Killing of Angel Street, 85–88, 226–27, 229, 231–32
Koch, C. J., 51–52, 228–29
Kotcheff, Ted, ix, 32, 38
Krejus, Kim, 147
Kurosawa, Akira, 176

Landis, Nina, 202
Lang, Joan, 149
Langton, Marcia, 131
The Last Days of Chez Nous, viii, 109–10, 225, 227, 230
The Last of the Knucklemen, 12, 23–25, 226–27, 231
The Last Wave, 4, 122–23, 226, 228–29, 232
Laseur, Carol, 66
Laurie, Piper, 192
Law, John Phillip, 50
Lawrance, Peter, 193
Lawrence, Denny, 60, 177
Lawrence, Ray, 179–80, 217
Lawson, Henry, 83
Lee, Christopher, 178
Lee, Mark, 46
Leigh, Michael, 122
Lemon, Genevieve, 204
Les Patterson Saves the World, 14
Lette, Kathy, 149
Levy, Sandra, 101
Lewin, Ben, 115
Lewis, Glenn, 6
Lewis, Tommy, 28, 124, 233
The Lighthorsemen, 68–71, 181, 227, 230, 234
Lindsay, Joan, 139
Little, Jimmy, 131–32
Little Women, x
Lohrey, Amanda, 48
Lonely Hearts, 195–96, 205, 226, 230, 233
Lonesome Dove, 68
Lovell, Patricia, 92, 227–28
Lowenstein, Richard, 6, 163
Lucas, Rose, 56–57, 107–8
Lucky Break, 115–18, 230, 232

Luhrman, Baz, 207, 210, 212

Mad Dog Morgan, 11–12, 19–21, 26, 34, 231–33
Mad Max, 6, 172–75, 181, 183, 192, 226–28, 231–32
Mad Max II, 3, 6, 9, 109, 172, 174–76, 181–82, 184, 223, 226–28, 230–33
Mad Max beyond Thunderdome, 172, 181–84, 226, 228, 230, 232–33
Malcolm, 6, 198–99, 202, 232
The Man from Snowy River, x, 6, 55–57, 60–62, 66, 70–71, 125, 156, 181, 226, 231, 233–34
The Man from Snowy River II, 62
Man of Flowers, viii, 196–98, 205–6, 226, 230, 232–33
Mann, Tracy, 84, 159
Manning, Ned, 183
Marawood, Charles, 21
Marsh, Marion, 75–76
Marshall, James Vance, 120
Martin, Adrian, 75, 176
Mason, Steve, 104
Mathews, Sue, 55
The Matrix, 3
May, Brian, 46, 191, 223, 231
Maynard, Sean, 122
McAlpine, Don, 35, 43, 81–82, 127, 145, 149, 191, 223, 229
McCausland, James, 228
McCullough, Colleen, 192–93
McCullough, Dorothea, 158
McElroy, Hal, 228
McElroy, Jim, 228
McFarlane, Brian, 4, 7, 21, 42, 45, 47–48, 51–52, 57, 78–79, 82, 124–25, 139–40, 142–43, 146, 159, 173, 191
McGregor, Angela Punch, 89, 124
McKenzie, Jacqueline, 166
McKimmie, Jackie, 98, 103, 114
McLennan, Don, 4–5, 84, 160, 164, 226
McMurtry, Larry, 68
Melvin: Son of Alvin, 14
Menelaus, Jane, 28

Mercurio, Paul, 210
Miller, Dr. George, 6, 172–74, 181, 226, 228
Miller, George, 6, 14, 55–56, 62–64, 226, 228
Mishra, Vijay, 8
Mitchell, Doug, 228
Moffatt, Tracy, 130–32
Monkey Grip, 90–92, 94, 227, 231–32, 235
Monton, Vincent, 230
Moorhouse, Jocelyn, 207
Mora, Philippe, 11–12, 19–21, 178, 189
Morice, Tara, 210
Morphett, Tony, 228
Morris, Meaghan, 65, 132
Morse, Helen, 42, 48, 50, 53, 76, 233
Moulin Rouge, 3
Mouth to Mouth, 147–49, 154, 158, 226, 228–29
Moving Out, 157–59, 230
Mulcahy, Michael, 6, 37
Mull, 164–65, 226
Muriel's Wedding, ix, 112–15, 230, 233
Murray, Bronwyn, 228
Murray, Scott, 3, 6–7, 131–32, 155
Murphy, Paul, 230
My Brilliant Career, vii–viii, x, 3, 6, 9, 78, 80–84, 94, 98, 112, 127–28, 144, 153–54, 205, 217, 223, 225, 227, 229–33
My Career Goes Bung, 84
My First Wife, 196
Myles, Bruce, 67

Ned Kelly, x, 12–14, 26–27, 34, 39
Nehm, Kristina, 127
Neill, Sam, 11, 27, 50–51, 81, 94–96, 110, 206, 233
Nelson, Margaret, 140
Nicholls, Bron, 164
Nielson, Juanita, 86
Night Cries, x–xi, 130–32
Nowra, Louis, 132
Noyce, Phillip, 5, 50, 86, 88, 163–64, 226

O'Donovan, Ross, 154
Ogilvie, George, 181, 226
O'Regan, Tom, 5, 7–8, 15, 18, 23, 37, 44–45, 47–48, 53, 56–57, 64, 80, 93–94, 98, 109, 111, 115, 125, 129, 131–32, 148, 166–67, 186, 191, 196, 206, 208, 210, 215–16
Oscar and Lucinda, 179, 217–18, 225, 228, 230
Otto, Barry, 180

Partridge, Dinah, 108
Pate, Michael, 192, 198
Patrick, 191–92, 230–31
Patterson, Banjo, 56–58
Pattinson, Michael, 4, 67, 157
Peat, Sonia, 147
Perkins, Rachel, 132, 134
Petersen, 3, 6, 31, 40–43, 50, 52, 226–27, 229–30, 232–34
Phar Lap, 5, 57–60, 156, 227, 229, 231–32
The Piano, ix–x, 6, 110–12, 206, 226–27, 233
Picnic at Hanging Rock, 5, 6, 139–44, 223, 226–29, 231, 233–34
Pike, Andrew, 3, 12, 14, 18–19, 34, 43, 122–23, 138, 146, 170–71
Pip, Chris, 75–76
Pleasence, Donald, 33, 67
Pollock, Daniel, 166
Popescu, Petru, 228
Post, Saki, 163
Preston, Michael, 24
Proof, 207–08, 232, 234
Puberty Blues, 3–6, 149–55, 223, 225, 230

Quigley, x, 6, 129–30, 132, 134, 227
Quinn, Karl, 208

Radiance, 132–36, 189, 223
Rattigan, Neil, xi, 7–8, 16, 19, 21, 24, 32, 35, 37, 42, 45, 47, 50–52, 57–58, 64, 70, 77–78, 82, 87–88, 92, 125, 127–28, 143–44, 148–49, 154, 156, 158, 171, 173, 176–77, 196

Razorback, 6, 37–39, 160, 228, 230–32
Rhys, Jean, 213
Reckless Kelly, 39–40
The Return of Captain Invincible, 19, 21, 178–79
Richards, Malcolm, 159
Richardson, Henry Handel, 143–45
Richardson, Tony, 12, 14, 26–27, 39, 78
Ricketson, James, 6
Rickman, Alan, 129
Rikky & Pete, 202–3
Robbery under Arms, x, 11–13, 26–30, 34, 48, 226, 233
Robson, Jocelyn, 75–76
The Rocky Horror Picture Show, x, 154, 169, 179
Roeg, Nicholas, ix, 120–22
Rohdie, Sam, 48
Romper Stomper, 3, 4, 6, 165–67, 232
Rowland, Bruce, 231
Rush, Geoffrey, 218
Ryan, Penn, 75–76

Said, Edward, 53
Sandow, Bruce, 60
Sands, Kate, 75–76
San Giacomo, Laura, 129
Savage, Georgia, 161
Schepisi, Fred, vii, ix–x, 14, 123–27, 130, 141, 226, 228
Schneider, Roy, 37
Schofield, Nell, 151
Scholes, Robert, 104
Schultz, Carl, 176–77, 208, 226
Scott, Jane, 228
Selleck, Tom, 129
Semler, Dean, 176, 230
Serious, Yahoo, 6, 31, 39, 70–72
Shakespeare, William, 67
Shame, 43, 106–9, 160, 162
Shane, 107–9
Sharman, Jim, ix–x, 154, 169, 171, 179
Shine, 207, 218–20, 228, 230
Shirley Thompson versus the Aliens, 169–70
Shorter, Ken, 138

Shute, Nevil, 48
Simpson, Geoffrey, 230
Simpson, Roger, 26
Slate, Wyn & Me, 160–61, 163, 226, 234
Smeaton, Bruce, 231
Smith, Kate, 178–79
Sokol, Yuki, 230
Spence, Bruce, 174, 190, 233
Squizzy Taylor, 12, 25–27, 31, 231, 234
Starstruck, 153–56, 158, 225, 229
Stead, Christina, 94
Stephens, David, 48, 228
Stever, Carl, 146
Stigwood, Robert, 227
Stitch, Rob, 31, 72
Stolen Generation, 131–32
Stone, 138–39, 156
Stork, 6, 190–91, 225, 227, 229, 233–34
Stratton, David, xi, 4–5, 29, 42, 46, 48, 50–51, 53, 57, 63, 67, 69–70, 86, 88, 92, 95, 97, 102–5, 107, 109, 125–27, 154, 156, 164, 176–78, 184
Street Hero, 4
Strictly Ballroom, 7, 207, 210–13, 232–33
Strikebound, 6
Sunday Too Far Away, 6, 12, 16–20, 23–25, 199, 223, 227, 229–30, 233
Surrender in Paradise, 34–35, 39, 40, 229
Sweetie, x, 3, 203–6, 226
Swift, Jonathan, 135

The Tale of Ruby Rose, 104–7, 112, 232
Tass, Nadia, 6, 198, 202, 206
Taylor, Noah, 162
Taylor, Ronnie, 212
Temple, Shirley, 204
Thompson, Jack, 17, 20, 40–43, 45, 50, 55, 124, 233
Thompson, Robert, 191
Thornhill, Michael, 145
Thornton, Sigrid, 55, 69, 161, 234

Tim, 192–93, 232
Tom Jones, 78
Tosi, George, 55
A Town Like Alice, x, 48–49, 75, 130, 229, 231, 233
Traveling North, 200–202, 226, 229
Trenchard-Smith, Brian, 155, 157, 179, 183, 185, 217
Truman, Jeff, 180
Tulloch, John, 8
Turner, Ann, 185
Turner, Graeme, 46, 64
Turner, Tina, 181–82

The Unbrella Woman, 96–98, 230–31, 233

Vidler, Steven, 28, 97
Vietnam War, 44, 53–54, 160, 200
Voltaire, 190

Wake in Fright, ix–x, 32–35, 38–39, 107, 223, 233
Waks, Nathan, 231
Walkabout, ix–x, 32, 120–22, 232
Wallace, Stephen, 94–96
Ward, Rachel, 97
Ward, Russel, 8, 32
Warner Brothers Studios, Gold Coast, 2
Waters, John, 50–51, 78
Weaver, Jacki, 26, 40, 42, 77, 190, 234
Weaver, Sigourney, 51–52
Weaving, Hugo, 94, 234
Weir, Peter, ix–x, 4–6, 46, 48, 51–52, 122–23, 139–41, 171–73, 226, 228–29
We of the Never Never, 5, 88–90, 230, 232
Whitcombe, Eleanor, 82, 144, 229
White, David, 3
White, Patrick, 169
Whiteley, Arkie, 37
Wide Sargasso Sea, 207, 213–15, 226, 228–29
Wignall, Louise, 115
Wild, Sue, 98

Williams, Huw, 94
Williamson, David, 35, 37, 42, 46, 48, 51, 58, 78, 190–91, 200, 223, 229
Wincer, Simon, 5–6, 57, 59–60, 68, 70–71, 129, 227
Winter of Our Dreams, 193–95, 205, 208, 226, 228–29, 231–32
Wood, Robin, 43
Woodcock, Tommy, 60
Woodward, Edward, 43–44

Wright, Andree, 75
Wright, Geoffrey, 4, 6, 165

The Year My Voice Broke, 161–63, 209, 226, 228–29
The Year of Living Dangerously, ix, 51–53, 55, 226, 228–29, 232
Yeats, William Butler, 140
York, Susannah, 78
Young Einstein, 6, 31, 70–72

Zalcock, Beverley, 75–76

About the Author

THEODORE F. SHECKELS is Professor of English and Communication at Randolph-Macon College in Ashland, Virginia. He is the author of many books, including *The Lion on the Freeway: A Thematic Introduction to Contemporary South African Literature in English* (1996) and *When Congress Debates: A Bakhtinian Paradigm* (Praeger, 2000).